TOWARD A SYNODAL CHURCH IN AFRICA

TOWARD A SYNODAL CHURCH IN AFRICA

Echoes from an African Christian Palaver

Ikenna U. Okafor ▪ Josée Ngalula

Nicholaus Segeja ▪ Stan Chu Ilo

editors

ORBIS BOOKS

Maryknoll, New York 10545

Founded in 1970, Orbis Books endeavors to publish works that enlighten the mind, nourish the spirit, and challenge the conscience. The publishing arm of the Maryknoll Fathers and Brothers, Orbis seeks to explore the global dimensions of the Christian faith and mission, to invite dialogue with diverse cultures and religious traditions, and to serve the cause of reconciliation and peace. The books published reflect the views of their authors and do not represent the official position of the Maryknoll Society. To learn more about Maryknoll and Orbis Books, please visit our website at www.orbisbooks.com

Originally published as *Journeying Together for a Synodal Church in Africa* © 2023 by St Paul Communications/Daughters of St Paul (Nairobi, Kenya)

This edition © 2024, published by Orbis Books, Box 302, Maryknoll, NY 10545-0302.

Manufactured in the United States of America

Library of Congress Cataloging-in-Publication Data

Names: Okafor, Ikenna U., editor. | Ngalula, Josée, editor. | Segeja, Nicholaus, editor. | Ilo, Stan Chu, editor.
Title: Toward a Synodal Church in Africa : echoes from and African Christian palaver/Ikenna U. Okafor, José'e Ngalula, Nicholaus Segeja, Stan Chu Ilo, editors.
Other titles: Journeying together for a Synodal Church in Africa.
Description: Maryknoll, NY : Orbis Books, [2024] | "Originally published as Journeying Together for a Synodal Church in Africa, 2023 by St Paul Communications/Daughters of St Paul (Nairobi, Kenya)"—T.p. verso | Includes bibliographical references. | Summary: "African Catholic theologians reflect on synodality and the church in Africa"— Provided by publisher.
Identifiers: LCCN 2023044258 (print) | LCCN 2023044259 (ebook) | ISBN 9781626985674 (trade paperback | ISBN 9798888660232 (epub)
Subjects: LCSH: Catholic Church—Africa. | Church renewal--Catholic Church. | Councils and synods. | Africa—Church history.
Classification: LCC BX1675 .J68 2024 (print) | LCC BX1675 (ebook) | DDC 282/.6—dc23/eng/20231127
LC record available at https://lccn.loc.gov/2023044258
LC ebook record available at https://lccn.loc.gov/2023044259

Contents

Final Statement of the Second Pan-African Catholic Congress
on Theology, Society and Pastoral Life 7

Message of His Holiness Pope Francis for the Second Pan-African
Catholic Congress on Theology, Society and Pastoral Life 15

Message to African Theologians Meeting at Nairobi (July 19, 2022) 17
    † Cardinal Mario Grech

Message of AMECEA at the Second Pan-African Congress
on Theology, Society and Pastoral Life 21

General Introduction 23
    Ikenna U. Okafor

Chapter 1
Proclaiming the Word of God to Young People in a Synodal
African Church 29
    †John Okoye

Chapter 2
Abraham, the Pilgrim: Three Paths for a Church on the Move 45
    Paulin Poucouta

Chapter 3
The Social Magisterium of Pope Francis and the Reform of the Church
in a Synodal Way: Latin American Perspectives 65
    Emilce Cuda

Chapter 4
Exploring the Possible Contributions of the African Palaver
Towards a Participatory Synodal Church 85
    Stan Chu Ilo

CHAPTER 5

Ubuntu and Synodality 123

   Josée Ngalula

CHAPTER 6

Chinua Achebe's *Arrow of God*: A Postcolonial Theological
Critique of Clericalism 137

   Ikenna U. Okafor

CHAPTER 7

The Social Dimension of Ecclesial Synodality in Africa:
A Call to Walk in Communion with the Laity in Doing Theology 161

   Nicholaus Segeja

CHAPTER 8

Contested Moral Questions in Africa Inspirations for Moral
Discernment in a Synodal Church 175

   Raymond Aina, MSP

CHAPTER 9

African Palaver and Interpretation of the Word of God with and for
the People of God: A Case for the Dialogical Construction
of the Homily in the Small Christian Communities in Africa 199

   Ignace Ndongala Maduku

CHAPTER 10

Five Key Lessons of Synodality for the Church-Family
of God in Africa 215

   Francis Appiah-Kubi

"THE TOMB IS EMPTY"

The Missionary Role of Communication in the Context
of the Synodal Church Today 229

   Lucio Adrian Ruiz

Selected Bibliography 235

Contributors 245

Final Statement of the Second Pan-African Catholic Congress on Theology, Society and Pastoral Life

PREAMBLE

1. Gathered at the Catholic University of Eastern Africa in Nairobi, Kenya for the Second Pan-African Congress on Theology, Society, and Pastoral Life from July 18–23, 2022, members of the People of God from the following African countries: Benin, Burkina Faso, Burundi, Cameroon, Cote d'Ivoire, Democratic Republic of the Congo, Equatorial Guinea, Ethiopia, Ghana, Kenya, Malawi, Mozambique, Nigeria, Republic of the Congo, Senegal, South Africa, South Sudan, Tanzania, Togo, Uganda, Zimbabwe, and people in solidarity from all other continents, we affirm the vitality of the Catholic Church in Africa as a sign of hope for the world.

2. Following the inaugural Pan-African Congress on Theology and Pastoral Life held at Bigard Memorial Seminary, Enugu, Nigeria from December 5-8, 2019, dedicated to sharing the inspiration to accomplish the works of God (*Jn* 6:8), the participants in Nairobi reflected on the theme: "Walking Together for a Vital Church for Africa and the World." This founding moment established new relationships, some of which have developed into ongoing collaborations and

common interests. This is the beginning of the Pan-African Catholic Theology and Pastoral Network (PACTPAN).

3. The vision of the Pan-African Catholic Theology and Pastoral Network is to bridge the gap between pastoral practices, scientific, and multidisciplinary works in the continent. It is about listening to God, the cry of our Mother Earth, and to the concerns of our people, in order to help them live flourishing lives rooted in our Christian faith and our African spiritual and religious traditions. Our active listening explains the choice of the theme of this second Congress "Walking together for a vital Church in Africa and in the world" which focused on Synodality; the experiences of African women and children; and the challenges and prospects of building a vital Church in Africa.

4. This Congress was significant because it was preceded by the General Assembly (July 16-18, 2022) of the Editorial Board of the international Catholic theological journal, *Concilium.* This is the first time that such a meeting has been held in Africa. *Concilium* was founded in 1965 by Catholic theologians to promote the theology of the Second Vatican Council and to contribute to new ways of doing theology in response to the signs of the times. We are grateful that the board members actively participated in the deliberations of this Congress.

The Harvest of the Pan-African Congress

5. We recognise the resilience of the African family amidst the challenges of COVID-19 pandemic. We mourn with many families who lost their loved ones. We continue to support our people with prayers and solidarity in these difficult times, and we call on all our churches, and governments to support families as they struggle to rebuild their lives.

6. We recognise the crucial role of women in society and the Church in Africa, as well as the priority of children who

suffer so much abuse and who are at the centre of family and community care as a sign of the new humanity for which we all hope.

7. We welcome with gratitude the message addressed to the Congress participants by His Holiness, Pope Francis at the Inaugural Mass for the opening of the Congress. We embrace fully his call for a synodal Church and commit our theological and pastoral reflections to advancing processes and practices for a synodal Church in Africa.

8. We also appreciate the messages of the Secretary-General of the Synod of Bishops, Cardinal Mario Grech, and the Association of Member Episcopal Conferences in Eastern Africa (AMECEA) in which they underlined the wisdom of African theology for a renewed humanity in its commitment to life, justice, and reconciliation for all.

9. We have reflected on the themes of synodality; concerns, aspirations, hopes, and achievements of African women; our African children and their hopes and aspirations aimed at the flourishing of their lives in society. We have also considered the ways of being a vital Church relevant to the context of Africa. As part of African life and thought, we commit ourselves to continue to develop these themes in the coming years.

10. We call on local Churches, social movements, universities, artists, and all persons to develop networks for mutual recognition, collaboration, and transformation of global society. This appeal will be actualised through local practices inspired by a culture of encounter, listening, discernment, and pastoral accompaniment in the spirit of the Church as Family of God and Salt and Light (*Mt* 5: 13-16).

11. Within this time together, the participants at the Second Pan-African Congress, through embracing the palaver and reverential dialogical process, were able to harvest the following fruits under the thematic focus of the Congress:

Synodality

12. In view of Pope Francis's invitation to the whole Church to embrace synodality, this Congress reflected on various aspects of being a synodal Church in Africa. The collective dialogues among the participants at this Congress have focused on multiple issues, among others; the mutual collaboration of institutes of religious life and Catholic universities in our countries; the developing processes of palaver and reverential dialogue in the local churches; the new models of leadership of communities and institutions that are so necessary for the renewal of the churches; the recognition of the place of the laity, especially the place of women; the social dimension of synodality that includes interaction with the protagonists of civil society; and the experiences of accompaniment with diverse human experiences marked by poverty and marginalisation in need of friendship and hospitality.

13. With joy, this Congress has identified many positive initiatives playing out in our ecclesial communities, and social contexts. However, we have also noticed how much road ahead we still have to traverse in order to reach that place of flourishing for all persons who call Africa their home. The "plague of clericalism" for example, in some of our ecclesial communities, is a major obstacle to walking together as a Family of God. It works against inclusion of all persons in the mission of the Church. The urgent and complex social problems that afflict us show how important it is that the synodal spirit – "walking together" – becomes a source of inspiration for ethical, ecclesial, and political commitments.

African Women

14. This Congress is impressed by the extraordinary ability of African women to embody resilience, perseverance, the ability to overcome hardship, and to bounce back from traumas and

adversities. These capacities are a response to experiences of violence that include domestic violence, wars, economic and ecological crises, and all forms of structural and systemic violence. African women are forced to bear the burden of life's trials and afflictions as they struggle to overcome obstacles to human flourishing and abundant life. This enduring resilience that defines the lives of African women is the path of hope for Africa, as the continent and its people look to the future. African women's resilience is where the courage to hope must find its expression as an affirmation of life, even in the face of death. Our task as a Family of God is to show solidarity in building a better society where African women will always flourish.

African Children

15. Our children are our present and future. As a people, Africans cherish the gift of life because it defines not only the continuity of our societies but also an expression of a life beyond the reality of death. This Congress is aware that life must be sustained, nurtured, and protected. However, for many reasons, the present and the future of Africa's children has long been mortgaged by conflicts, corruption, and all forms of abuses, and recently, by unguarded adhesion to unethical globalisation. In light of these, this Congress actively listened to child education actors, and agents of early child development to help foster the growth and flourishing of our children. This Congress also celebrates the contributions of Africa's pastoral workers in helping to bring about a better life for our children today and tomorrow. Finally, this Congress calls attention to the need for the Church in Africa to embrace policies that are intended to protect our children henceforth from all forms of abuses in families, churches, and society. This includes child sexual abuse, modern-day slavery, and human trafficking playing out both in the continent of Africa and beyond.

Vital Church

16. The vitality of the Church in Africa is the fruit of a long process of reception of the Word of God as a seed of new life to be cultivated. This Congress explored five areas where people and churches in Africa are flourishing: new leadership in society and in the churches; corporate accountability; peace building; political *diakonia*; and the need to hear God speaking through family stories, through music and drama. In these fields, African society and churches are contributing to imagining a new humanity and opening up perspectives of liberation from the wisdom of *Ubuntu* rooted in family spirit and reverential dialogue.

17. We, the participants at this Congress, have succeeded in shedding light on the critical problems of the structures that produce suffering and death. But above all, we have recognised the experiences that strengthen processes of social, ecclesial, and political responsibility as signs of the new world coming from the love of God for the whole creation and all the peoples on earth.

A Call to Commitments

18. In accord with our collective African palaver and discernment, we make the following commitments:

Synodality

- We commit to the full participation of the whole People of God in the life of the Church. In particular, we call for a Gospel-driven servant leadership in our churches that overcomes clericalism and samaritanises the wounded, the broken and those at the existential peripheries.
- Our vision of synodality must also include a prophetic collaboration with our African societies, and their particular

ecological and social challenges, guided by the wisdom of *Laudato Si'* and *Fratelli Tutti*.

- We commit to a synodal relationship with the world at large. This includes collaborating with partners around the world who work towards justice, peace, and reconciliation as seeds of the Kingdom of God.

African Women

- We commit to a critical engagement with the cultural structures playing out in our African societies that limit the rights of women to self-actualisation.

- We commit to advocating for the eradication of the practices of different kinds of abuse of women and girls, for example, sexual abuse, forced marriages, gender mutilation, new forms of slavery, and human trafficking.

- We commit to fully supporting, promoting, and advocating for the flourishing of women and girls in our African societies and churches.

Our Children

- We commit to embracing policies that are intended to protect our children henceforth from all forms of abuses in families, churches, and society.

- We commit to celebrating the gifts and talents of our children and empowering them to a full realisation of their dreams.

Vital Church

- We commit to developing networks of collaboration between churches in Africa and beyond to enhance prophetic Christian witness in the world.

- We commit to advancing a healthy dialogue between churches, religions, and African spiritual traditions for the purpose of mutual growth and peace.

- We commit ourselves to listening, dialoguing, and collaborating with other churches, faith communities, civil authorities, and social actors to promote a sustainable way of life in our continent and world.

Conclusion

19. As members of the Family of God in Africa, we pray and resolve to work together towards building a synodal and vital Church in Africa. We pray that God through his Son will lead us to see the surprises of the Holy Spirit in our uniqueness and diversity.

Our Lady, Queen of Africa, pray for us.

Message of His Holiness Pope Francis for the Second Pan-African Catholic Congress on Theology, Society and Pastoral Life

[Nairobi, July 19–22, 2022]

Sisters, Brothers of the Pan-African Catholic Theological and Pastoral Network:

I am delighted to hear about this meeting at the Catholic University of East Africa in Nairobi. I know that you are meeting for the Second Pan-African Catholic Congress on Theology, Society and Pastoral Life. It is a sign of hope that theologians, laity, priests, men and women religious, Bishops have taken the initiative to walk together.

Coming together to discern what God is telling us today, not only to meet challenging needs with certainty, but also to make African dreams come true (social, cultural, ecological and ecclesial dreams) is already a sign of an outgoing African Church. Continue your efforts.

In my visits to Africa, I have always been impressed by the faith and resilience of these peoples. As I commented during my trip to the Central African Republic in 2015, "Africa always surprises us." Bring out the best of you in these reflections so that the result will be a surprise, so that that African creation that surprises us all can be born. Because Africa is poetry. The wisdom of the African ancestors reminds us for this important call that "mountains never meet, but people do." Let us continue on.

Together. Accompanying one another, helping one another, and growing together.

May a wisdom theology, as you propose, be the good news of mercy for the poor and nourish people and communities in their struggle for life, peace and hope.

May the Holy Spirit inspire you - may paths emerge from this congress that the Church needs: paths of missionary, ecological conversion, peace, reconciliation and transformation of the whole world.

And I bless you all. God bless us all.
May the Blessed Virgin be with us.
And please don't forget to pray for me.
Thank you.

Message to African Theologians Meeting at Nairobi (July 19, 2022)

† Cardinal Mario Grech

According to Yves Congar Catholic ecclesiology over the last two millennia can be divided into two distinct periods. The first millennium operated out of what he called a *communio-*ecclesiology. The Church of the second millennium shifted, to operating out of a top-down ecclesiology, which he summarised as "hierarchology." Today I want to share my hope that, in the wake of Vatican II and its reception by Pope Francis, historians will look back on the Church of the third millennium as one characterised by an ecclesiology of "synodality." Whether this will become the reality depends on how Vatican II, and Pope Francis's conception of what it was envisaging, becomes deeply embedded into the daily life and mission of the Church. In this process of ongoing reception, theologians will play a vital role. And this is my challenge to you all today. The Church in Africa, Madagascar and the Islands possesses significant resources to enrich and contribute to the process of synodality. The religious, cultural and philosophical traditions of Africa have rich examples, resources, values and practices that correlate with the concept of synodality.

As *Dei Verbum* 8 teaches: "God, who spoke in the past, dialogues without interruption (*sine intermissione colloquitur*) with the spouse of his beloved Son. And the Holy Spirit, through whom the living voice of the Gospel rings out in the Church leads believers to the full truth and makes the word of Christ dwell in them in all its richness." Reflecting on *how* the Church can access this guidance of the Holy Spirit brings us to the very heart of synodality—the means through which the Holy Spirit communicates and enlightens the Church. *Lumen Gentium* 12 teaches that the conduit between the Church and the Holy Spirit is through a special gift which the Spirit gives to all baptised believers – "the supernatural *sensus fidei* of the whole people." This is a gift given to all baptised individuals and to the Church as a whole. The Spirit not only grants the gift of *fides*, but also a special gift for interpreting revelation, a *sensus fidei*. There is, however, a tension created through this gift from the Holy Spirit, an ecclesial tension which is of the Spirit's making. This is the tension between an individual's sense of the faith (*sensus fidei fidelis*) and the community of the faithful's sense of the faith (*sensus fidei fidelium*).

This dynamic tension between individual and communal discernment characterises the dynamism at work in what the council calls "the living tradition" (*DV*, 12). *Dei Verbum* 8 states that "the tradition that comes from the apostles makes progress in the Church *with the help of the Holy Spirit*." It then speaks of three interrelated means through which the Holy Spirit works. Firstly, theological scholarship: "the contemplation and study of believers who ponder these things in their hearts." Secondly, the *sensus fidelium*: "the intimate sense of spiritual realities which [believers] experience." And thirdly, the episcopate: "the preaching of those who, on succeeding to the *episcopatus*, have received the sure charism of truth." This "sure charism of truth," when understood in the light of this whole paragraph, and indeed all of the Vatican II documents, presupposes the search for truth as a dialogue between all of the three interrelated ways in which the Spirit guides the Church: theological scholarship, the *sensus fidelium*, and the Magisterium. Accordingly, Walter Kasper speaks of Vatican II's call for "a new form of ecclesiality: orthodoxy through dialogue." And, for Pope Francis, this new form of ecclesiality is best captured in the term "synodality."

In one sense, the Synod of Bishops is one way in which this threefold dialogue can occur between theological scholarship, the *sensus fidelium*, and the Magisterium. Thus, for synodality to be received deeply into the life and mission of the Church, theological investigation and theological education into a synodal imagination will be needed. It is for this specific reason that I feel honoured to address your assembly today! You African theologians have an important task and a vital contribution to make for the renewal of a synodal Church. An African theology of synodality would be a lasting contribution to the development of a synodal Church in the third millennium. Your (African) contribution in your continent can bring a solid contribution to the whole Church. African Bishops need your expertise in all the fields or areas of theological studies to deepen their understanding and practice of synodality. You may also place your expertise at the service of Bishops to prepare continental Bishop delegates to the Synod based on the Document for the Continental Stage (DCS).

In this process of synodality, you also have an indispensable role to play in the subsequent phases of implementation and in ensuring that synodality becomes a way of life "which God expects of the Church of the third millennium." For this to happen, your work as theologians entails studying and promoting *the spirituality of journeying together* so that it becomes *an educational principle for the formation of the human person and of the Christian, of the families, and of the communities.* I encourage you to develop formation programmes in your respective institutions of higher learning for "people, especially those who hold roles of responsibility within the Christian community, to make them more capable of 'journeying together'" and imbibing the cardinal principles of synodality, such as discernment in common, listening to one another and engaging in dialogue.

The synodal spirit is alive in Africa. It is rooted in the diverse and inculturated ways of being Church in local contexts. As stated in the "Vision of Synodality Rooted in an African Ecclesial Context," a document produced by the International Colloquium on Synodality that was convened by ASI in April 2022, Nairobi, Kenya, "Our contribution to the Synod on Synodality must include our African cultural values (expressed in terms like Ubuntu, Ujamaa, Baraza, Palaver, etc.), reverential dialogue that is inspired by the family spirit and related to nature, our ancestors, and the desired future for Africa."

My dear brothers and sisters, thank you for your love for the universal Church! You have a noble mission because theological reflection can explore the broad implications of a theology of synodality. But, whatever the issues still to be explored, one thing is clear from Pope Francis's vision: conceiving the Church in a synodal way brings to the fore the importance of listening to the *lived* faith of all the baptised, what *Dei Verbum* calls "the intimate sense of spiritual realities which [believers] experience" *DV*, 8). This means that for theology to serve the mission of the Church it must be grounded in the *sensus fidelium*, the sense of the faithful, with all their "joys and hopes, griefs and anxieties" (*GS*, 1). And so, I leave with you with words Pope Francis has addressed to theologians: "Do not settle for a desktop theology. Your place for reflection is the frontier... Even good theologians, like good shepherds, have the odour of the people and of the street and, by their reflection, pour oil and wine onto the wounds of mankind. Theology is an expression of a church which is a 'field hospital', which lives her mission of salvation and healing in the world."

Message of AMECEA at the Second Pan-African Congress on Theology, Society and Pastoral Life

Greetings to the organisers of this Second Pan-African Congress on Theology, Society and Pastoral Life on the theme: *Walking Together for a Vital Church in Africa and in the World.* We thank you for coming to the AMECEA region. We feel greatly honoured for your choice of Kenya, the seat of the AMECEA Secretariat, and of the Catholic University of East Africa (CUEA) as the venue for this important event. We will do our best to make you comfortable.

AMECEA, which stands for Association of Member Episcopal Conferences in Eastern Africa, is a Catholic service organisation for the national Episcopal Conferences of the nine countries across Eastern Africa which include Eritrea, Ethiopia, Kenya, Malawi, South Sudan, Sudan, Tanzania, Uganda and Zambia. Djibouti and Somalia are affiliate members. AMECEA is one of the regional Episcopal Conferences that form part of the Symposium of Episcopal Conferences of Africa and Madagascar (SECAM). The mission and mandate of AMECEA is to inspire and empower the family of God for credible witness by promoting unity, justice and solidarity.

AMECEA is well known for its pastoral structure of well-organised Small Christian Communities (SCCs). This structure domesticates theology at the grassroots among the people at the periphery, whose voices are often not heard in major theological discourses. As theologians, it will interest you to learn about the efforts AMECEA has put in place to promote theological discipline at the grassroots (Small Christian Communities). They are efforts which correspond to the vision of the synodal process—to reach out and listen to the forgotten voices. I do believe that together we can achieve this dream. As YOU theologise at a high intellectual level, which is what this congress provides, WE, in the AMECEA region through SCCs will diffuse that theology to meet the needs of the common people on the ground. The SCCs provide a conducive environment and fertile ground for consultation, listening, discernment, participation and taking everybody on board as the Church walks together guided by the Holy Spirit.

We have a *Training Handbook for Facilitators on Strengthening the Growth of Small Christian Communities in Africa.* English and Swahili copies are available at the Paulines Publications Africa Bookshops at an affordable price. E–version and paper back copies in English and Swahili are also available for sale at Amazon online store. We look forward to spending the next 5 days in theological engagement with you. Thank you once again and I wish you a very enlightening and successful Congress.

Rev Fr Anthony Makunde,
Secretary General, AMECEA
19 July 2022

General Introduction

Ikenna U. Okafor

W hat initially began as a preparation for a Synod of Bishops on Synodality gradually, and one would say positively, metamorphosed into a global synodal process involving all the faithful in a journey to develop a new ecclesial lifestyle that will guide the Church of the twenty-first century. This process is not better understood by an intellectual definition, but rather through the mutual and fraternal engagement of Christians with one another and at all levels in charting the course of the Church's mission in contemporary society. The synodal approach which Pope Francis is promoting through this process is one that has awakened a lot of enthusiasm among Catholics all over the world, and one that will redefine our way of being Church. It is an approach that is characterised by deep involvement such as speaking out, listening with interest, and being open to the novelty of the Spirit. Inspired by the Holy Spirit who is the driver of this process, many African theologians and pastoral agents gathered in Nairobi, Kenya from 18th to 23rd July 2022 with their colleagues from all parts of the world to discuss among other things, the theme of synodality. The Congress, which was akin to a family discussion, received the blessings of the Holy Father, Pope Francis, through a video message. It also enjoyed the cordial encouragement of the Secretary General of the Synod of Bishops, His Eminence Mario Cardinal Grech, who acknowledged that "the religious, cultural and philosophical traditions of Africa have rich examples, resources, values and practices that correlate with the concept of synodality."[1] The treasures of the African traditions are precious

---

[1]   Grech, Mario Cardinal, "Message to African Theologians Meeting at Nairobi", 17.

gifts which the continent does not hesitate to present to the universal Church with joy and pride. The essays published in this volume are the academic fruits of that synodal encounter in Nairobi.

African Christians feel happy about the African cultural heritage which are believed to have the potentials of immensely enriching the Church's mission and Christian practice beyond the boundaries of the African continent. And one of those invaluable cultural goods with which Africa is blessed is the traditional practice of reaching communal consensus through a process of participatory dialogue widely known as palaver. This tradition is known to provide many African communities the social climate for maintaining justice, peace and harmony, and for promoting sound ethical choices for human and cosmic flourishing. It is a practice that is so widespread in Africa and known under various designations, like *shikome* among the Sukuma people of Tanzania, baraza/indaba in South Africa, *enkiguena* among the Maasai of East Africa, *ibori uka*[2] among the Igbo of West Africa, etc. In fact, from their earliest contact with missionary evangelisation, the Igbo people designate Christians as *ndi uka* (which literary means the palaver people), and the Church or liturgical assembly is known as *uka*. Sunday is translated as *ubochi uka* and the church building as *ulo uka*, which mean 'the palaver-day' and 'house of palaver' respectively. So intimately was the practice of palaver associated with the identity of the Church from earliest missionary days that it has become imperative to explore deeper into this African cultural heritage and its connection with Christian culture, and to find ways of appropriating its theological and pastoral potentials for the good of the Church in the modern world. The contributions in this volume are committed to such a creative appropriation. The methodology cuts across field researches and analyses, inductive reasonings about the efficacy of palaver, phenomenological hermeneutic of cultural literature,

---

[2]   See Stan Chu Ilo, "Exploring the Possible Contributions" in page 85 below.

biblical exegesis, and case study methods, which give this work a rainbow colour of diversity and richness.

As the entire Church journeys on a pilgrimage with eyes on the Church's missionary horizon, eager to hear what the Holy Spirit is saying to the Church at this moment, theologians and pastoral agents in Africa are confident that the African perspective to synodality will be crucial and beneficial to the life of the Church. The peculiar history of Africa's missionary experience and the inclusion which the practice of synodality compels, combine to make Africa's voices akin to voices from the manger, "because there was no room for them in the inn" (cf. *Lk* 2:7). The inclusion of Africa in the world of the third millennium is the challenge not only of the Church but also of the entire human community. As African scholars grapple with the nuances and lived experiences and challenges of synodality, they only echo the many marginalised voices of the African humanity that are yearning to be heard and acknowledged. The essays are developed from different backgrounds which includes interdisciplinary hermeneutics that are relevant to the theology and pastoral life of the Church in Africa. The diverse perspectives that are arti-culated in this volume reflect the hope of African people and the actions of the Holy Spirit who enkindles that hope and turns it into a transformative energy for the work of building God's kingdom. All these perspectives enrich the synodal conversation on the building of a new culture in the Church, a culture that will become a leaven of inclusive humanism for the whole world.

As we turn the chapter pages, John Okoye leads us through a lived experience of synodality as a diocesan Bishop, highlighting the potentials of a local Church to unlock the evangelical energy of young people, especially when mutual collaborations are unified, visions are clear, goals set, and practical applications are widespread. Paulin Poucouta then recapitulates biblical literature, where we contemplate the ancestral legacy of Abraham whose weaknesses, doubts, turpitude, and family saga, did not overshadow his steadfastness in walking with Yahweh.

Abraham's calling and life are thus presented as a witness of a daily adventure with a God who constantly leads us beyond our familiar borders. Abraham's example is showcased as a lesson for all lay men and women to help them discover the importance of their own calling.

From a Latin American perspective, Emilce Cuda underscores the point that any authentic contemporary theology must be a political theology of the people. That is, a theology that promotes grassroot organisation that challenges the imperialism of liberal capitalism. Such a theology must not be content with an "option for the poor" which stops at giving the poor food handouts without giving them a signature in the decision-making process. The theology of the people is then further explored from an ecclesiological point of view by Stan Chu Ilo who investigates the theological developments on synodality between the Second Vatican Council and Pope Francis and some of the contributions of the reforms of Pope Francis to synodality in the Church. He introduces the African palaver as a model for participatory dialogue that could contribute to promoting consensus-building and inclusiveness in the Roman Catholic Church. Josée Ngalula, on her part, draws insight from African social anthropology which is expressed in the spirituality of Ubuntu. She attributes the success of African ecclesiology (both in theory and practice) to this spirituality of communion which underlies the structure of Small Christian Communities (SCC), where mutual respect and promotion of the human dignity of the other are primarily cultivated.

In chapter six, Ikenna Okafor steers the conversation into a discourse in interdisciplinary terrain which x-rays the postcolonial narrative of Chinua Achebe in his *Arrow of God*, a novel that articulates the intimate bond between the priesthood and the religion as well as the intricate web of interdependency between the deity, the priest, and the people in any religion. Okafor's interdisciplinary hermeneutic warns of the danger posed by clericalism in obscuring the culture of "walking together" and thereby undermining the mission of the Church. It also argues for the relevance of African literatures as important sources of theological deposits and loci of divine inspiration that are hitherto insufficiently explored by academic theology in Africa.

In chapter seven, Nicholaus Segeja argues for how the involvement of the laity in doing theology can promote synodality for new evangelisation, especially in Africa. Segeja contends that the articulation of the social dimension of ecclesial synodality sub-sisting in the practice of reverential dialogue is capable of activating a process of conversion toward a renewed way of evangelisation in Africa. And this can better be achieved if the laity becomes more involved in the production of theological knowledge. He proposes that an orientation and focus in theology which accommodates the secular character of the laity should be encouraged, especially in relation to some key areas of the apostolate in the life of the Church, like education, health care and information technology.

In chapter eight, Raymond Aina raised questions and made recommendations about how to deal with contested moral issues. According to Aina, the contestations which centre on the tensions between sin and conscience—between objective good and lesser evil arguments; between pragmatism (what works) and normativity (what's given); or the hermeneutical clash on given doctrinal positions–concern important moral, social, and political decisions. In exploring the tensions, it is important to know how to navigate our way together through an atmosphere of toxic emotions when we passionately disagree on moral grounds. Two case studies involving the children of an orphanage and students of a major seminary reveal how important it is to all respondents to identify with a Church of communion that promotes equal opportunities and practices accompaniment. Aina's study is followed by an experiment carried out in the parish of Sainte-Trinité in the archdiocese of Kinshasa (DR Congo) which centres on the significance of the role of the laity in active evangelisation. In line with the decolonisation of theological knowledge and the co-construction of knowledge in the sense of a *pastorale d'engendrement*, Ignace Ndongala reports how a synodal shift from a monological authority of interpretation of the Word of God to a polyphonic praxis in homiletics in tune with the culture of palaver and fraternal dialogue associated with a Church–Family of God has yielded good results at the grassroot level of the Basic Christian Communities.

Finally, Francis Appiah-Kubi appreciates the Synod on Synodality as a *Kairos moment of grace* for the Church in Africa to critically re-examine herself and her internal mechanisms. He identifies five key lessons which the African Church can draw from the process. These include the need for good formation of agents of evangelisation; rethinking the hierarchical ministry to involve active sacramental participation of the laity; promoting vocation and responsibility of lay faithful; encouraging a synodal ecumenical learning process; and rejecting all ideologies of exclusion, like ethnicism or racism while affirming unity in diversity in the Church–Family of God. What is not clear, however, is the level of sacramental participation that will satisfy the desires of those who believe that the laity are not sufficiently included in the pastoral ministry of the Church. Herein lies one of the major challenges of the synodal process. But we hope that this is a challenge that can be turned into an opportunity for progress in the Church.

The humble contributions of the African Church which are reflected in this volume surely do not exhaust the perspectives from the numerous African voices that are engaged with this theme. But even without pretensions of offering a silver bullet against the problems associated with synodality, this work will help seminarians, theologians, and pastoral agents in the work of evangelisation in Africa. Its findings and recommendations will remain an important driver of theological and pastoral debates on the path to achieving a better and more inclusive approach in the ecclesial pilgrimage of the People of God in our time. It is expected to animate the praxis of synodality in Africa with vision and orientation in many levels.

CHAPTER 1

Proclaiming the Word of God to Young People in a Synodal African Church

†John Okoye

E xperience, we hear, is the best teacher. Therefore, I prefer to adopt a methodology here that is typical of Wisdom Literature, which is autobiographical narrative. It consists in using one's personal life experiences to teach others. Hence, my experiences as a teacher of Scripture to young candidates to the priesthood and as a diocesan Bishop is the background to the thoughts in this work. It reflects on what we have done and what we are doing, our challenges and a proposal on what I think should be done to make for effective proclamation of the word of God to young people in a synodal African Church. My reflection in this brings together a number of interesting elements which includes the following:

1) the proclamation of the Word of God,

2) young people in Africa,

3) the Church in Africa, and

4) synodality.

I will begin by clarifying the important keywords contained in the title of this chapter.

Explication of Concepts

A brief examination of some keywords that are central to the discussion at hand is important to facilitate the understanding of my reflection, and to situate it within a specific context. First is "proclamation of the Word of God," classically known as the *Kerygma*. This consists in announcing the Good News of Jesus Christ. The proclamation of the Word of God is the principal task of the Church in her mission of evangelisation. In the context of our reflection, proclamation of the Word of God could take place in the form of teaching in classrooms, catechising in pastoral settings, preparation for participation in the celebration of the sacraments, homilies during public worship, and continuing formation programmes of the faithful.

The second keyword is "young people". It is difficult to define those who fall into this class because it is a fluid category.[1] However, in the present discussion, young people are considered to be those who are in the period of transition from the dependence of childhood to the independence of adulthood. Hence, the term "young people" does not necessarily refer to a group of people of a particular age bracket, but a group of people who are in this period of transition from the dependence of childhood to the independence of adulthood and yet, are aware of the interdependence that exists between them as Christians.

Next is the phrase "African Church." One may be tempted to think that the use of the terminology "African Church" connotes a different Church for or in Africa. No, for there is only one Church of Jesus Christ that "subsists in the Catholic Church, which is governed by the successor of Peter and by the bishops in communion with him."[2] Therefore, when I say, "the African

---

[1]   The United Nations, for example, defines a young person (a youth) as one between the ages of 15 and 24. The Nigerian Youth Policy of 2009 defined youth to be people who fall within the age bracket of 18 and 35. In Brazil, youth refer to people from 15 to 29 years.

[2]   Second Vatican Council, *Lumen Gentium*, no. 8.

Church," I mean the one Church of Jesus Christ which exists in the African soil and as it is lived by the people in the continent.

Finally, we have "a synodal Church." The words "synodal" and "synodality" are derivations from the word synod. "Since the first centuries, the word "synod" has been applied, with a specific meaning, to the ecclesial assemblies convoked on various levels (diocesan, provincial, regional, patriarchal or universal) to discern, by the light of the Word of God and listening to the Holy Spirit, the doctrinal, liturgical, canonical and pastoral questions that arise as time goes by."[3] Usually, synods played the role of advising Bishops or the Popes on how to govern the Church. Sometimes, they are convoked to discuss and proffer solutions to controversial issues in the Church. Whereas a synod refers to an assembly of the People of God, particularly their leaders and representatives, convoked for the purpose of performing the consultative role described above, synodality denotes a process of living and doing things as a Church which lays emphasis on the participation, collaboration, and journeying together of all the people concerned or at least their representatives in the process of discernment and decision making.

While synods, synodal and synodality are not new in the Church, there is, however, a new and strong emphasis that the Holy Father, Pope Francis, has introduced into synodality in the Church of today. The novelty consists in the Pope's declaration that the Church is by its nature synodal, that synodality "is an essential dimension of the Church," and that "it is precisely this path of synodality which God expects of the Church of the third millennium."[4] Saint Pope Paul VI instituted the Synod of Bishops to be a permanent feature of the Church, and Pope Francis has taken it further to this point where the People of God are made to see synodality as essential to the Church's life and mission.

---

[3] International Theological Commission, *Synodality in the Life and Mission of the Church*, no. 4.

[4] International Theological Commission, *Synodality in the Life and Mission of the Church*, no. 1.

Synodality aims at ensuring that the voices, opinions, views, and thoughts of different persons from the various segments of the community of believers (priests, religious and lay faithful) are heard, particularly as it pertains to the way things are and how they would like things to be. In the synodal Church, everybody is part of the discussion and the voice of everyone counts. Synodality emphasises mutual listening, talking and sharing of ideas, experiences, faith, love and hope. It is an exercise in collaboration, communion, sharing, mutual listening and discernment. The young people in Africa form the primary focus of our presentation as it pertains to how the word of God is proclaimed to them and with them as participants and collaborators in the process.

Lessons from my Teaching Experience and its Relevance for the Proclamation of the Word of God in a Synodal African Church

My experiences as a seminary formator and a teacher of Sacred Scripture to young candidates to the priesthood, as well as my pastoral experiences as a diocesan Bishop have given me ample opportunities of active involvement in the proclamation of the Word of God to young people. Those experiences contain in them important lessons for the Church in Africa.

The Word of God and the Existential Reality of Young People

For about 27 years I taught Wisdom Literature in various seminaries. This academic function exposed me to the challenges which our young people face in understanding the Sacred Scripture. I realised that one of the greatest challenges which young people face in their effort to understand the Sacred Scripture is the hurdle created by language, culture and worldview. As a result, I through the years developed various strategies of assisting them to overcome some of these difficulties. As already mentioned, knowledge of the Bible presupposes knowledge of the original languages in which the Bible was written; hence, knowledge of Ancient Hebrew, Greek and Aramaic. Young students, especially of African extraction, usually find these languages difficult to master, not simply because of the difficulty of mastery of a foreign language, but because some of the ideas, words and expression belong to specific socio-cultural and religious contexts which are, sometimes, alien to the African culture and understanding.

In an attempt to find a solution to the linguistic difficulty, I discovered that translating the ideas behind a particular word to the traditional language of the students has often led to a better understanding and appreciation of the Bible. Sometimes, they are encouraged to find folklores, adages and proverbs from their specific cultural backgrounds to explain the same biblical concepts without, however, downplaying or removing its original biblical meaning and message. Once a student grasps the idea behind a particular concept in their own traditional language and from their own cultural worldview, the biblical text becomes easier to understand and interpret. This approach is important for African young people for at least two reasons: first, it helps in making the biblical message easily conceivable from the context of their cultural and existential worldview. Thus, they have a better appreciation of the biblical message and can translate it to their personal lives. Second, the methodology is synodal – it is participative, interactive and communal. They get involved in the process of developing and understanding biblical imageries. It teaches us that proclaiming the Word of God does not have to be from the pulpit. It requires close and interpersonal contact. There is no doubt that young people have the capacity and the desire to learn, but sometimes, we lack the methodology and capacity to teach them.

Collaboration, Participation, and Communion

Another experience which has helped me immensely in the work of evangelisation, not only of young people but also of the entire diocese is the involvement of the entire People of God in the task of shaping the life of the diocese. By divine providence, I was appointed the pioneer Bishop of our diocese. Being a new diocese, my first responsibility was to set up a road map for the diocese by putting in place a pastoral initiative called "Future Search Conference." This was basically a forum for brainstorming and creative dialogue that sought to encourage people to actualise their capacity to transform ideas into goal-oriented actions. The meeting was task-focused, bringing together a number of people from different walks of life to engage in open-minded dialogue and creative thinking. The Conference had in attendance priests, religious, lay faithful from all corners of the diocese, professionals, artisans, young and old alike. The goal was simple: to determine and set a road map for the diocese. A committee made of people from various walks of life was charged with the task of organising and moderating the Conference.

One of the distinguishing features of this initiative is the emphasis on diverse representation and equal participation. In order to ensure comprehensive representation, participants were drawn from every section and organ of the diocese. Particular attention was given to the participation of young people in the whole exercise. Throughout the one-week exercise, the Bishop, just like every other person was allowed 15 minutes of talk. The Conference allowed everyone equal opportunity to express his/her expectations from the new diocese, the problems that needed to be addressed, and the direction the diocese was to go. At the end of this exercise, the committee's report proposed two major projects for the diocese, namely, grassroots evangelisation through catechesis, and economic self-reliance. These two projects proposed by the committee constituted the operative road map of our diocese.

The lessons drawn from that Future Search Conference are considered relevant for the topic of our discussion here. First, the Church in Africa, in order to achieve her mission of evangelisation, has to be synodal in character. She has to involve the People of God in the life of the Church. Second, no one has monopoly of the Holy Spirit. The more synodal the African Church is, the more she is open to the voice of the Spirit. Third, when the People of God in Africa feel that they are part of the life of the Church, they become co-actors and not mere spectators. Finally, proclaiming the Word of God to our people especially young people requires their active involvement and participation. This last point ushers me into the next experience I would like to share with you.

The People of God as Protagonists of Evangelisation

My experience as the first Bishop of a new diocese gave me a clearer understanding of the need to make the whole People of God participants and not spectators in the work of evangelisation. When it was clear that our road map was evangelisation through catechesis, it took us a long process of discernment to figure out how to go about it. It dawned on us that the traditional practice of Sunday evening instructions could not yield the desired fruit, mainly because it always recorded poor attendance. In the wake of 2015, we were able to formulate a diocesan program of catechesis known as "Diocese, Evangelise Yourself!" It turned out to be a highly effective and efficient system of catechesis that truly reflects synodality. Permit me to explain how it works.

Each year, the Bishop proposes a common theme for catechesis throughout the diocese. For example, we have such themes as *Worshipping God in Spirit and Truth; Repent and believe the Gospel* etc. Some years we had to combine themes. For example, in the year 2017 the choice of the diocese to reflect on the Holy Spirit was combined with the decision of the Church in Nigeria to dedicate the year to the Blessed Virgin Mary. Thus, we chose as our theme of catechesis: *To the Holy Spirit in Union with Mary.* In 2019 we had to combine the theme of strengthening our relationship with God in prayer with that of the celebration of the year of St Joseph.

The process of evangelisation takes the following steps:

i) The topic is given to three different experts to study. One is expected to delineate the theological and biblical import of the topic; the second focuses on how reflection on the topic could help in the pastoral and liturgical needs of the diocese, as well as how the People of God could live out the fruits of the reflection in their day-to-day Christian life; the third reflects on how the topic could solve specific pastoral problems in the diocese.

ii) All priests and religious working in the diocese gather on a stipulated date for the lecture to be delivered by the experts charged with the task of studying the selected theme in advance.

iii) After a week of individual reflections, the priests and religious gather once again to share the ideas they got from the lectures. They further discuss the topic and agree on the various points that will be taught in all parishes of the diocese.

iv) On a specific day, at a specific time, all the priests of the diocese are sent to the different parishes, each assigned a parish different from his place of apostolate, to share with the parishioners what they learnt from the deliberations and reflections on the selected theme. The message will be the same for all the parishes. Usually, the various organs of the parish (Catholic Men Organisation, CMO; Catholic Women Organisation, CWO; and Catholic Youths of Nigeria, CYON) have their separate days of catechesis. The priest exposes the topic, answers their questions and ministers to them with the sacraments.

v) Subsequently, each statutory body in the parish – CMO, CWO, CYON – organises a meeting under the guidance of their parish priest to deliberate on how their reflection on the theme and the message they received could address their specific existential situations. They take the catechesis to the grassroots.

vi) This process is repeated in three cycles of teaching by the various experts, and the subsequent catechesis at the grass-root. It lasts all-year round. The entire process – lecture on the selected theme, reflection by the priests, sending the priests to different parishes to engage the statutory bodies in grassroots catechesis and deliberations by the people on how to apply the fruits of their reflection to specific circumstances – all these are repeated in three cycles of teaching by the different experts designated to study the selected theme for the liturgical year.

vii) Before the end of the liturgical year, a day is set aside for the solemn celebration of the close of catechetical year. On this day, the whole diocese gathers to reflect on and assess the fruit of the catechetical year, as well as declare the theme for the next liturgical year.

This method of evangelisation has eloquent lessons for us on synodality. In the first place, evangelisation is more effective when the lay faithful do not sit on the sidelines as spectators but rather see themselves as engaged actors and co-operators with the clergy in the task of the dissemination of the good news. In this whole process, the work of evangelisation is not seen as the work of the Bishop. The entire People of God (priests, religious, lay faithful) are actively involved. The success of the entire programme hinges on collaboration and active participation. Both the clergy and the lay faithful seek to understand the message of the selected theme together. The search for understanding and the task of applying the message to lived experiences become shared responsibilities of both the clergy and the lay faithful. The involvement of young people in the whole exercise is quite encouraging. On days slated for the catechesis of youths, they often come out in large numbers when reflections and messages drawn from the process are tailored to suit their situation in life. This methodology is at the same time truly African and biblical. It "emphasises care for others, solidarity, warmth in human relationships, acceptance, dialogue and trust."[5]

Challenges to Proclaiming the Word of God to Young People in a Synodal African Church

1. Influence of the Traditional Religion

One of the disturbing trends we are witnessing in African Christianity today is the increasing drift of the youths towards traditional religion beliefs and practices. What started as religious syncretism is fast turning into full scale return to paganism. There seems to be two main causes of this resurgent attraction to African Traditional Religion (ATR): first is the unfounded fear of deities. Some youths have been brainwashed by cultural revivalists into believing that pre-Christian traditional practices form part of their culture, and that failure to adhere to those practices will bring deadly consequences. Secondly, so many youths are easily exasperated by Christian understanding of faith, resignation to divine will and patient endurance of trials and difficulties as a sign of participation in the cross of Christ. They want what works here and now. The African Traditional Religion conceives of its deities from a pragmatic/utilitarian perspective. They are made to believe that the gods of traditional religion will immediately solve all their existential problems.

---

5   John Paul II, *Ecclesia in Africa*, no. 63.

2. *Socio-Political and Economic Factors*

Another difficulty in reception of the Word of God by the youths is that majority of the youths have lost faith in the socio-political order. Unfortunately, this loss of faith extends to different forms of authority including the authority of the Church. Many are losing faith and going back to paganism. This systemic collapse and the consequent loss of hope on the part of the youths have contributed to the craze for "prosperity gospel" which seeks to give unrealistic hope to the youth. Selective scriptural interpretations aimed at making the Word of God attractive to the youth often become the order of the day. In the face of such aberrations, it becomes harder to convince them on the right interpretation and understanding of the Word of God.

3. *Influence of the Media*

The anti-clericalism of some parts of the Western world as well as antipathy to the Church and God is subtly influencing young Africans via social media. Hence, some of the things that were regarded as taboos are now overlooked or treated as part of everyday life that raises no eyebrows: attacks on the clergy; gross immorality, criminality, fraud and all sorts of indecency.

Listening to Young People and Hearing with them the Word of God Anew in a Synodal Church: The Way Forward

Here, we wish to make some observations about possible steps to take in order to effectively proclaim the Word of God to young people in the Church in Africa in a synodal way.

1. Encounter:

Every meaningful listening begins with a genuine encounter. As Pope Francis has constantly demanded, ours today must be a ministry of encounter: going out in search of the sheep that has gone astray. The era of remaining in the Church waiting for the youths is over; the Church must find them where they are, speak the language they understand, understand and appreciate their many challenges, give them hope by genuine empathy and convince them that we care.

The more I interact with youths in my pastoral visits as a Bishop, in classroom as a biblical lecturer, in the course of my pastoral activities, it dawns on me that the Church must creatively rethink our youth apostolate.

Nevertheless, there are two extremes to be avoided:

i) Allowing the youth apostolate to degenerate into another social jamboree without biblical and theological depth, all in the name of following the youth at their pace and meeting them where they are;

ii) Remaining insensitive to the new vision, new approach the youths are yearning for. The Church needs to understand and encourage the youths as they seek for a new approach, since they are no longer satisfied with doing things the old way. Far from stifling their enthusiasm, the Church must find creative ways to accompany them and take advantage of their zeal and innovative spirit.

2. Strategies:

Some strategies that can be adopted in leading the youth to a deeper knowledge of the Word of God may include:

i) Educating them on the many websites where they can download different versions of the scripture and other sites where they can freely and easily have access to daily reflections on the Word. In this age of social media and internet, the Church must not shy away from meeting the youths at this all-important public forum of the 21st century.

ii) Promoting diverse manners of sharing the Word: drama, quiz, outreach etc.

iii) Prayer and accompaniment: grooming the youths in understanding the indispensable role of prayer for any authentic Christian engagement is absolutely essential. Prayer remains the most crucial pathway towards understanding the mysteries of God hidden in the Scripture. Youths need committed pastors who they will look up to as a role model. This was the pastoral style of John Paul II when he was the chaplain of undergraduate students. George Weigel, his biographer, comments: "Accompaniment was a way of walking with young adults, of helping them unveil their humanity by living through their problems with them. Just like God accompanied man even unto death, the Cross is the final justification of pastoral accompaniment."

3. Being Sensitive to Change:

The *Vademecum* for the Synod on Synodality notes that "Synodality entails receptivity to change, formation, and ongoing learning. How does our Church community form people to be more capable of 'walking together', listening to one another, participating in mission, and engaging in dialogue? What formation is offered to foster discernment and the exercise of authority in a synodal way?"[6] In view of this, the priests who are the ministers or the proclaimers of the Word need to be

---

[6] Secretary General of the Synod of Bishops, *Vademecum for the Synod on Synodality, Official Handbook for Listening and Discernment in Local Churches* (Vatican City: Libreria Editrice Vaticana, 2021), no. 10.

sensitive to the changing landscape of the work of evangelisation. The emphasis on synodality calls for more participation of the lay faithful in the life of the Church. They need to be trained to become agents of the Good News. Seminars and ongoing formation need to be organised for the lay faithful, especially the youths to form them and provide them with the correct and orthodox interpretation of the Word of God so that they, in turn can become agents of the Good News to reach as many as possible. The Church in Africa must learn to listen to the young, to speak to authority on their behalf, to fight for their interests in society especially in a world where the political elites are stealing their future. The Church can no longer afford to remain indifferent; when the young understand that the Church is looking out for her best interests in areas that pinch them most materially, only then would they believe that the teachings of the Church are also for their best interest – spiritual interest.

4. Re-education:

Re-education is required in order to realise the desire of Pope Francis about synodality. The clergy, the religious and the lay faithful need to be re-educated in order to play their roles effectively in a synodal Church.[7] Through re-education, people would develop more capacity for listening, collaboration and sharing. The clergy will understand ministry differently and the laity will be empowered for collaboration and communion. In all, care must be taken to ensure that synodality is not applied as "a move toward a more democratic or parliamentary way of governing the Church and teaching doctrine."[8] This means that synodality is open to possible misunderstanding and misinterpretations and extra care should be taken to guard against it. Synodality does

---

[7]   For the need for re-education see Elochukwu E. Uzukwu, *A Listening Church: Autonomy and Communion in African Churches*, (Maryknoll, New York: Orbis Books, 1996), 98.

[8]   This is one of the fears of critics concerning synodality as expressed in "What is Synodality?", http://secretariat.synod.va.

not mean that the experience, opinion, and view of the people determines the truth of faith. It does not compromise but rather promotes the authority of divine revelation through the Scripture and tradition, and the Magisterium.

Conclusion

The future of the Church in Africa lies very much on the youth, and it is expected that they would rise up to the challenge if only they are formed well in the Word of God. In the light of the signs of the times, this formation will yield the best results if it is carried out in the context of a synodal Church guided by the process of synodality. Synodality challenges everybody in the Church to let go of some of the ways of the past and present to embrace a new way of evangelisation where mutual listening, solidarity, collaboration, participation, togetherness and sharing is the order of discernment and decision-making. This would be done without compromising the place and authorities of divine revelation and the Magisterium. By building on existing elements and practices of synodality in the African Church and creatively responding to the demands of new challenges, the way to the future filled with hope will be fashioned. When the teeming population of young people in Africa get transformed from being observers to agents of evangelisation, the African Church would indeed become the expected hope of the universal Church in the third millennium.

CHAPTER 2

Abraham, the Pilgrim:
Three Paths for a Church on the Move

Paulin Poucouta

The central question for us as God's people and as Church in Africa is namely, "how can we walk together in the construction of a living and life-giving Church?" This important question is at the heart of the synodal dynamic to which Pope Francis has invited the universal Church. Indeed, the XVI Ordinary General Assembly of the Synod of Bishops, which will be held in Rome in October 2023/24, will have as its theme "For a synodal Church: communion, participation and mission."

Already, the Second Vatican Council reminded us: the Church is communion. She is a people-on-the-go. The Word of God presents the Church to us as a community of believers with a vocation to live and journey together, to walk in unison, as the etymology of the Greek name *sun-odos* suggests.[1] In order to reawaken this major intuition of Vatican II, Pope Francis invited all Christians on the path of synodality.

This synodal march is rooted in the paradigmatic experience of the great pilgrims who populate biblical history, and particularly Abraham, the Father of Believers. At one of the important turning points in its history, probably during the Persian period, the sons of Israel were tempted to unite themselves and get out

---

[1]   Yves-Marie Blanchard, "Synode et Synodalité dans le Nouveau Testament", *Spiritus 241* (2021), 409-421.

of the way. So, they were invited to rediscover in Abraham a unifying and founding figure of the future. And this because he accepted the call to move to a strange land when God asked him to: "leave, go." This transhumance is a common march, caught up in the dynamic of covenant. This was a covenant founded on openness and trusting fidelity to the unexpected that comes from God. It is a covenant that leads us to relativise our roots to attach ourselves to a people "as countless as the stars of the sky and the sands of the seashore" (*Gn* 22:17).

The figure of Abraham announces that of Jesus and the Apostles. It suggests to the Church of Africa many avenues in its synodal adventure. In this chapter, I will focus on three aspects because they continue and consolidate the messages of both the Synodal Exhortation *Africae Munus* and the Kampala document, namely: listening, creative solidarity, and the march for life.

Abraham, The Ancestor of Ancestors

The Founding Ancestor

Abraham is venerated by the three monotheistic religions as a founding ancestor. For the Hebrews, he is the Father, for the Muslims, the First of Believers, the Friend of God and for Christians, the Father of Believers. But, as in African traditions, the face of the founding ancestor retains a certain mystery, linked to his aura. It is difficult to pin down. Many questions are raised around this important biblical figure (Abraham Ségal, 1995).

According to *Gn* 11-25, Abraham was part of a nomadic people of Semitic origin.[2] He enters into biblical history as belonging to the clan of the Terachites which would have been established in the vicinity of Ur in Chaldea, at the beginning of the 2nd millennium, around 1850, in the Middle Bronze Age. At the time

---

[2]   Bertrand Lafont, "30 idées reçues sur la Bible", *Le Monde de la Bible*, 207 (2013).

of Hammurabi, Abram, son of Terach, emigrated with his family to the north of Mesopotamia. After a stay in Harran (north of the Euphrates, in upper Mesopotamia), he went to Canaan, to Hebron in southern Palestine. It is there that he concludes a covenant with Elohim, an essentially Semitic divinity. He takes the name of Abraham, "Father of Nations." Until the 1960s, it was in this very vast territory that the majority of biblical scholars and historians of the ancient Near East located the setting of Abraham and his tribe, in relation to the major population movements attested by Mesopotamian sources.

For scholars, such as the American William F. Albright or the Frenchman Roland de Vaux, this saga seemed all the more historically plausible since, on the whole, the pastoral life of the patriarchs of the Bible resembled that of the Bedouins of the Near East, as it was still unfolding before their eyes. Moreover, clear references to large Mesopotamian sites like Ur or Harrân seemed to correspond to the results of excavations undertaken from the beginning of the 20th century in the Mesopotamian part of the Fertile Crescent.

However, today, archaeologists and historians question these assumptions. Researchers now place the founding history of Israel, as related by the Hexateuch, as that of all the patriarchs, in the Persian period. J. L. Ska summarises the situation as follows:

> (…) For these authors, current research on the history of Israel is faced with a double insurmountable gap. First of all, it is impossible to reconcile the way in which the biblical books present to us the history of Israel, on the one hand, and the history of Palestine which a historian tries to reconstruct today on the basis documents at his disposal, on the other. Secondly, and this is in fact a corollary of our first point, a considerable gap separates the biblical writings which all or almost all come from the post-exilic period, the Persian or Hellenistic period, and the pre-exilic Israel of which these books speak to us.[3]

---

[3] Jean Louis Ska, "L'histoire d'Israël", ACFEB, *Comment la Bible saisit-elle l'histoire ?* (Paris: Cerf, 2007), 19.

The Unifying Ancestor

In this new perspective, the story of Abraham, as reported in the book of Genesis, would have been written between the 7th and 5th centuries BC. Admittedly, as Römer points out, the traditions that underlie it probably came into being long before, for example during the monarchical period.[4] The final editors combined accounts from various sources gathered by multiple editors and traditions.

Would Abraham then be a mythical figure, constructed from scratch, as some critics suggest? In our opinion, in a context of "oralness", the strength of oral tradition and memory should not be overlooked. Along with scholars like J. Briend and Römer, we believe that Abraham is a founding hero. Israel has kept a vivid memory of it. But it is not possible to have the exact picture. The different traditions have tried to paint his portrait, the size of his stature and the place he occupies in the memory of the people.

But, as in our African traditions, there are several founding ancestors. And when families and villages want to federate and project themselves together towards a more solid future, one of the founding ancestors takes precedence over the others, because of his unifying and mobilising qualities which have strongly captured the imagination.

Thus, it is very likely that there existed in Israel several founding patriarchs. We can even think with Römer that the figure of Jacob, which comes from the traditions of the North, is prior to that of Abraham, from the tradition of the South.[5] Abraham is certainly less quoted than Jacob, but the Judean tradition makes him the first patriarch. Why?

---

4   Thomas Römer, "D'Abraham à la conquête", *Recherches de Science Religieuse*, 103/1 (2015), 41.

5   Thomas Römer, "D'Abraham à la conquête" *Recherches de Science Religieuse*, 103/1 (2015), 42-48.

In the Persian period, once the post-exilic euphoria was over, the return to the country proves to be more difficult than expected. Stuck in the management of daily life, in the tensions, the problems of the division of goods, the people struggled for a new beginning. Dreams of greatness and exclusion of other peoples continued to haunt them. In order to give life to the people and stir in them the momentum for a new beginning, the Lord raises up three characters from Babylon: Zorobabel, one of the last descendants of the Jewish kings, the priest and scribe Esdras, as well as Nehemiah, a Jew from the court of the Persian king appointed governor of Judea. But this is not enough. It needed a federating patriarchal figure, a real founding ancestor who summons the image of a new movement; a pilgrimage.

Thus, the journey of the patriarch from his distant Chaldea, with the Sumerian pantheon comprising gods of the world, astral deities, gods of nature, and national gods, challenges Israel in its faith. This leads this great patriarch to rediscover the true face of God and make the leap from monolatry to monotheism, from the God of the nation to the Lord of all peoples.[6] The figure of Abraham also raises questions about God's project: divine election is not a privilege, but a mission at the heart of the world, under the sign of service and no longer of power, as demonstrated in the image of the servants of Deutero-Isaiah. The sacrifice of Isaac on Mount Moriah confirms the need to rebuild the temple of Jerusalem, the sacrificial place par excellence (*Gn* 22:1f). Nevertheless, with Abraham, the founding experience of Israel is not that of a sacred place, but that of a God who meets a person and a people and sets them on the march towards utopia.

In sum, for post-exilic Israel and that of all times, the remodeled and magnified figure of Abraham becomes the paradigm of a foundation or a refoundation, of an opening to the possibility of a new beginning, of another adventure with God into the unknown.

---

6   André Lemaire, *Naissance du monothéisme,* (Paris: Bayard, 2003).

Refoundation, As Transhumance

Abraham, The Wandering Aramaic

The refounding experience must be perceived and lived as a transhumance. Indeed, the experience of Abraham is that of a traveller, a pilgrim. Thus, according to the book of Deuteronomy, the offering of the first fruits of the harvest to the Lord was accompanied by a solemn profession of faith: "My father was a refugee Aramean who went down to Egypt with a small household and lived there as a resident alien" (*Dt* 26:5).

While taking into account the reservations of critics on the historicity of this origin and the epic genre used by hagiographers, it is possible to think that the ritual formula "My father was a refugee Aramean" is the affirmation of the historicity of Israel's migratory dynamic. It is a question of understanding and entering into the human and spiritual adventure of this chosen one of God and father of believers. With Abraham, biblical history and spirituality are part of an itinerant perspective, roaming both geographically and spiritually.

This insistence on the nomadism of the patriarch is certainly linked to the socio-economic experience of the people which strongly marks this memory. In the antagonism between the agricultural world and the pastoral world, pastoral life is idealised. The farmer Cain kills his brother Abel, the shepherd, the just (*Gn* 4:4; *Heb* 11:4). The God of Israel is often presented as the pastor of his people. The socio-political and religious leaders of the people are invited to behave like pastors, like David, the ideal and idealised king.

Religiously and ethically, nomadism embodies strict fidelity to God. This is why the Rechabites, the brother-prophets, by settling in the desert and adopting the lifestyle of the environment, intend to denounce the vices of the society that the Hebrews were in the process of building by settling in Canaan. They challenge the idolatry, gentrification, inequalities and power shifts associated with this way of life. They want to be witnesses of fidelity to Yahwism and its demands.

However, the prophet Hosea, also rooted in the spirituality of the desert, will propose the challenge of living the radicality of fidelity to God in the heart of Canaan. The experience of Hosea shows that it is not nomadism in itself that allows refoundation. It is adherence to God, following a call, a departure, a rupture and fidelity.

Abraham, A Patriarch Who Listens

Apart from the Bible, it is the human person who, in various ways, seeks his God. In the biblical tradition, it is God who is in search of the human person; seeking for humans to listen and to respond to the One who calls. Abraham is a good example of that right way of listening, responding and following God.

This is how the biblical story of the patriarch begins abruptly with a call, and a marching order: "The Lord said to Abram: Go forth from your land, your relatives, and from your father's house to a land that I will show you" (*Gn* 12:1). Without flinching, Abraham leaves. He agrees to leave his ties, to renounce his certainties and his securities and pursue this adventure; a project which was not his own choosing, but that of God:

> Abram went as the Lord directed him, and Lot went with him. Abram was seventy-five years old when he left Haran. Abram took his wife Sarai, his brother's son Lot, all the possessions that they had accumulated, and the persons they had acquired in Haran, and they set out for the land of Canaan (*Gn* 12:4-5).

Using the light of statistics, Jean-Michel Poirier judiciously points out that "48 of the 121 occurrences of the verb to go in Genesis appear in the cycle of Abraham (40 percent) and 29 of the 36 occurrences of the verb 'to go out' (i.e. 80 percent) are in these same chapters."[7] However, in the Bible, the verbs "to go" and "to leave" are linked to mission.

This is indeed the case here. Abraham leaves to give life, to become a father. His departure is the event, the place of a genealogical refoundation, not from the land or the ethnic group, but from a call, a vocation. Thus, at the call of God, Abraham leaves the land of his ancestors to find new roots in unexpected pathways and perspectives. The entire life of the patriarch will henceforth unfold under the sign of divine initiative.

It is often said that to leave is to die, however, to leave with God is to allow oneself to be transfigured by him. So, Abraham must strip himself of his name. He will no longer be called Abram (the Father is exalted), but Abraham (the Father of the multitudes), depending on the context, even if it is only a dialectal variant. We know the importance of names in the Eastern and African tradition. It designates the person themself. Changing your name is like a kind of dispossession to belong to someone else. It is also the sign of a new existence.

This new walk is linked to a blessing for Abraham and for the whole earth. Blessings are not a reward for leaving. However, there are no blessings if one does not leave, if one does not come out of oneself, of one's home; if we do not enter into God's plan.

We understand that the biblical experience of migration finds a broad echo in the festivals of pilgrimage where three important moments in the history of Israel are commemorated: Passover (pesah), the Exodus from Egypt (pesah); Pentecost the covenant and the gift of the Law (shavôot); and the walk in the desert (sûkkôt). Migration is celebrated there as a quest and encounter with God.

Thus, Abraham initiates the network of walkers who follow God as believers. Following the example of their founding

---

[7]   Jean-Michel Poirier, "De campement en campement", Aguilar Chiu, José Enrique; O'Mahony, Kieran J.; Roger, Maurice, eds., *Bible et Terre Sainte*, (New York/Bern/Berlin/ Bruxelles/Frankfurt am Main, Oxford, Wien, 2018), 31.

ancestor, these pilgrims can bring about the blessing of the whole earth, change the deserts into springs (cf. *Ps* 84:6-8). For this, they reject any form of fatalism. They are always ready to get going again, as is summed up so well by J. -M. Poirier:

> The responsibility of Abraham and his descendants according to the flesh as well as according to the spirit is immense: God wanted to save a humanity running towards its perdition by the choice of a few walkers in the faith. Sometimes affected by discouragement, doubt or quite simply fatigue, also held back by the fear of the unknown that any undecided future dispenses, they may be tempted to sit down, or even worse still, to look back to a past idealised (…). Biblical faith warns them against such deadly decisions.[8]

Entering into a Covenant

The Father of Many

By adhering to God's call, Abraham accepts to enter into a covenant with this Other who speaks to him. This is mentioned twice. In Genesis 15, the faith of our ancestor is put to the test. Promises are slow to be fulfilled. They are then renewed and sealed by a covenant: "On that day the Lord made a covenant with Abram, saying: To your descendants I give this land" (*Gn* 15:18).

According to an old oriental rite (cf. *Jer* 34:18), the contracting parties passed between the bloody flesh and called upon them the lot done to the beasts if they transgressed their commitments. The fire symbolised the presence and passage of God. A way of showing the seriousness of the covenant that God sealed with Abraham and, through him, with all the people.

Indeed, the covenant, *Berit* in Hebrew, is the key experience that will summarise the biblical history of salvation. The particularity of Israel is not its political, military or even scientific

---

8   Jean-Michel Poirier, "De campement en campement", 44.

strength, but the particular relationship with its God who has made a covenant with it. With Israel, God chooses a pilot people who will show all humans the type of relationship that God wants to establish with them. As in covenants between peoples, the covenant includes clauses. It includes a charter, a set of commandments and institutions that testify to this pact.

By calling him, God promises to make Abraham a "great nation." (*Gn* 12:2) The covenant no longer makes him the chief of a clan or a tribe, but the Father of a multitude. By tying the fortunes of the other patriarchs (Isaac, Ishmael, Jacob, Moses, Joseph) and matriarchs (Sarah, Hagar, Rebecca, Leah and Rachel) to Abraham, as well as the entire history of Israel, tradition makes him the first in this line of solidarity that nothing can defeat.

After exile, new perspectives open up. The covenant is no longer reserved for the few. In Isaiah 56, the prophet shows that no one is excluded from the covenant either because of his socio-religious affiliation or because of his national or ethnic affiliation. Only the interior dispositions count, a real obedience which is impossible solely through the efforts of the human will. Only the grace of God can make us capable of this, by encrusting it in our hearts. This is the way that could arise, what Hélder Câmara called "Abrahamic minorities."[9]

Abraham, the Pillar in the Middle of the House

The second mention of the covenant is found in Genesis 17: "He was ninety-nine years old, the Lord appeared to Abram and said: I am God the Almighty. Walk in my presence and be blameless. Between you and me I will establish my covenant, and I will multiply you exceedingly" (*Gn* 17: 1-2).

This new account is linked to the same promises as in chapter 15. But this time, God imposes moral requirements on

---

[9]   Hélder Câmara, *Le Désert est fertile*, Paris, Seuil (1977).

the chosen. This was a religious bond with him symbolised in the prescription of circumcision. Very judiciously, Antonio Abela points out that the circumcision on which the text seems to insist is in fact only one of the signs of the covenant.[10] Moreover, the structuring elements of the text make it a unique piece whose central theme is that of the covenant, which translates into companionship with the Lord. Recognising the authority of God, Abraham fell face down: "Abram fell face down, and God said to him (…)" (*Gn* 17:3). This gesture which usually marks the vassalage of the vanquished towards the new masters, is here the sign of a friendship and intimate union which will be verified day after day.

Witness the meeting of the two friends at the oak of Mamré and the beautiful prayer of intercession in favour of the inhabitants of Sodom and Gomorrah (*Gn* 18:17-32). At first glance, it looks like the markets of the East and Africa where you negotiate and do a palaver for a long time before buying any item. Is such market place bargaining not also a way of creating, weaving and maintaining links? But this bargaining, if we can call it that, can only be understood in the relationship of friendship that unites the patriarch to his God.

Henceforth, Abraham espouses the very gaze of God. He can thus see what is good in the midst of the general explosion. He believes that a few righteous people can help save the world. Hasn't he already understood God's whole plan? Abraham confirms God's creative project in Genesis 1 which makes man and woman in his image, as his partners.

On the other hand, in the parable of Genesis 2-3, Adam and Eve testify to the human will to enter into competition, even in dissidence, with their God, conceived in the image of the terrifying pagan divinities who crush and infantilise the human. This

---

[10]   Antonio Abela, "Abramo camina davanti al Signore (Esegi di Gen 17)", Francesco Viatoni (éd), *Sangue e anthropologica biblica nella patristica*, I, (Roma: Edizioni Pia Unione Preziosissimo Sangue, 1982), 23-55.

will to power destroys the covenant relationships with God, within the couple, between brothers and sisters, but also with creation. We enter a cycle of violence contrary to God's plan.

In fact, Adam and Eve symbolise our daily refusals to enter into a covenant with God, refusals which engender death in the spiritual, ethical, socio-political and ecological sense of the term. Abraham is the anti-Adam. By its liberating and invigourating partnership with God, it becomes for all peoples the solid pillar, placed in the middle of the construction, according to the Palestinian architecture of the time. On it, it is possible to build a common future, in the dynamics of the covenant. This is what a Jewish tale says, reported by Alain Marchadour:

> Abraham deserved to be created before Adam, but the Lord said: If I had created Abraham before Adam, and the world was corrupted, no one could have come to bring him salvation. I want to let Adam come first as the first man so that when he stumbles Abraham will come after him and again can fix everything. If someone has a solid pillar, where do they place it? Simply in the middle of the construction so that it protects the walls placed above and below it. This is what the Lord did with Abraham: he placed him in the middle of time so that he would carry the generations before and after him.[11]

Three Pathways for the Church of Africa on a Synodal Path

Listening

Listening is indeed the starting point of the covenant adventure between God and Abraham. We understand that the biblical tradition makes listening the first spiritual and theological moment. This is expressed by the *shema Israel*, listen to Israel (*Dt* 6:4-9), the profession of faith that every son of Israel proclaims as soon as he gets up and which punctuates his whole day. Here,

---

[11]   Alain Marchadour, *Genèse*, (Paris: Bayard/Centurion 1999), 143.

to listen is to root oneself in the Word of God, to adhere to it by entering into God's projects. To listen is to make oneself totally available to God.

Listening is also an important part of African wisdom. As the proverb says: "God gave us one mouth and two ears to tell us that we must listen more than speak, that we must speak once and listen twice." The wise child is the one who listens, obeys and puts into practice what was learned. But do we still know how to listen in a noisy world, which even invades our Churches?

In the synodal walk, listening opens up to the others, to the world, to hear "the cry of the African man, (sic)"[12] but also the Africans' immense capacities for resilience. Badly used, the New Communication Technologies can, of course, interfere with this listening. But when used responsibly and wisely, they are valuable means of connecting to the historical, cultural and socio-economic reality of our peoples. Similarly, the various analytical tools made available to us by both endogenous and exogenous sciences enlighten and sustain our attention. They also make us listen to the creation that we are called to serve as guardians in the manner of God, and not as predators. Birago Diop proclaims: "listen more often to things than to beings."[13]

Following the example of Elijah, we must learn to die to the din of storms and hurricanes or even to luminous tinsel. We must let God purify our listening in the "light breeze." Then, we can pursue our mission, no longer dithering to the rhythm of our human agitations and impatience, but to that of the peaceful patience of God.

In short, it is in prayer and the Word of God that our listening to others, to the life of our peoples and our Churches, is refined. This listening makes us truly and fully servants of God and of others. Our synodal walk can be truly fruitful if we followed the

---

12   Jean-Marc Ela, *Le cri de l'homme africain*, (Paris: L'Harmattan, 1980).

13   Birago Diop, *Le souffle des ancêtres*, (Paris: Présence Africaine, 1960).

example of Abraham. On the occasion of its 50th anniversary, SECAM invites the Church of Africa to a spirituality of Christian efficiency that is rooted in the sacraments, the Word of God and prayer which is an important conclusion to this section on listening:

> This spirituality of Christian efficiency is particularly nourished by the sacraments of the Eucharist and reconciliation. It is also based on silent and contemplative prayer, meditation on the Word of God, adherence to its truth and the fundamental option for a life of fidelity to the Gospel. Also, this spirituality allows the baptized to become the witnesses of the Gospel which the Church needs so that Africa (...) is not infected by all forms of the virus of spiritual, cultural, economic and political impoverishment.[14]

Future-Creating Solidarity

By convening the Vatican Council—a Council whose spirit and message we are still drawing from—Pope John XXIII invited all Christians to a listening attitude to others and to the world which engenders creative solidarity with the whole of the human family:

> The joys and hopes, the sadness and the anguish of the men of this time, especially of the poor and of all those who suffer, are also the joys and the hopes, the sadness and the anguish of the disciples of Christ, and there is nothing truly human that does not resonate in their hearts. Their community, in fact, is built up with men, gathered in Christ, led by the Holy Spirit in their journey towards the Kingdom of the Father, and bearers of a message of salvation that must be offered to all. The community of Christians therefore recognises itself as truly and intimately in solidarity with the human race and its history (*Gaudium et spes*, 1).

This was already Abraham's experience. By his yes to God, he inaugurates solidarities which largely go beyond the clan, ethnic, political and religious divisions between the kingdom of the north and that of the south.

---

14   SECAM, *Document de Kampala*, (Accra: Bayard, 2020), 149.

Of course, we can consider that solidarity is obvious for Africans, as we sing about it. However, our continent is also plagued by contempt for others, pride, selfishness, discrimination, injustice, poverty in all its forms, even abandonment and marginalisation of brothers and sisters. Africa beats the sad record of outbreaks of violence and displaced persons due to insecurity. Was it not the endemic violence on the continent that led Pope Benedict XVI, following John Paul II, to convene the synod on "reconciliation, justice and peace?"

The covenant demands a society of justice, equality and law. The Church is the first witness to this. It is the place where new solidarities are invented which, without renouncing them, go beyond ethnic, racial or religious affiliation. It is about solidarities that cannot be reduced to day-to-day management or to ecclesial, family, national or international conviviality. It is also time to reactivate intergenerational solidarity largely mortgaged by susceptibilities, misunderstandings and violence.

The Church must arouse and encourage solidarities which are real signs of walking together, a mobilisation around a common project, which does not rule out the fight against all forms of injustice. It must be the place where men and women set out to imprint on the history of the continent deep marks of liberating and future-creating solidarity. We need a solidarity that is part of organisations, institutional reforms, and projects that are part of history. This requires audacity and inventiveness, both in terms of reflection, action and strategies.

The next synod will be a turning point in the history of the Church on the continent. Does she take the measure? Are our Christian communities, our dioceses, our episcopal conferences ready for this Abrahamic transhumance? Isn't it up to SECAM and our various institutions to set the tone? It is therefore imperative that SECAM pursues with greater lucidity, solidarity, determination and audacity the path travelled since 1969:

The path thus travelled since the founding of SECAM in 1969 until today is cause for thanksgiving. If at the level of organization and structures, much remains to be done, as evidenced by the periodic return of the question of "restructuring," at the level of the emergence of an African ecclesial subject, a significant path has been done. The option of building a Church-Family of God, which makes living ecclesial communities, true theological places, and which puts itself resolutely at the service of reconciliation, justice and peace, has offered the Church in Africa a historic opportunity, to contribute in an original way to the reflection on synodality and its implementation within the universal Church.[15]

The March for the Service of Life

Abraham experiences throughout his journey: the God of the Covenant is the God of life. Anything that kills or destroys people, peoples or creation is contrary to the covenant. Moreover, life is a long chain: Yahweh is the God of Abraham, Isaac and Jacob. He is not the God of the dead or of death, but of the living. We understand that in the Bible, life sums up the ideal of happiness and well-being. Thus, in Ezekiel 37, the spirit of the Lord raises the dry bones and transforms them into forces of life.

The African universe is also marked by the theme of life, as expressed in proverbs, rites, literature and art. It is expressed in terms of struggles, physical, social and spiritual healings. We understand the importance of healing in pastoral work in Africa, but also in the post-synodal exhortations *Ecclesia in Africa* and *Africae Munus*.

Indeed, *Ecclesia in Africa* compared Africa to the unfortunate man who fell into the hands of brigands and who needs "good Samaritans." Isn't this a pessimistic vision on a continent that is full of so many material, human and spiritual resources? Despite its wealth of life, Africa cannot forget the many wounds that poison its sources of life. Nevertheless, like any people, the

---

15   SECAM, *Document de Kampala*, 50.

African can be at the same time sometimes the bandit, sometimes the victim, but also sometimes the good Samaritan.

In *Africae Munus*, Africa presents itself as sick. This is why the post-synodal exhortation makes us relive many stories of healings. All insist not on the healing that Jesus brings about, but on the fact that the Lord of life raises the sick, makes them leap and invites them to walk.

Thus, the conclusion of the exhortation (172-177) is illuminated by a word addressed to the blind man of Jericho: "Take courage; get up, he is calling you" (*Mk* 10:49). Then, Bartimaeus throws off his coat and leaps towards Jesus who restores his sight. Already, before, during the healing of a paralytic reported by Mark (2:1-12) and Luke (*Lk* 5:17-26), Jesus asks the cripple to get up. This miracle announces the healing of the paralytic of the pool of Bethesda in John 5. It is the most abundantly quoted Johannine passage (*Africae Munus*, 147-149).

In 2009, at the end of the second African synod, the Bishops of Africa, drawing inspiration from this Johannine episode, particularly from John 5:8, had invited Christians to stand up to walk in the footsteps of the Risen One: "Church of Africa, get up, take up your pallet and walk" (II Special Assembly for Africa of the Synod of Bishops, 2019, 43). Because, as Irenaeus of Lyon said, "The glory of God is the living man; the life of man is to contemplate God" (*Adversus haereses*, IV, 20, 7).

So, from the Christian perspective, life is not just a cultural given that we gargle in the name of African culture. The fight for life is multidimensional. It is a requirement of walking that is rooted in God. To achieve this, the Kampala Document proposes to open up to the strength of the Spirit of the Risen One who guided and supported Abraham and the martyrs of Uganda:

> The pastoral strategy promoting the life of communion with Christ leads the faithful to a greater presence of the Holy Spirit who acts and transforms people and social situations. Under the breath of the Spirit, the disciples of Christ will manage to depart from the mentality of fatalism

and resignation, indifference, the spirit of passivity, idleness and lack of inventiveness in the work as well as the search for solutions to life's problems.[16]

Abrahamic Walkers

This is an important time for us in Africa to actively participate in the synodal process initiated by Pope Francis. The term "synodality" suggests," the specific *modus vivendi* and *operandi* of the Church, the People of God, which manifests and concretely realises its communion of being by walking together, gathering in assembly and actively participating of all its members to its evangelising mission" (International Theological Commission, 2018, 6).

Our synodal journey can be enlightened by the experience of Abraham. The critical reading we made of his figure allowed us to situate the function of this ancestor in the Old Testament tradition and allow him "to visit Africa."[17] The pilgrim Abraham is the witness of a transhumance and a daily adventure with a God who constantly leads us beyond our borders. It opens us to the dynamics of the covenant, which will be definitively sealed in the death and resurrection of Jesus, the new Abraham.

By inviting us to "listen to what he says to the Churches" (*Rv* 2-3), the Spirit of God guides us on the paths of universal brotherhood and inspires us to give the free gift of oneself "to the extreme." He heals us and enlivens us. He guides us and makes us witnesses of the covenant of life, with God, with the Church-family serving everyone, especially the most disadvantaged.

For this, it is necessary to instill synodal spirit and attitude in the countless places of formation in our Churches. Whether in universities, religious or parish centres, training must stimulate

---

16   SECAM, *Document de Kampala*, 131.
17   Paulin Poucouta, *God's Word in Africa*, (Nairobi: Paulines, 2015).

reflection, a sense of history, creativity and daily commitment. They are places where we learn to let ourselves be guided and healed by the Spirit of the Risen One, in the words of Pope Francis:

> The Synod is a path of spiritual discernment, of ecclesial discernment, which takes place in adoration, in prayer, in contact with the Word of God. (…) The Word opens us to discernment and enlightens it. May it guide the Synod, so that it is not an ecclesial "convention", a study colloquium or a political congress, so that it is not a parliament, but an event of grace, a process of healing led by the Spirit. In these days, Jesus calls us, as he did with the rich man of the Gospel, to empty ourselves, to free ourselves from what is worldly, and also from our closures and our repetitive pastoral patterns. It calls us to ask ourselves what God wants to tell us at this time, and in what direction he wishes to lead us.[18]

---

[18] Pope Francis, *Opening of the synodal Path. Holy Mass*, (Rome, 10 October 2021).

CHAPTER 3

The Social Magisterium of Pope Francis and the Reform of the Church in a Synodal Way: Latin American Perspectives

Emilce Cuda

Pope Francis has undertaken a reform of the Church which is in tune with his social Magisterium. This reform is not about a change in organisational structures but about a commitment to living in a synodal way. In his two social encyclicals, *Laudato Si* and *Fratelli Tutti*, the Pope anticipated this reform by denouncing a crisis of civilisation facing today's world, while proposing a new lifestyle with a gospel flavour that lead us to social dialogue as a better option to the current forms of social policies that continue to generate so much suffering and inequality in the world. In this chapter, I will present the way of organising the ecclesial and political community proposed by the Latin American pontiff to meet the needs and dreams of the People of God in the world. That path is synodal, which means walking together. It must be noted that the action of walking together, in this sense, does not begin with a clear plan and strategy. On the contrary, it is unity first among the People of God, then strategy. The ecclesial and political decision to unite despite the differences precedes the actual walking. Feeling the same needs and dreams together comes before concrete, conjunctural decisions are made, which at the end of the road make up, like a symphony, the strategy. That strategy will be evangelical to the extent that it moves people to ethical action in stewardship and care for the earth in order to bring about the reign of God in history.

The tragic reality of our world today is that we are presently in the middle of a war, which is not just a war between Ukraine and Russia, but is our war too. As the poet John Donne says: "Ask not to see for whom the bell tolls. The bell tolls for you." In the encyclical *Pacem in Terris* after the First and Second World Wars, Pope John XXIII promoted social justice by speaking about the economic problems of his time. In that document, it is clear that the way for peace has to be charted through politics. Pope Francis toed the same line as he published his social encyclical, *Fratelli Tutti*, speaking about the best politics in the actual productive model. There, he shows us the path that we all must follow in journeying together to the future that God wishes for humanity and the entire cosmos. It is the path of social dialogue that guarantees the conditions for a good life. The contrary is bad politics. Some theologians may think that supporting one part of the conflict is catholic, while speaking about the best politics is tantamount to "populism." But the truth is that we cannot shy away from politics.

The *Curia Romana*'s new constitution which took effect on the 5th of June 2022 is a great tool for the synodal path which focuses on "the reform" of the Church. This reform is not about a structural reform at the Vatican, but rather a conversion. The reform of the *Curia Romana* is at the service of the reform of the Church, and that reform is "conversion." It is not an individual conversion but a communal conversion which entails a new model for the organisation of the People of God in history. It is an ecclesiological, social, cultural and ecological conversion, like Pope Francis proposed in *Querida Amazonia's* four dreams. Doing that concretely is to do politics, because it is a community decision where everybody — *tutti* — has the authority to see, judge and act, in living the spirituality of *Fratelli Tutti*. This way of living and acting is also very synodal. If we were to ask the question: which is the best politics? The answer would be love, communication, and the recognition of the human in everybody. The human being is the one who has the capacity to participate in some elements of divine wisdom because of the *sensus fidelium* that God in God's generosity has given to all the baptised. So, each human being can judge. This is the best politics, and the rest is business.

Synodality *ad extra*

It is important to clarify, in relation to the social Magisterium of Pope Francis, the second approach to synodality, which refers, in my opinion, to the *ad extra* dimension. This will allow us to see the connection between synodality and the social doctrine of the Church. The Preparatory Document for the Synod on Synodality makes clear that its second perspective "considers how the People of God walk together with the entire human family. The gaze will thus focus on the state of relations, dialogue and possible common initiatives with believers of other religions, with people far from the faith, as well as with specific social environments and groups, with their institutions (the world of politics, culture, economy, finances, work, trade unions and business associations, non-governmental organisations and civil society, popular movements, minorities of various kinds, the poor and excluded, etc.)" (*DP*, 29).

The same document chastises the world for lacking initiatives that bring together all of humanity. For this reason, it affirms that "the option to 'walk together' is a prophetic sign for a human family that needs a shared project, capable of achieving the good of all. A Church capable of communion and fraternity, of participation and subsidiarity, in fidelity to what she announces, will be able to stand beside the poor and the least and lend them her own voice" (*DP*, 9). In tune with this vision we have the affirmation contained in the *vademecum* of the Synod on Synodality which points out unequivocally that "in fact, synodality is not so much an event or a slogan, rather it is a style and a way of being, with which the Church lives its mission in the world" (*Vad*. 10).

Following these texts, we can see that this mission essentially comprises two levels. On the one hand, dialogue with society, on the other hand, ecumenical and interreligious dialogue. Therefore, we must avoid "the temptation not to look beyond the visible confines of the Church. By expressing the Gospel in our lives, lay women and men act as leaven in the world in which they live and work. A synodal process is a time to dialogue with the people from the world of economics and science, politics and culture, the arts and sports, the media and social initiatives. It will be a time to reflect on ecology and peace, on the problems of life and on migration. We must consider the big picture to fulfil our mission in the world. It is also an opportunity to confirm the ecumenical journey with other Christian confessions and to deepen our understanding with other religious traditions" (*Vad*. 21-22).

Although the role of the laity is emphasised, religious men and women should also feel like "fellow travellers" with humanity and enter into dialogue with it (*Vad*. 40). All of us must bear in mind that, as the lyric by Mario Benedetti puts it: "I love you because your hands work for justice" and "in the street side by side we are much more than two." This is an expression that happily articulates the spirit of the *vademecum* which states that: "In the Church and in society we are side by side on the same path" (*Vad*. 40).

The Holy Father himself encourages us not to neglect this perspective, when on the eve of the opening of the Synod he pointed out that "it is an itinerary of effective spiritual discernment, which we do not undertake in order to give a beautiful image of ourselves, but to collaborate better with the work of God in history."[1] At this level, the discernment to which we refer

---

1   Francis, "Address of the Holy Father Francis on the occasion of the Moment of Reflection for the Beginning of the Synodal Journey." https://press.vatican.va/content/

is rather social, rather than communal or personal (although it shares a spiritual character with them). As Juan Carlos Scannone taught, such discernment is at the core of the social ethic of Pope Francis, who for his part draws our attention to the fact that in this synodal process we are faced with the "opportunity to be a Church of closeness." Let us always return to God's style, for God's style is closeness, compassion and tenderness.[2]

Bearing in mind these preliminary considerations, I will proceed to develop the themes in this chapter. First, we begin with this important quote: "The Church exists to evangelise. We can never concentrate on ourselves. Our mission is to bear witness to the love of God in the midst of the entire human family. This synodal process has a deep missionary dimension. Its goal is to enable the Church to better witness to the Gospel, especially with those who live on the spiritual, social, economic, political, geographical and existential peripheries of our world. In this way, synodality is a path through which the Church can more fruitfully fulfil her mission of evangelisation in the world, as leaven at the service of the arrival of the Kingdom of God" (*Vad.* 13).

Here, I want to dwell on the statement, which associates evangelisation with the fundamental, distinctive mission of the Church. I consider it pertinent to remember that the Holy Father, on the one hand, asks us to be "the Church that goes forth," understood as "the community of missionary disciples who begin, who get involved, who accompany, who bear fruit and celebrate." The evangelising community experiences that the Lord has taken the initiative, has first given it love (cf. 1 *Jn* 4:10); and, for this reason, she knows how to get ahead, take the initiative without fear, go out to meet, look for the distant and reach the crossroads to invite the excluded. He lives an inexhaustible desire to offer mercy, which is the fruit of having experienced the infinite mercy

---

salastampa/en/bollettino/pubblico/2021/10/09/211009a.html.

2   Francis, "Address of the Holy Father Francis on the occasion of the Moment of Reflection for the Beginning of the Synodal Journey."

of the Father and his diffusive force (*EG*, 24). On the other hand, he warns against "spiritual worldliness, which he defines as seeking human glory and personal well-being, instead of the glory of the Lord. Closely linked to this, he points out that the mission of the Church "is not a business or a business project, nor is it a humanitarian organisation, it is not a show to count how many people attended thanks to our propaganda; it is something much deeper, which is beyond measure" (*EG*, 93 and 279).

The *vademecum* does the same, although the analysis of the "context in which this synod is taking place" is more detailed, with *ad-extra* and *intra*-ecclesial situational description: "a global pandemic, local and international conflicts, the growing impact of climate change, migrations, different forms of injustice, racism, violence, persecution and the increase in inequalities in humanity," just to name a few factors. In the Church, the context is also marked by the suffering experienced by minors and vulnerable people "because of sexual abuse, abuse of power and conscience committed by a significant number of clerics and consecrated persons." Having said this, we find ourselves at a crucial moment in the life of the Church and of the world. The context of the Covid-19 pandemic will undoubtedly affect the development of the synodal process" (*Vad.* 8).

It seems pertinent to complement these remarks by drawing attention to the following. If in the 19th century Victor Hugo led literature to deal with the social question of the miserable conditions of the working class at the wake of industrialisation and the rise of the bourgeoisie; in the 20th century, Mother Teresa of Calcutta put love into action towards the poorest of the poor (inhabitants of the underdeveloped Third World), in whom she saw Christ hidden under an anguished disguise (as she liked to say from an open-eyed mystique). In the 21st century, in the framework of an unprecedented technological revolution, the god of money that has taken hostage the economy, and rampant inequality, Pope Francis places the priority of pastoral care on the discarded, those who are deprived of land, shelter, decent work and technology. That is, those who Toni Catalá, would describe as "without the roof" which refers to the symbolism of rejection, "without the bread" (material and cultural deprivation), and "without the word" (communication and social isolation). This reality of suffering which is a product of the culture of discarding or the tipper-culture, is something new, a negative sign of the time. Describing this "throw-away culture" in his programmatic document, *Evangelii Gaudium*, the Pope says:

> Today everything falls within the game of competitiveness and the law of the strongest, where the powerful eat the weakest. As a consequence of this situation, large masses of the population find themselves excluded and marginalised: without work, without horizons, without a way out. The human being in itself is considered as a consumer good, which can be used and then thrown away. We have started the culture of "disposal" which is also promoted. It is no longer simply a question of the phenomenon of exploitation and oppression, but of something new: with exclusion, belonging to the society in which one lives is affected at its very roots, since one is no longer down there, in the periphery, or without power, but you are outside. The excluded are not "exploited" but waste, "leftovers" (*EG*, 53).

This prophetic denunciation has become central in the Social Magisterium of the first Latin American Pope, something that makes it a point of reference even for non-Christian sectors, but which coincides with the Holy Father's proposals on the need for a shift in the socio-cultural paradigm. His remarks on this subject invite us to consider the emergence of a new principle of the Social Doctrine of the Church: the preferential option for and with the poor. As we know, this is an important topic for theological reflection in, from and for Latin America, but under the current pontificate it receives emphasis on the leading role of the poor, architects of their own destiny and, even more, many times our evangelisers. Pope Francis himself expresses this with a forceful statement that, in my opinion, is the most well-developed teaching in the last 130 years of the Pontifical Social Magisterium in clearly capturing the relevance of the poor in the social mission of the Church. For the Church, the option for the poor is a theological category rather than a cultural, sociological, political or philosophical one. God places them in the first place in God's offer of mercy. This divine preference has consequences in the life of faith of all Christians, called to have the same sentiments as Jesus Christ (cf. *Phil* 2:5). Inspired by it, the Church makes an option for the poor understood as a special form of primacy in the exercise of Christian charity, to which the entire tradition of the Church bears witness.

This option, Benedict XVI teaches, "is implicit in the Christo-logical faith in the God who made himself poor for us, to enrich us with his poverty."[3] That is why I want a poor Church for the poor. They have much to teach us. In addition to participating in the *sensus fidei*, in their own pain they know the suffering Christ. It is necessary that we all allow ourselves to be evangelised by them. The new evangelisation is an invitation to recognise the saving power of their lives and to place them at the centre of the path of the Church." We are called to discover Christ in them, to lend them our voice in their causes, but also to be their friends, to listen to them, to interpret them and to gather the mysterious wisdom that God wants to communicate to us through them" (*EG*, 198).

It is from this perspective that it is appropriate to read Francis's proposal of humanity's need for a conversion to the paradigm of integral ecology (*LS*, Chapter 4). It is no coincidence that to illuminate this he resorts to his former teacher, Juan Carlos Scannone (the only Latin American author cited in *Laudato Si*) to point out that this change is already taking place, in the making, among the poor and in a salvific, concrete and organised form, using the expression "community salvation experience" (*LS*, 149).

---

[3]   Benedict XVI, "Address Of His Holiness Benedict XVI at the Inaugural Session of the Fifth General Conference of the Bishops of Latin America and the Caribbean" (Sunday, 13 May 2007) https://www.vatican.va/content/benedict-xvi/en/speeches/2007/may/documents/hf_ben-xvi_spe_20070513_conference-aparecida.html.

This should challenge us! As Saint Paul VI teaches, "only the Kingdom is absolute, and all the rest is relative" (*EN*, 8). Hence, in the spiritual discernment of human history its ambiguous character emerges, a mixture of grace and sin. For this reason, Saint Augustine warned of two cities founded by two loves (the anthropocentric and the theocentric), Saint Ignatius of Loyola distinguished two opposing flags (that of Being, raised by Christ, and that of Non-Being, the banner of the evil one) and Pope Francis lucidly sees the contrast between the culture of discarding and the culture of care, one excludes while the other includes (*LS*, 22 and 231). In the words of Kierkegaard, all discernment is done with fear and trembling, which expresses that we are not infallible. I, therefore, invite you to ask ourselves with total frankness and evangelical freedom to which of these polar dynamics we belong personally and communally in our religious families. If the answer is that we are doing little or nothing to "seek paths to liberation together" (*LS*, 64), which we can translate as working side by side in pursuit of the "integral human development of all" (*FT*, 133), let the good spirit encourage us to correct our course. It must be borne in mind that "when someone recognises God's call to intervene together with others in these social dynamics, they must remember that this is part of their spirituality, and that it is an exercise of charity that in this way mature and sanctifies" (*LS*, 231).

To better illustrate what I want to convey, I take these words from Pope Francis when he appeals to examples that we all know: "Who intends to lock up in a temple and silence the message of Saint Francis of Assisi and Saint Teresa of Calcutta? They couldn't accept it. An authentic faith, which is never comfortable and individualistic, always implies a deep desire to change the world, to transmit values, to leave something better behind when we pass through the earth. We love this magnificent planet where God has placed us, and we love the humanity that inhabits it, with all its dramas and weariness, with its longings and hopes, with its values and weaknesses. The earth is our common home, and we are all brothers and sisters. Although "the just order of society and of the state is a main task of politics," the Church "cannot and must not remain on the sidelines in the struggle for justice" (*EG*, 183).

Thus, given the epochal context that we have analysed, to help our examination of conscience or our pause for internal and external listening, we can recover the questions raised by the *vademecum*, when it refers to "sharing the responsibility of our common mission." "Synodality is at the service of the Church's mission, in which all members are called to participate. Since we are all missionary disciples, how is each baptised person called to participate in the mission of the Church? What prevents the baptised from being active in mission? What areas of mission are we neglecting? How does the community support its members who serve society in different ways (social and political engagement, scientific research, education, promotion of social justice, protection of human rights, care for the environment, etc.)? How does the Church help these members to live their service to society in a missionary way? How is discernment about missionary options carried out and who does it?" (*Vad.* 41). I believe that it will do us good that, both personally and as a community, we try to answer these questions, always remembering that we are required to be a Church that goes forth.

Regarding the theme of the social implications of the synodal process, the remarks of the International Theological Commission are illuminating, when in the section "Synodality and social *diakonia*" it highlights what we can do in terms of promoting justice, solidarity and peace, within the framework of cementing the culture of encounter: Today, when awareness of the interdependence between peoples forces us to think of the world as a common home, the Church is called to show that the catholicity that qualifies her and the synodality in which it is expressed are ferment of unity in diversity and of communion in freedom. This is a contribution of fundamental importance that the synodal life and conversion of the People of God can offer for the promotion of a culture of encounter and solidarity, of respect and dialogue, of inclusion and integration, of gratitude and freedom. The synodal life of the Church is offered, in particular, as *diakonia* in the promotion of a social, economic and political life of peoples under the sign of justice, solidarity and peace. "God, in Christ, not only redeems the individual person, but also the social relationships between men (sic)." The practice of dialogue and the search for shared and effective solutions for those who are committed to building peace and justice are an absolute priority in a situation of structural crisis in the procedures for democratic participation and mistrust in their inspiring principles and values, for the danger that they lead to authoritarianism and technocracy. In this context, there is a priority commitment and a criterion in each social action of the People of God: it is the imperative to "listen to both the cry of the earth and the cry of the poor," claiming urgently, in determining the options and projects of society, the position and privileged role of the poor, the universal destination of goods, the primacy of solidarity, the care of the common home" (*CTI*, 118 and 119).

Synodality and Social Discernment

Pope Francis maintains that the social evangelical discernment has as its subject the organised community as a people (*pueblo*) of God as against peoples of the earth. This expands the Latin American Catholic social principle of option *for* the poor. It is not just about opting for the poor, standing on their side and being the voice of the voiceless. It is, as expressed by Pope Francis in *Querida Amazonia*, mainly a matter of choosing *with* the poor (*FT*, 119), that is, creating a space for them at the table of economic decisions (*QA*, 26 and 37). For, to work for development means to care for creation and guarantee abundant life to all People of God which is all the human family, which is the mission of Christ as stated in the Gospel of St John (*Jn* 10:10). In that sense, politics is the organisation of the people, for the people, to the people, and the best politics is being "with" the poor, and not just "for" the poor. For Pope Francis, it is important not to fall into the diabolical trap of separating synodality from universal political participation. To avoid this, it is pertinent to remember that we are *fratelli tutti*, (that is, we are all brethren) walking together in the parishes and in the Roman curia, but also in the governments, the universities and the neighbourhoods.

According to the current Pontifical Social Magisterium, it is not only a matter of helping the poor by distributing part of the income and to care for the planet, but also of acknowledging the poor. Politics for the people means for the state, a recognition of them in their communities as agents of economic decision regarding the processes of production, distribution and reinvestment of income and the care of natural wealth. For the Church, it means acknowledging communities as agents of social evangelical discernment, especially with regard to the value placed on their human dignity as contributors through creative labour to the care and development of creation, ensuring universal access to common goods, universal political participation, and institutionalised forms of social organisation. Without this consciousness on the part of the state and the Church, peace, understood as social peace, which is the only possibility of a true peace, will remain elusive.

The new *Curia Romana Constitution* places evangelisation at the centre of its vision. Evangelisation is everyone's task, of the entire Church as the People of God, of which the Roman Curia is a part. To walk together is to walk preaching the gospel, with the Word, the liturgy and the concrete action of healing and caring for creation. But what does it mean to recognise the community as an evangelical subject? What does it mean to see the People of God as an evangelical social community whose discernment is essential to valuing the impoverished, marginalised, and discarded bodies from the existential peripheries, to establishing the true peace as the social peace? It will mean to struggle against different forms of individual and particular interests, which are almost always economic interests. Walking together is not walking through the Garden of Eden, as if we were on vacation. Walking together is working for the Kingdom.

The best politics, in an evangelical way, is recognising the people as the People of God politically, not only at election season when their votes are needed, but also through active participation in decision-making regarding the forms of production and their degree of morality. Giving them a place at the table is much more important than adding a plate of food. They are not pets. Giving them a place at the table is sharing bread and economic decisions; it is to give them a signature in the directories and in the ministries. The main social conflict is not only moral because no Christian could refuse to help the poor without falling into evangelical moral contradiction. The main conflict is juridical, since it is not about helping those who are in some form of economic, academic, and moral deficiency, but about "discerning" and "deciding" with them how to develop and to care for creation, because we are all created free and equal by a God who is not only a creator but also a provident and merciful father.

If we Christians would like to stop wars and guarantee peace, if we must do away with the different covert modes of warfare that have become naturalised as part of the system, we must understand that the only true peace is social peace, understood as social justice, economic justice, and educational justice. To establish such a peace, we must undergo a process of conversion and accept that all the People of God are agents in the process of discernment about the common good. Such discernment is not only about how to distribute the goods, but also about how to produce, how to consume, and how to invest. The requisite conversion is impossible without unity, and without a commitment to journeying together through embracing the process of synodality.

It is important to emphasise that the change that the Church and her members require is conversion. This foregrounds our judgement and the choices we make based on that judgement.

This conversion is necessary in order to make it possible for an inclusive world and an inclusive Church where we accept all the human family as subject of discernment in social and ecclesiastical matters. In summary, we can say that the changes the Church needs are: first, the acknowledgement of the reality of suffering, second, fidelity to the Gospel as source of discernment, and lastly, applying the principles of Catholic Social Teaching, that is based on historical reality and not on ideological prejudice.

Pope Francis affirms that the word "people" is necessary, because it refers to a real social phenomenon, which means that a group of people, with common needs and dreams, make the decision "to unite to save themselves." They come together to initiate a long-term process conceived as a collective dream, and appear as a people, in unity (*FT*, 157). According to the categories of the Latin American liberation philosophy, the people "are" not (*es*), but rather "is" (*esta*). A people, according to the Theology of the People, is a myth because it constitutes their common identity in memory of the injustices suffered as a community and of the community's decisions to confront them. It is a historical myth, says Pope Francis, because it is not an invented story, but a lived memory. It is a community's mystical experience of salvation (*FT*, 158; *LS*, 149). As a mystical community, the People of God from the peripheries are already walking together, because there they find "community salvation" in an ecclesial and social sense. The basic ecclesial communities are, in Latin America, a synodal experience. According to it, the people is a community subject, an ecclesial and political subject; it is the People of God between the peoples of the earth. The people discern and decide as "one" subject, regardless of whether this is recognised or not. The people "is" always there. Except if someone affirms that they are not the people, they "stay" and they "are". If we can't recognise it, we are not in the conversion that Pope Francis wants for the Church. To proclaim it is to proclaim the Gospel. *Fratelli Tutti* is in a juridical way, not in the quasi-caritative way. It is not welfare; it is democracy in a popular sense.

Being a popular leader is not a question of being an individual from the pópular constituency who is exercising authority on what should be done, but rather of being an organised community acting as a collective political subject. In the same way, preaching the Gospel is a personal and communal work, done together as a Church. The people, as People of God, as community subject, as Church, is a concrete expression of synodal unity. Church and synodality are synonymous as understood in this ecclesiological sense.

To maintain that the people as an organised community has the 'know how' to evangelise means that they can take charge of curing and caring for the common home, that is, the planet and the human beings. This is clearly explained by Francis in the 2020 Social Catechesis, *To care for the world*. There he says that, just as faith is the theological virtue that allows a person to believe in God, and to believe that they are a creature of God, the Father, in his image and likeness, this also allows them to develop an awareness of human dignity. Similarly, they develop trust in the community to become one together, and save themselves. For Pope Francis, the popular conscience is not class conscience, but brotherhood because it believes that all people are sons and daughters of the same Father. For him, popular conscience is a Christian conscience; it is a "lifestyle with flowers to gospel" (*FT*, 1).

Understanding Pope Francis's initiative to walk together implies acknowledging the beauty of our unity in diversity. Pope Francis understands the people as being dynamic (*FT*, 160), and as having the capacity to decide to unite themselves. It is about unity in difference, which does not presuppose a partisan indoctrination on common interests, but rather faith in a divine economy of salvation, faith in the community as a faithful People of God. Synodality is thus a necessary conversion from individual position (political and ecclesiastical) to a community position. It is the "creed," to take a position as People of God, motivated by a deep conversion, and with commitment to the reform of the Church. It is necessary that the people move themselves by communal memory of historical injustice, and by the theological virtue of hope as a dynamic principle of the political decision.

Synodality is also the mode of social relationship as a community of people who remain united even in their differences. In their "symbolic union" the sense is manifested, not only as a political speech, but as a body present with its dreams in the public space. From the moment we gather as God's people to walk together we are already on the path of synodality, the rest is a process that is built over time, through generations and among the peoples of the earth.

Regarding the challenges of social conflict or social injustice, *Fratelli Tutti* recommends dialogue that eschews a "dialectical war" but embraces communication (*FT*, 4). The Philosophy of Liberation, of Latin American origin, whose founders were Enrique Dussel, Juan Carlos Scannone and Mario Casalla, developed a method called "analectic." They understood communication as a being or "staying" in the earth, rather than as a transmission of information. Communicating is an act of "staying" in unity. For Pope Francis, it is, like conversion, an act of "turning passion into community action."[4]

Social communal discernment is not a question of the people deciding technical questions, but rather of being able to discern, according to the principles of evangelical faith, between fair options for all. For that the *sensus fidelium* present in each of us is enough, and at the same time it is necessary to prevent the social injustice that, at the end, is the cause of the economic war and of the liberation revolution. And this is the same history in Africa, America, Asia and Europe.

We must apply synodality in all cultural fields because it is a process over time. In the current productive conditions, and

---

4   Papa Francisco, "II Discurso a los Movimientos Populares, Santa Cruz de la Sierra", 11 de Julio de 2015.

democratic politics, understood as the best policy in any form of government, we do not yet see the liberation of the poor or the creation of conditions for human and cosmic flourishing. We need conversion in an economical sense also. We need to infuse the economies of the world with the leaven of the Gospel. The current productive form not only compels unemployed workers to live in unworthy conditions, but also obscures politics as social dialogue, displacing it with politics as power relations, or directly replacing it with anarchy. The best policy implies communication between all the productive sectors, because all are in different degrees and modes of collaboration. This communication supposes action of reciprocal recognition of all productive value, and of care, as well as economic and cultural inclusion of a people as a way of constitution of personal identities. This economic inclusion is very important since unemployment makes political communication, that is, social dialogue, impossible, because it atomises labour activities. Work is no longer collaborative, and the popular cliché—"it is politics"— creates no space for social justice to thrive. If there are different parties that cannot communicate, the symbolic people as a unit cannot emerge, and the diabolical administration replaces the symbolic politics. As a result, the Church must intervene by preaching the Gospel of universal fraternity (*fratelli tutti*).

It is indeed remarkable that chapter 5 of the social encyclical *Fratelli Tutti* is titled "The best politics." It is the collective conversion to the best politics that yields social peace. This is the reform of the Church, not as an organisation but as People of God living in the historical structures. It is what synodality is all about. We need an ecological conversion as a Church, as People of God living in history. *Laudato Si* clearly states that the ecological crisis has two faces, environmental and social, and that the environmental crisis has social roots, which is why the solution is anthropological. This point is reiterated in *Fratelli Tutti* where the Pope says that "Saint Francis, who felt himself a brother of the sun, the sea and the wind, knew himself even more united to those who were of his own flesh" (*FT*, 2). It would seem that it is necessary to insist that ecological spirituality, even in Saint Francis, must be understood as socio-environmental. Pope Francis says that the saint of Assisi "sowed peace everywhere and walked close to the poor, the abandoned, the sick, the discarded, the least" (*FT*, 2). Even, and not for nothing, he emphasises that in Saint Francis "his fidelity to the Lord was proportional to his love for his brothers and sisters" (*FT*, 3).

The current system of productive relationships need conversion because it has commoditised and objectified the human bodies and wounded human agency. The second person of the Trinity paid his ransom in blood. People are body and soul that are manifested in the flesh as human form; They are sons and daughters of the same Father and are sisters and brothers in the flesh (*FT*, 8, 128, 227 and 247). Therefore, conversion starts at the flesh, it is not purely spiritual, for it is an act of body and soul. The incarnation, death and resurrection of Jesus Christ, valued the flesh.

We also need conversion in the family. What does it mean today? *Fratelli Tutti* mentions the nature of the social conflict in the time of St Francis of Assisi. In that world, the cities lived in bloody wars between powerful families, and at the same time, the miserable areas of the excluded peripheries grew. At the fall of the empire, the political form that emerged was that of the *pater familias*, according to Gianbattista Vico in *Ciencia Nova*. And it would not hurt to take into consideration in this historical moment where income is concentrated in a small number of families identified by first and last name. According to the economist Thomas Piketty in his book *Capital in the 21st Century*, it can be seen very well through data from tax collection how wealth is increasingly concentrated in the hands of a few families, and how unemployment disorganised the social field thus destroying politics.

This is why Pope Francis recommends that in the face of different and current ways of eliminating or ignoring others, we should be able to react with a new dream of fraternity and social friendship that does not stop at words (*FT*, 6). Faced with the current socio economic forms that make up a system that kills, he proposes another form of political engagement as a way of life. He proposes an alternative to the current productive form that tends to eliminate or ignore, that tends to devalue, to remove bodies, from the value chain. The alternative that he proposes is the acquisition of the "capacity", habit, virtue or knowledge, to "react", that is to say, to set in motion in order to actualise a new social —not individual— dream of fraternity and of social friendship. That fraternal and friendly political form does not remain in words, but is passion turned into community action, as previously said. Herein lies the great conversion of the Church as People of God, the fulfilment of the dream of *Fratelli tutti*.

Political love is not an intimate, individual feeling, but a concrete communal love, effectively realised (*FT*, 164-165), which aims to give value to bodies; social institutions that value bodies and natural wealth guarantee just productive relationships and concrete expression of social love. The conversion must touch social, cultural, economic, and ecclesiastical structure. The four dreams of *Querida Amazonia* must not be seen as illusions that are impossible to be realised. Dream is not ideology. Dream implies hope, a theological virtue, and the only possibility to move at the unity in differences.

Conversion presupposes participation. The organised community tactically reflects the principle of subsidiarity proposed by the Social Doctrine of the Church, understood as political and economic participation (*FT*, 175). Thus, political love is a vocation, called to the common good, and this is identified with the essence of Christian preaching: the Kingdom of love and equality (*FT*, 180).

Conversion is love, and concrete love is political love. It is a love that touches and heals the flesh; touches and heals body and soul, it is "tenderness" (*FT*, 188 and 194), it is effective love.

The politician is the one who knows how to care for and heal the flesh; they can do it and they can take care of people's body and soul. A politician who works for business is not a politician, they are a businessman, they are very different from the "ideological Samaritan" (*FT*, 183). The best politics is love, not business. We need conversion in politics. Countries are not companies, persons are not human resources, and the planet is not natural resources. Each of them has their own dignity.

CHAPTER 4

Exploring the Possible Contributions of the African Palaver Towards a Participatory Synodal Church[1]

Stan Chu Ilo

T his essay argues for a participatory synodal Church and the possible contributions of the African palaver as a model for participatory dialogue in the Roman Catholic Church. The African palaver is the art of conversation, dialogue, and consensus-building in traditional society that can be appropriated in the current search for a more inclusive and expansive participatory dialogue at all levels of the life of the Church. I will develop this essay first by briefly exploring some theological developments on synodality between the Second Vatican Council and Pope Francis and some of the contributions of the reforms of Pope Francis to synodality in the Church. Secondly, I will identify how the African palaver functions through examples taken from two African ethnic groups. I will proceed to show how the African palaver could enter into dialogue with Pope Francis's teaching and the limitations identified in Pope Francis's teaching and practices within the larger context of the synodal tradition of the Church. The essay will conclude by showing how this palaver approach could guide the develop-

---

1   This is a revised essay originally published as: Stan Chu Ilo, "Exploring the Possible Contributions of the African Palaver towards a Participatory Synodal Church." *Exchange*, 50 (2021): 209-237.

ment of a process of participatory dialogue in the Church today and how it can offer an expansive sacred space for the voices of the voiceless, and *the invisibles* in our Church. This way, the Church will become a site for a culture of encounter, and for the celebration of the gifts and wisdom of the whole People of God.

A Participatory Synodal Church? From Vatican II to Pope Francis

The forthcoming 2023 Synod on Synodality offers Catholic scholars the opportunity to deepen and appraise some of the theologies, methods, praxis, and processes for a synodal Church, developed since Vatican II. Particularly for theologians from the Global South, this is a special moment to make a case for a recognition and appropriation of the traditions of synodality in the non-Western cultures and spiritualities. From an African perspective, I will propose the palaver tradition as a process for participatory dialogue that can enrich the current synodal process and methods.[2]

The synodal tradition is very ancient in the Church, but our concern in this article is to examine how the current synodal process that emerged since Vatican II has functioned in advancing or hampering the Church's mission of bringing the light of the Gospel to the ends of the earth.[3] Between Pope Paul VI's

---

[2]   See the analysis of the views of some of the African Bishops on the Eurocentric nature of the synodal process in Molly Jackson, "African Bishops Criticize Vatican's Priorities as Eurocentric," available from: https://www.csmonitor.com/World/Global-News/2015/1025/African-bishops-criticize-Vatican-s-priorities-as-Eurocentric. accessed on 15 July 2021.

[3]   On the meaning of the words, 'synod' and 'synodality', its biblical and historical development, and current theological and ecclesial understanding of these two concepts in the Church particularly in the papacy of Francis, see the International Theological Commission, *Synodality in the Life and Mission of the Church*, https://www.vatican.va/roman_curia/congregations/cfaith/cti_documents/rc_cti_20180302_sinodalita_en.html. (accessed 14 July 2021). Massimo Faggioli provides a very helpful summary of this document and its limitations. He notes that the document fails to integrate synodality with the new ministries and movements that have developed since Vatican II; and the document is vague on how to develop the synodal character of

promulgation of *Apostolica Sollicitudo (1965)* through which he instituted the Synod of Bishops as a permanent instrument of papal governance in the Catholic Church, and Pope Francis's promulgation of *Episcopalis Communio* (2018), both the synodal process and the *Ordo Synodi* have been updated and modified by several popes. However, the episcopal, hierarchical, and clerical structure of synods in the Church have remained the same. The changes in the process have not substantially altered this structural misalignment in Catholic ecclesiology. This is why I advance a case for a participatory synodal church in this article. I will demonstrate how this structural problem in Catholic ecclesiology can be reformed through an appeal to traditions of participatory dialogue from a non-Western tradition capable of generating new practices for a more expansive and participative synodal process that involves the whole People of God.

According to the International Theological Commission's Document, *Synodality in the Life and Mission of the Church,* "although synodality is not explicitly found as a term or as a concept in the teaching of Vatican II, it is fair to say that synodality is at the heart of the work of renewal that the Council was encouraging. The ecclesiology of the People of God stresses the common dignity and mission of all the baptised, in exercising the variety and ordered richness of their charisms, their vocations and their ministries."[4] The central synodal principle operative at the Council is the openness of the Church to the world, the Church's internal dialogue in her search for her identity and mission, and dialogue with the modern world.[5] The hermeneutics

---

the Church and the needed reform of the Roman Curia See. Massimo Faggioli, "From Collegiality to Synodality: Promise and limits of Francis's 'Listening Primacy,'" *Irish Theological Quarterly* 85/4 (2020): 360.

International Theological Commission, *Synodality in the Life and Mission of the Church,* 6.

Stan Chu Ilo, "Dialogue in African Christianity: The Continuing Theological Significance of Vatican II," *Science et Esprit,* 68/2-3 (2016): 343.

4   International Theological Commission's, *Synodality in the Life and Mission of the Church,* 6.

5   Stan Chu Ilo, "Dialogue in African Christianity: The Continuing Theological Signifi-

of dialogue is a central key for understanding both the synodal character of Vatican II and the spirit that animated the Council and the subsequent, albeit contested reception of the teachings of Vatican II in the Church.[6] In other words, Vatican II was synodal because of its dialogical character, and the synodal processes that are true to the spirit of Vatican II ought to embrace the needed "participatory processes" (*EG*, 31) through dialogue in bringing about the fruits of the eschatological reign of God in history and in building up the People of God (*EG*, 224).

An examination of the synodal process from Vatican II to Pope Francis reveals three perennial tensions that remain unresolved. First, is the tension between episcopal collegiality, the synod of Bishops, and ecclesial synodality. Second, is the failure to heal the divisions in the Church through these synods. Rather than being a depolarising space for deep encounter and communion, the recent synods of bishops have widened divisions; hence the need to explore what Judith Gruber calls, "the theological role of conflict in a synodal Church."[7] Third, is the marginalisation of the voices of the laity, and minorities in contemporary synods. In addition, old and new forms of ecclesial colonialism continue to reinforce a mindset in the Catholic Church that neglects the

---

cance of Vatican II," *Science et Esprit*, 68/2-3 (2016), 343.

[6] This is the conclusion of many scholars including Gerard Mannion, who writes: "I would suggest that the enduring legacy of Vatican II, in accord with John XXIII's call for *aggiornamento*, is its unswerving commitment to *dialogue* among the human family." See Gerard Mannion, *Ecclesiology and Postmodernity: Question for the Church in our Time* (Collegeville, Minnesota: Liturgical Press, 2007), 110. See also Dermot Lane's argument that dialogue was the fundamental achievement of Vatican II and he argues further that "if there is a tension surrounding the reception of Vatican II and the proper interpretation of Vatican II, is partly due to the fact that insufficient attention has been given to the development of a theology of dialogue, and in particular to the hermeneutics that should inform the practice of dialogue. See: Dermot Lane, *Stepping Stones to Other Religions: A Christian Theology of Inter-Religious Dialogue* (Maryknoll, New York: Orbis Books, 2011), 115; see also John W. O'Malley, *What Happened at Vatican II* (Cambridge, MA: Harvard University Press, 2008), 10-11.

[7] Judith Gruber, "Consensus or Dissensus? Exploring the Theological Role of Conflict in a Synodal Church," *Louvain Studies*, 43 (2020): 239-259. For a counter argument to Gruber's see William T. Cohen, "Doctrinal Drift, Dance or Development: How Truths Take Time in the life of Communion," *International Journal of Systematic Theology*, 20/2 (April 2018): 209-225.

contributions of the Global South, who now constitute the centre of gravity of Catholicism. Conscious of this unfortunate situation, Bradley Hinze makes a strong case for "decolonising synodality" because "the fact that the legacy and power of colonialism and neo-colonialism remain influential in and through the Church necessitates a decolonial approach to ecclesial power, authority, epistemology, work, race, gender, and art."[8]

In explicating the tension between episcopal collegiality and ecclesial synodality, one could look at the unresolved tension in how the ITC's document narrows the ecclesial synodality of the whole People of God to episcopal collegiality when it states: "Collegiality is thus the specific form in which ecclesial synodality is manifested and made real through the ministry of Bishops on the level of communion of the local Churches in a region, and on the level of communion of all the Churches in the universal Church. An authentic manifestation of synodality naturally entails the exercise of the collegial ministry of the Bishops."[9] This conclusion is also advanced by Pope Francis in *Episcopalis Communio* where he affirms that synods in the Catholic Church are *structurally and essentially* "configured as an episcopal body" (par 6), that there is "a supra-diocesan dimension" (par 2) to the office of the Bishop. Francis's teaching here is in continuity with the implication of John Paul II's *Apostolos Suos*' (20) teaching which gives the impression that local Bishops are really like legates of Rome and that dioceses are outposts of the Pope. Thus, episcopal conferences owe their authority to the Pope who as Supreme authority grants them particular mandates based on universal laws and also "entrusts determined questions to the deliberation" of local Bishops and also approves the outcome of such deliberations.

---

8   Bradford Hinze, "Dreams of Synodality, Specters of Constraint," *Louvain Studies*, 43 (2020), 299-300.

9   International Theological Commission, *Synodality in the Life and Mission of the Church*, 7.

At the core of this complexity is what Hervé Legrand calls "a universalist perspective on the episcopacy" and a "minimalist interpretation of Vatican I" on papal primacy which has carried through to Vatican II and beyond.[10] Legrand argues that this lack of clarity and structural reforms of episcopal collegiality and ecclesial synodality stems from the interpretation of chapter three of *Lumen Gentium* and the "elaboration of the concept of the college of Bishops in its relation to the papal primacy defined by Vatican I."[11] This has affected the way the Church has functioned with regard to the relationship between the local Churches and Rome in such areas as doctrine, pastoral life, liturgy, and laws.[12] This raises some important questions: How could the dioceses or regional Bishops undertake a synodal path if they need the approval of Rome to do so and if decisions reached at diocesan and regional synods must in fact be approved by the Pope? How could diocesan Bishops engage in contextual pastoral and moral dialogues with the faithful to find solutions to particular problems that pertain to the local Church if as *Apostolos Suos* (12) affirms, they first belong to a universalist episcopal college which in reality precedes the office of being the head of a particular Church? How could an ecclesial synodality be carried out by all the People of God without the lay faithful being passive recipients (*EG*, 120) who are simply invited to make up the number?

Richard Gaillardetz, rightly argues, for instance, that Vatican II's positive appreciation of the role of cultures in the expression of the Christian faith demonstrates the recognition by the Council that the local Church is "the place where the universal Church was concretely realised."[13] This vision of Vatican II of a Church

---

[10]   Hervé Legrand, "Communio Ecclesiae, Communio Ecclesiarum, Collegium Episcopo-rum," in *For a Missionary Reform of the Church: The Civilta Cattolica Seminar*, eds. Antonio Spadaro and Carlos Maria Galli (New York: Paulist Press, 2017), 162, 176.

[11]   Legrand, "Communio Ecclesiae," 160.

[12]   Legrand, "Communio Ecclesiae," 160.

[13]   Richard Gaillardetz, *Ecclesiology for a Global Church: A People Called and Sent* (Maryknoll, NY: Orbis Books, 2008), 117.

of Churches—*pars pro toto* (Tillard)[14] where each local Church is the Church of God with its own unique character and identity based on its contextual experience of the faith means, as Elochukwu Uzukwu puts it, "that the one Church of God is fully realised in diverse locations with its own autonomy. This requires mutual recognition, respect for difference of each local Church vis-à-vis the Church of Rome in order to create room for the realisation of the specific mission and contextual nature of the pastoral life of local Churches."[15] However, this vision of a *Church of Churches* was hampered by series of centralising rules and practices aimed at interpreting and implementing the wishes of Vatican II for the establishment of Synod of Bishops.[16] Legrand lays the blame for this situation on the curial interpretation of *Lumen Gentium*, and the priority given in the revised Code of the Canon Law of 1983 to "the concept of a particular Church over the diocesan Church, of the episcopate of apostolic succession over the diocesan episcopate, and finally of the universal Church over the particular Church."[17]

Pope Francis recognises this tension and in *Evangelii Gaudium* (32) expresses the wish for a reform of the papacy and the central structures of the universal Church as part of the missionary and pastoral conversion required in the Church. Pope Francis proposes granting episcopal conferences a juridical status,[18]

---

[14] Jean-Marie Tillard, *L'église Locale: Ecclésiologie de Communion et Catholicité* (Paris: Cerf, 1995), 284-285.

[15] Elochukwu Uzukwu, "A Theology of Christian Unity for the Church in Africa," in *The Church We Want: Foundations, Theology and Mission in the Church in Africa*, ed. Agbonkhianmeghe Orobator (Nairobi: Paulines Publications Africa, 2015), 286.

[16] See the detailed development of this debate in Walter Kasper, *Leadership in the Church: How Traditional Roles Can Serve the Christian Community Today* (New York: Crossroad, 2001); and Joseph Ratzinger, *Called to Communion: Understanding the Church Today* (San Francisco, CA: Ignatius Press, 1996). See the analysis of this debate in Kilian McDonnell, "The Ratzinger/Kasper Debate: The Universal Church and Local Churches," *Theological Studies* 63 (2002), 227-250.

[17] Legrand, "Communio Ecclesiae," 165.

[18] See for instance, Francis's revision of Canon 838 through the promulgation of the Motu Proprio, *Magnum Principium* which modifies the competences of the Holy See, local Bishops and episcopal conferences on the interpretation of liturgical texts.

"which could see them as subjects of specific attribution, including genuine doctrinal authority" (*EG*, 32) so that they could, as *Lumen Gentium* 23 teaches, "contribute in many and fruitful ways to the concrete realisation of the collegial spirit."[19] The tension over the "synodal path" undertaken by the German Church, and some regional decisions by episcopal conferences on same-sex marriage, and denial of communion to politicians among others are important developments that will test the conversion of the papacy under Pope Francis. This conversion of the papacy will also naturally bring into closer scrutiny the needed conversion of a universalist supra-diocesan dimension of the episcopacy that will give birth to Bishops who are more accountable to the laity of their particular dioceses. This conversion of the papacy and the synodal process will bring about a participatory synodal process, where the local Churches and local needs are being addressed using resources from that particular context and not simply as an externally imposed ecclesial colonial deliberation determined, moderated and mediated through the Roman centre with the local Churches as outposts of the Roman Church.

The second tension in the synodal process is the continued exclusion of the voices of the laity and particularly of women in the Catholic Church. Anyone who looks at the picture on the official site of the Secretariat of the Synod of Bishops and does not cringe at that image of all-male participants discussing the future of the Church, fails to grasp how far the Church's understanding of synodality is from the vision of the Church as the gathering of all of God's people, where everyone is a first-born child (*Heb* 12:22). Carmel McEnroy wrote of the women participants at Vatican II as "guests in their own house." Sadly, that imagery is still true today. It is important to state clearly that any synodal process dominated by men and which continues to ignore the voices of women and their full participation in both *decision-making and decision-taking* in the Church is not only unjust,

---

19   Legrand, "Communio Ecclesiae," 186.

but also sinful. This is because such a defective synod is only a gathering *of some People of God*, and not of the *whole People of God*. It also defeats the mission and will of God that it is through journeying together as equal children of God that the Church can find her way to realising her mission in the world today.[20]

The third tension is that the synodal process in the Catholic Church has remained within a Western paradigm of participation which continues to overlook the power differentials in the synodal process itself between the Bishops and the laity, male and female voices, the Global North and the Global South. Particularly, significant here is the fact that the Roman Church has not expanded the method, process, and orientation of the synodal process by appropriating creative approaches to participatory dialogue and engagement from the Global South and participatory practices being developed in the social sciences, democratic institutions, and international development.[21] Modern synods in the Catholic Church—except perhaps the synodal path of the German Church—are still a very top down approach: Rome sets the theme, chooses the structure of the dialogue, appoints the key functionaries for the synod, chooses the place for the conversation to take place. It seems to me that the method, process, and orientation of synods in the Catholic Church since Vatican II have not offered the Church a strong framework for an "interactive participation" of all the members of the Church, beyond functional participation and tokenism. In an *interactive participation*, all the members of the Church or dialogue partners are equal stakeholders, and each person is learning with and in the presence of one another, governed by a key principle of participation—*nothing about me, without me* which is another way of restating the ancient ecclesial

---

[20]   See Carmel McEnroy, *Guests in Their Own House: The Women of Vatican II* (Eugene, Oregon: Wipf and Stock, 2011).

[21]   See for instance, Samuel Hickey and Giles Mohan, eds., *Participation: From Tyranny to transformation? Exploring New Approaches to Participation in Development* (London: Zed Books, 2004); See also Andrea Cornwall, "Unpacking 'Participation:' Models, Meaning, and Practices," *Community Development Journal* 43/3 (July 2008): 269–283.

maxim for councils, *quod ad omnes tangit ab omnibus tractari et approbari debet* — what concerns all, must be examined by all.[22]

These three shortcomings in the synodal process and goals — a reductionist interpretation and application of Vatican II's teaching on collegiality, the neglect of the participation of women and the laity in the synodal process because of the baggage of clericalism in the Church, the failure to find a way of managing diversity, dissensus, and conflicts in World Catholicism; and the neglect of the voices of the Global South in the synodal process and in the choice of issues and themes for the synod — are some of the challenges which Pope Francis has tried to engage through his reforms. There are limitations in his approaches which I argue could be addressed through the African palaver for the emergence of a more inclusive and expansive method for the 2023 synod and beyond.

Pope Francis on a Synodal Church: People, Process, and Praxis

In his address at the ceremony commemorating the 50th anniversary of the institution of the Synod of Bishops (17 October, 2015), Pope Francis goes beyond the reductionist limitation of synod in the Church to episcopal collegiality.[23] He begins a process of recognising ecclesial synodality as something that is much more than the gathering of Bishops to an understanding of the Church as synodal in its essential dialogical constitution as Trinitarian.[24] A synodal Church, in this sense embraces the anointing of the whole People of God as a prophetic unction of the

---

22   Cornwall, "Unpacking 'Participation,'" 271.

23   Pope Paul VI, *Apostolica Sollicitudo*, 2, https://www.vatican.va/content/paul-vi/en/motu_proprio/documents/hf_p-vi_motu-proprio_19650915_apostolica-sollicitudo.html.

24   Pope Francis, "50th Anniversary of the Institution of the Synod of Bishops," 17 October 2015, https://www.vatican.va/content/francesco/en/speeches/2015/october/documents/papa-francesco_20151017_50-anniversario-sinodo.html.

Spirit from which arises the *sensus fidei* which "prevents a rigid separation between the *ecclesia docens* and an *ecclesia discens*, since the flock likewise has an instinctive ability to discern the new ways that the Lord is revealing to the Church."[25] It is impossible in a short essay of this kind to fully develop the magisterial teaching of Pope Francis on a synodal Church, but as a preliminary summative account, I have reduced his teaching to **3 Ps**: People, process, and praxis and offered some principles identifiable in Pope Francis's magisterial teaching on a synodal Church.

People: The key to understanding Pope Francis's teaching and practices on a synodal Church is his ecclesiology of the People of God which he captured in his speech commemorating the 50th anniversary of the institution of the Synod of Bishops this way: A synodal Church is a Church which listens, which realises that listening "is more than simply hearing." It is a mutual listening in which everyone has something to learn. The faithful people, the college of Bishops, the Bishop of Rome: all listening to each other, and all listening to the Holy Spirit, the "Spirit of truth" (*Jn* 14:17), in order to know what he "says to the Churches" (*Rv* 2:7)."[26] For Pope Francis, if there is one way in which Christianity has gone astray, "It is to forget that we belong to a people. To set yourself above the People of God is to ignore that the Lord has already come close to His people, anointing them, raising them up."[27]

People, for Pope Francis, is not a sociological or economic concept, nor is it a collection of individuals or simply a population. According to Guzman Carriquiry Lecour, Pope Francis locates

---

[25] Cf. Pope Francis, "Address to the Leadership of the Episcopal Conferences of Latin America during the General Coordination Meeting," Rio de Janeiro, 28 July 2013, 5,4; ID., "Address on the occasion of a meeting with Clergy, Consecrated Persons and members of Pastoral Councils," Assisi, 4 October 2013.

[26] Pope Francis, "50th Anniversary of the Institution of the Synod of Bishops."

[27] Pope Francis, *Let Us Dream: The Path to a Better Future* (New York: Simon Schuster, 2020), 106.

the people[28] in the awareness of the origin of each individual, the historical circumstances in which each person lives and a constellation of the social, religious, and cultural traditions and histories of each person. People is inherently a way of capturing the shared spaces that we occupy; our common journey on the path of hope and truth; and the uniqueness of particular experience and the mutual connections and implications in each other's life and the life of the earth all of which form "the deepest fibres of the identity of a people."[29]

I find two images very useful in capturing Pope Francis's teaching here. First, is the principle which he enunciates in *Evangelii Gaudium*, 235 when he writes, "the whole is greater than the part, but it is also greater than the sum of its parts." He uses the image of a polyhedron to demonstrate the diversity, distinctiveness and convergence that should exist between all parts which he applies to world systems, the Church and to our common home. Everyone belongs; everyone is invited to the table; everything belongs, and no one should be excluded or overlooked and there should be "a place for everyone" (*EG*, 237).

He applies this image of polyhedron in *Querida Amazonia* (29-40) to show the rich diversity in creation as the basis for dialogue reflected in the "great human diversity" in the Amazon through which "God manifests himself and reflects something of his inexhaustible beauty" (*QA*, 32). While emphasising the need for respect for the unique history and treasures of the Amazonian peoples and rejecting "a false openness to the universal" (*FT*, 145), he makes an important appeal that "starting from our roots, *let us sit around the common table, a place of conversation and of shared hopes* (my emphasis). In this way, our differences, which could seem like a banner or a wall, can become a bridge. Identity and

---

28   Guzman Carriquiry Lecour, "The 'Theology of the People' in the Pastoral Theology of Jorge Mario Bergoglio" in *Discovering Pope Francis: The Roots of Jorge Mario Bergoglio's Thinking*, eds. Brian Y. Lee and Thomas L. Knoebel (Collegeville, Minnesota: Liturgical Press Academic, 2019), 46-47.

29   Lecour, "The 'Theology of the People,'" 47.

dialogue are not enemies. Our own cultural identity is strengthened and enriched as a result of dialogue with those unlike ourselves" (*QA*, 37).

It is, however, in *Fratelli Tutti* that he develops fully the idea of the theology of the people. He uses the term "people" 95 times in *Fratelli Tutti* and 164 times in *Evangelii Gaudium*. He develops the core element of the idea of people this way, "each of us is fully a person when we are part of a people; at the same time, there are no peoples without respect for the individuality of each person" (*FT*, 182). However, belonging to a people or a community means that the person becomes part of a shared identity that has both cultural and social bonds (*FT*, 158). In *FT*, "people" is an open-ended fact, "a living and dynamic people, a people with a future… constantly open to a new synthesis through its ability to welcome differences" (*FT*, 160). Person, within the context of people, in the vision of Pope Francis, evokes relationality. It is to be understood, not as something external, but as a constitutive identity marker of being human within the webs of relationships that build the community as a people.

This explication of "people" at the natural order, offers a theological aesthetic for the ecclesiology of the People of God, the mission of the Church, and a participatory synodal Church. God has chosen to gather a people through the free act of grace to be united with God and with one another (*EG*, 112-113). The Church is "a people for everyone." The Church is the People of God of all those who have been called forth by the love of God the Father and enabled by the Spirit to participate in diverse ways in carrying out the mission of Salvation accomplished by the Son. The Church, then is a site for "the complex interweaving of personal relationships entailed in the life of a human community" (*EG*, 113). This People of God is a community of many faces with diverse cultures (*EG*, 115-116); no single culture captures the whole of the gifts and dimensions of God's love; no single group within the Church has a monopoly of the gifts because "God furnishes the totality of the faithful with an instinct of faith—*sensus fidei*—

which helps them to discern what is truly of God" (*EG*, 119). Every member of the Church is, therefore, a missionary and has a part to play in bringing the joy of the Gospel to the ends of the world (*EG*, 120). This Church is invited to go into the world "unprepared", with no pre-packaged plan, rigid and static design, but through a synodal spirit of dialogue, consultation, prayer, and openness to the Spirit, to engage human experiences and changing human condition with a listening ear.[30]

The second image of the People of God is that of the Church as *an inverted pyramid* [31] where "the top is located beneath the base."[32] This reversal of the dualism between the college of Bishops and the rest of the People of God is significant in terms of emphasising the ministerial and servant role of the hierarchy, while de-emphasising the hierarchy of power and privilege that has often rendered the laity invisible in the Church's synodal process except when they are protesting or objecting to policies and teachings that cause them grief. The rich development of the baptismal denominator of ecclesiality in Vatican II as the basis for ecclesial synodality that involves the whole People of God has not led to any structural changes of the power dynamics in the Church's synodal process. In that light, the inversion of the pyramid remains largely at the predilection of a Pope or Bishop, the necessary changes in the Canon Law and the final decision-taking at the end of a synod. Thus, one sees that this inverted pyramid is still a structured clerical formula which the International Theological Commission has retained in its preferred interpretation of synodality as an expression of *communio* ecclesiology, rather than an ecclesiology of the People of God (54-56).

---

[30]   Anthony Spadaro, "Francis' Government: What is the Driving Force of his Pontificate?" *La Civiltà Catholica*, 14 September 2020, 5-6, https://www.laciviltacattolica.com/francis-government-what-is-the-driving-force-of-his-pontificate/. (accessed 23 January 2021).

[31]   Congar made a similar analogy in these words, "The church is not a pyramid whose passive base receives everything from the apex." See Yves Congar, "Pneumatology Today," *American Ecclesiastical Review* 167 (1973), 443.

[32]   Pope Francis, "50th Anniversary of the Institution of the Synod of Bishops."

In this framework, ITC affirms the circularity of communal discernment, consultation, and joint exercise of discernment in "decision-making." This distinction between "decision-making" and "decision-taking" process relating to the ministerial authority of the Bishop within the governing structure of the Church does not involve the laity in determining the final outcomes of a synod's consultative process. This is one of the limitations where the African palaver offers a helpful corrective as we shall demonstrate later in this essay.[33] Let me be clear, the African palaver is far from an ideal type or a flawless process. In its worst expression, it has fostered an androcentric, patriarchal (clericalist), and gerontocratic (hierarchical) reading of African history.[34] Thus, my allusion to the resources the African palaver can offer the Church does not exclude the possibility of reform in palaver itself so as to make this ideal type more inclusive for women. By the same token, Pope Francis's teaching on the People of God also has limitations when we look at the process and praxis which he offers for realising this vision of the whole People of God journeying together.

Process, and Praxis: The images of a polyhedron and an inverted pyramid help to clearly develop four fundamental ecclesiological principles in Pope Francis's teaching on a synodal Church. First, synodality is an ecclesial process central to the mission of the Church and reforming the synodal process in the Church is central to realising the central impetus of Pope Francis's call for missionary conversion needed for bringing the joy of the Gospel and the mercy of God to a wounded and broken world.

Second, synodality, is a journey of the whole People of God and not an exclusive gathering of Bishops. It is a dialogue of the whole of the faithful (*LG*, 23). The reform of Pope Francis has centred around removing those institutional obstacles and

---

[33] International Theological Commission, *Synodality in the Life and Mission of the Church*, 69.

[34] My thanks to the anonymous reviewer who pointed out this flaw.

ecclesial mindset and culture that have made it impossible for an expansive dialogue to take place in the Church.[35]

Synodality is a journeying together in which everyone is to be carried along. It is a communal process of deliberating, engaging, listening, and discerning the signs of the times. It is the breath of the Spirit that leads the whole Church into the whole truth; it is the Church's compass for seeing the footprints of God in history in the concrete life of the Church and of the world. According to Pope Francis, synodality invites the Church and her members to a humble spiritual disposition and turning towards the Holy Spirit for the gift, "to listen to God, so that with him we may hear the cry of his people; to listen to his people until we are in harmony with the will to which God calls us."[36]

The dynamics of listening is key to the synodal process in Pope Francis and key to the synodal praxis. Listening leads us to go beyond the claims of our personal, cultural, ecclesial powers and fixation with protection or defence of time-worn positions and claims. Listening is an invitation to pay attention to the "heart of the matter" (*FT*, 50) in the cries and contestations of our times. Listening opens us to a wider horizon for dialogue, debate, contestation, and disagreement in a spirit of charity but with a firm commitment to allowing the Spirit to lead us to a higher perspective and greater unity. Listening leads the Church to see and imagine things as God would see them (St Ignatius); it leads to a shared wisdom, and when carried out in the freedom of the Spirit (*FT*, 49), it releases people from attachment to fixed positions; stubborn idolatry of systems, institutional claims, and defence of doctrinal fortresses to a new experience of a new creation and openness to new things.

While one sees that under Pope Francis, the Synod of Bishops is becoming "the dynamic point of convergence for mutual listening to the Holy Spirit at every level of the Church's life,

---

[35]   Pope Francis, "50th Anniversary of the Institution of the Synod of Bishops."

[36]   Pope Francis, "50th Anniversary of the Institution of the Synod of Bishops."

by all the members of the Church", the process is still very hierarchical, clerical and male dominated. It has failed to address the marginalisation of the laity or the problems identified by the ITC in its June 2014 document, *Sensus Fidei in the Life of the Church* on the need to carry the laity along and how to honestly deal with the fact that "certain decisions have been taken by those in authority without due consideration of the experience and the *sensus fidei* of the faithful, or without sufficient consultation of the faithful by the magisterium."[37] The problems of clericalism, polarisation in the Church, and marginalisation of the laity, the voices of women, minorities, and the non-Western Christian voices still remain unresolved. This is why I think that we need to look at new models from the South which could challenge the Church to live with multiple standpoints; to sometimes suspend judgement and embrace diversities in the contextual pastoral discernment that is needed to celebrate Catholicity in its different forms of emergence in the world today. What the African palaver offers in meeting these challenges and furthering Pope Francis's teaching and practices for a participatory synodal Church will occupy us in the rest of this article.

The African Palaver Process

The African palaver (*l'arbre à palabre*) is a unique art of conversation and participatory dialogue in the common search for practical solutions to everyday challenges and conflicts in personal, family, communal, and intercommunal relationships. It aims at building a community spirit, and consensus in both decision-making and decision-taking. What has been translated in the English language as "palaver" is a poor rendering of a rich socio-ethical ancestral religious tradition found in many African ethnic groups. This tradition provides the tools in the

---

[37] International Theological Commission, "*Sensus Fidei* in the Life of the Church," https://www.vatican.va/roman_curia/congregations/cfaith/cti_documents/rc_cti_20140610_sensus-fidei_en.html (accessed: 14 July 2021).

traditional setting for maintaining justice, peace, social cohesion, and for promoting those sound ethical choices for human and cosmic flourishing. Among the Maasai of East Africa, palaver is what is designated by the tradition of *enkiguena*. Among the Igbo of West Africa, there are cognate terms which designate this tradition (*ịkpá ńkàtá, ịchịkọtá úchè ọnụ, ọgbákọ, ịbọrị ụka*). The process and praxis of the palaver is captured in this Igbo proverb, *ótù áká ànághị èké ńgwùgwù, one hand does not tie the parcel*. In his African classic, *Things Fall Apart*, set in pre-colonial Igboland in Eastern Nigeria, Chinua Achebe writes: "Among the Ibo the art of conversation is regarded very highly, and proverbs are the palm oil with which words are eaten."[38] In *Things Fall Apart*, there are many examples of the application of the process of the African palaver—how war was averted through dialogue between Umuofia and Mbaino following the murder of an Umuofia woman; the settlement of domestic violence in the family of Uzowulu through restorative justice; the dialogue between an Umuofia man, Akunna, and the white missionary, Mr Brown, on God and religious tolerance; the resolution of the indebtedness of Unoka to Okoye among others. These many episodes in this African classic reveal significant aspects of the African palaver among the Igbo of West Africa which we also see among the Zulu of Southern Africa, in the dialogic tradition called *Indaba*. A short analysis of the roots of "palaver" in two ethnic groups in Africa will shed light on the profound meaning and methods of this tradition that has been designated in the writings of African scholars as *the African palaver*.[39]

---

[38]   Chinua Achebe, *Things Fall Apart* (New York: Anchor Books, 1994), 7.

[39]   Whereas one can identify different variants of the palaver in most ethnic groups in Africa, the two ethnic groups chosen here, represent the palaver practices that have been applied in recent times in Africa and globally in promoting dialogue on climate change (indaba), and on developing participatory practices and models in international development, conflict resolution, and promoting dialogue in the global Church. On the application of palaver to other African ethnic groups in Central Africa, and East Africa, see Bénézet Bujo, *Foundations of an African Ethic: Beyond the Universal Claims of Western Morality*, Trans. Brian McNeil (New York: Crossroad, 2001), 42, 54. See also Elochukwu E. Uzukwu, *A Listening Church: Autonomy and Communion in African Churches* (Maryknoll: Orbis Books, 1996), 126-127.

Metumo ildonyo kake ketumo iltunganak (Mountains cannot meet, human beings can)

Mara J. Goldman and Saningo Miliary have offered a helpful study on the use of *enkiguena* among the Maasai, which I employ here in unpacking this rich tradition for consensus building.[40] After an extensive case study of the Maasai pastoral people of East Africa, they concluded that *enkiguena* was for the Maasai a participatory tool for communication, dialogue, and consensus-building "in recognition of multiple, complex, and overlapping power dynamics." An analysis of power in any social system from the simplest family relations to the most complex human communities like clan, state, corporation, churches, and institutions shows that there is always the danger of asymmetries of power based on different kinds of social hierarchies which particular societies and institutions have developed over time.

Goldman and Miliary argue that creating a participatory space for dialogue does not guarantee even in modern institutions that more power will not be appropriated by the rich and powerful at the expense of the poor. This is why even in the most advanced democracies, there still exist unjust institutions which leave the weak with less power and in many instances make them vulnerable to exploitation, oppressive and unjust laws and different forms of abuse of their rights and their persons. Therefore, it is not enough to recognise power dynamics and how they affect and determine life outcomes for individuals and groups. It is important then to pay particular attention to how power even within formal processes of dialogue and consultation can be manipulated by individuals and systems to perpetuate injustice and marginalisation of the poor and the voiceless.[41]

---

[40]   Mara J. Goldman and Saningo Miliary, "From Critique to Engagement: Re-Evaluating the Participatory Model with Maasai in Northern Tanzania," *Journal of Political Ecology* 21 (2014), 408-423.

[41]   Goldman and Miliary, "From Critique to Engagement," 412.

Enkiguena emerged in the course of history among the Maasai because of the need to open wider the space for open discussion and dialogue in order to resolve conflicts and balance individual and common interests in a just manner. At the same time, *enkiguena* was applied to avert the manipulative instinct of individuals or groups which might imperil the good of the community and of individuals, especially the poor and the less powerful. When viewed from the roots of the word, *enkiguena*, means any of these three things:

(i) A *communitarian process* for the healthy and harmonious functioning of society where discussion, meeting, consultation, debate or counsel take place among clan leaders, age-grades, women's groups, youth, family or a *boma* (Maasai homestead).[42]

(ii) A *quality that is valued* among leaders and followers for the good functioning of community which includes: ability to speak and communicate in a respectful manner, listening to others, delegating responsibilities to others in a shared and participatory manner, and openness to including others in deliberation on things that concern them.

(iii) A *calling together of people usually under the shade of a large tree (l'arbre à palabre)* to make a joint decision on a matter which concerns the community, or a meeting convoked primarily to resolve a conflict or arbitrate between families and individuals.

In either case, what is sought is a consensus—there is no voting or horse-trading which could create camps or leave some people feeling defeated and humiliated. The consensus reached has been described as "an imaginative synthesis" arrived at through dialogue and debate in a non-linear path, rather than through a formal construction of a compromise.[43] Consensus

---

[42] Goldman and Miliary, "From Critique to Engagement," 413.

[43] Paul Spencer, *Time, Space, and the Unknown: Maasai Configurations of Power and Providence* (New York: Routledge, 2000), 249.

emerges through a rigorous and winding participatory discursive exchange which Goldman and Miliary describe this way: "It circles around and meanders off in different directions as different speakers contribute new ideas, knowledge and opinions to the topic at hand. People will often draw on memory to discuss how a similar problem was tackled in the past, what they decided then and if it is relevant to current discussion."[44]

Indaba: mkono mmoja haujikuni mgongoni (A hand does not scratch its own back)

When the Anglican Church accepted the proposal of the Archbishop of Cape Town, Thabo Makgoba to adopt *indaba* as a possible format for the 2008 Lambeth Conference, he was offering to the Church and the world a Zulu variant of the African palaver, which was practiced in African social life, even if imperfectly, many centuries ago.[45] Archbishop Makgoba had warned against the continued use of a synodal method in the Anglican Church which was structured around the Western parliamentary processes characterised by the kinds of combative debates which could "feed destructive attitudes of competitiveness, dominance, and power, over and against one another, that then run through our common life."[46] Paula D. Nesbitt has described the *Indaba* Zulu tradition as "a process rather than an end in itself. This type of journey involves leaving comfortable assumptions behind and stepping into the cultural context of others who may have very different habits, expectations, and assumptions."[47]

There are three main ways through which *Indaba* has been interpreted today among other forms of interpretation and application identified by Paula Nesbitt:

---

[44]   Goldman and Miliary, "From Critique to Engagement," 415.

[45]   Paul D. Nesbitt, *Indaba: A Way of Listening, Engaging, and Understanding Across the Anglican Communion* (New York: Church Publishing, 2017), 3.

[46]   Cited in Nesbitt, *Indaba*, 8.

[47]   Nesbitt, *Indaba*, xviii.

(i)   *it is the gathering together of the community* for a purposeful discussion on the common concerns of all in the community.[48] Everyone is welcomed to the *indaba*; everyone is encouraged to speak so that the community can listen to the matter at hand from different perspectives and begin to seek common grounds and a way forward even where there are still some unresolved questions and difficulties. *Inbada*, in this understanding, is a way of reconciling differences, enhancing social cohesion in the community, and a means for strengthening the bonds of life in the community through a greater commitment to a shared purpose—the common good.[49]

(ii) *Indaba is a tool for engaging the community in reconciling differences*: Nesbitt writes as follows with regard to *Indaba*'s traditional application as a tool for community engagement: "*Indaba* as a form of community engagement comes out of a particular cultural context where both the community and its members have a strong mutual identity and commitment. It assumes that everyone belongs and that differences can be worked out even if not resolved."[50]

(iii) *Indaba as a tool for conflict transformation*: Nesbitt proposes that *Indaba* is also a tool for healing wounds in the society especially "long-standing deep wounds, and trauma."[51] The process of healing begins when the community in the spirit of *ubuntu*—I am related, therefore we are; I am a person through other people—recognises itself in those who are suffering in the community as a result of physical or spiritual ailments, poverty, injustice, exclusion or prejudice.

---

[48]   Gregory K. Cameron, "Lambeth Indaba 2008 and its Ecumenical Implications," *One in Christ* 42/2 (2008), 364.

[49]   Nesbitt, *Indaba*, 3.

[50]   Nesbitt, *Indaba*, 6.

[51]   Nesbitt, *Indaba*, xii.

Benezet Bujo writing with reference to the practices in both Central Africa and among the Ashanti of Ghana identifies a process of transformation of conflict and therapeutic similar to *Indaba's* when he writes: "In concrete terms, the cause of an illness lies primarily in interpersonal relationships. It is always a sign that something is wrong in the community, in its two dimensions of the living and the dead, and this means that the re-establishing of the broken interpersonal relationship cannot be a matter for doctor and patient alone: it demands the participation of the entire community. This is why a palaver is indispensable."[52] Palaver thus seeks to provide a reverential space for hearing the voices of everyone, including the invisible ancestors as well as those who might be made invisible because of disability or other acts of injustice in the community that need to be healed, so that all will participate in the bond of life to which all must draw as from a well pool.[53]

African Palaver and a Participatory Synodal Church

It is now possible to demonstrate the possible contributions of the African palaver to addressing the three limitations in Pope Francis's teaching on synodality in the Church. The palaver model offers a "how" for a synodal Church. I will concentrate on three areas—the expansion of the understanding of people or community, a more inclusive participation of every member of the Church in the synodal process at all levels of church life, and overcoming the dualism and binary thinking that is at the heart of the polarisation in today's Church.

First, the African palaver invites all people in the community to a sacred space for a *creative dialogue* on how to realise abundant life, human and cosmic flourishing and combat those vices or unjust

---

52   Bujo, *Foundations of an African Ethic*, 46.

53   Bujo, *Foundations of an African Ethic*, 55.

acts which hamper the participation of all in the bond of life. The emphasis is on *all people rather than some people*. The palaver is representative, but it devolves the responsibility for decision-making and decision-taking to intermediate groups like women's groups, age-grades, clans, and family groups. Masamba ma Mpolo sees the African palaver as a gathering space for sharing the Word which gives life. Life is understood in this sense in many ways—a vital principle with an unbroken chain of being from God and ancestors to humanity and all creatures; flourishing, being who one is meant to be; being in a right relationship, participating and contributing to the common good, and sharing in the common good. Life also refers not simply to the human life, it refers not only to the living (the gathered assembly), rather to the community—a rich and expansive notion which includes the living, the ancestors, the not-yet born, all spiritual realities, the visible and invisible creatures, ecological life, the planet, and the entire cosmos. Everyone in the community has something to contribute to the shared bond of life. This is why Mpolo identifies the freedom and right to speak and the inclusiveness of the palaver space to hearing everyone's opinion as decisive. So, everyone is allowed to speak in their own manner, whether by words, dance, stories, symbols, and in mimes.

Indeed, Mpolo argues strongly that the African traditional society created this inclusive space for dialogue because "everything revolves around the word, for to speak is to live, to recognise and to affirm the existence of the other person. To be speechless is to be naked, to be deprived of oneself. Loss of freedom to communicate and to transmit life biologically are synonymous with death. Speech is creative because it often engenders life."[54] Given the importance of speech, truth-telling is of vital importance; and lies and falsehood are frowned at: "Ability to have recourse to speech and to assess the acts of life

---

[54]   Masamba ma Mpolo, "Jesus Christ—Word of Life: An African Contribution to the Theme of the Sixth Assembly," *The Ecumenical Review* 35/2 (April, 1983), 168.

is therefore essential. God becomes flesh in human speech and acts. When it is a matter of blessing and reinforcing life, *mpova* (speech) becomes *Nzambi*, i.e., the human word becomes the Word of God. It is word which brings peace, reconciliation, health, life, the word which re-establishes the equilibrium of the community when it is in danger of disintegration."[55] The palaver is a space for truth-telling, because the truth heals, binds, and restores the community; the depths, diversity and ramifications of truth are found in the traditional African community through a patient listening, long and often laboured deliberation, and openness and attention to the spoken word—spoken in freedom. This is why "the dynamic of palaver permitted free expression; it was possible to pour out one's heart, to give testimony or to analyse together a conflict which might endanger the existence, i.e., the life, of the community. The chief was obliged to listen to everything, even if this took a whole week.... Here we have the discourse of the people, the word which liberates."[56]

Second, *the African palaver method with its emphasis on the participation of all in the community in dialogue can help the Church today to move away significantly from a top-down approach to synodality.* This can happen by strengthening and simplifying the synodal process and devolving the power to make decisions to local Churches and other intermediate ecclesial bodies in matters that are specific to their context, following the age-old principle of subsidiarity. The bureaucratic nature of synods in the Church even in local Churches, and the centralisation of power in Rome, or in the hands of diocesan Bishops and local parish priests, limits the ability of local Catholic communities, lay groups, and Small Christian Communities to make decisions and find solutions and approaches to addressing most of the issues that they face in their daily witnessing to the Gospel. Seeking the approval of the Vatican for local Church Bishops and episcopal conferences,

---

55　Masamba ma Mpolo, "Jesus Christ—Word of Life," 168-169.

56　Masamba ma Mpolo, "Jesus Christ—Word of Life," 169.

and seeking the approval of the Bishops for parish priests and lay groups means that decisions made at these levels are often a waste of time. Those decisions cannot be implemented without the approval and consent of a higher authority who can reject those decisions or impose his own decision on the rest of the ecclesial family. We can see an example of this in the tension in the current effort of the German Church in developing a synodal path for its local Church and the tension between the U.S. episcopal conference and the Vatican on a document on the Eucharist.

The third contribution of the African palaver is in overcoming dualism and creating a depolarising space for conversation, creative conflicts, and conversion of world views. The African Palaver *is an ethic for consensus-building in the common and dynamic search for how to preserve, promote, and protect the common good from which all should draw as from a well pool. It is also a means for healing divisions and hurts and wounds inflicted on people.* It proceeds from the acceptance of the inherited practice of traditional African communities that the resolution of moral or existential complexities is not achieved through stubborn attachment to a single viewpoint, or the narrow reduction of one's purview to a preconceived idea or a limited horizon of meaning. The palaver is thus a depolarising space for listening, conversation, and the fusion of individual subjective horizons in the ever expansive and dynamic horizon of the communal wisdom of the ancestors in the search for justice and peace. The goal is not to shut anybody's opinion down or to drown individual perspectives, concerns, and insight in certain prefabricated communal answers to existential questions or ultimate concerns.

In this way, the community is enriched by the multiple perspectives brought to the table of dialogue by everyone concerned by the matter at hand. As an Igbo proverb has it: *úchè bu àkpà, onye o bula nya nke ya* – human opinion is like a bag of treasure which everyone carries with him or her at every time. In the African palaver, therefore, everyone is invited to bring from their bags of wisdom, the treasures of truths and insights to enrich the communal wisdom. The goal of the palaver is to make possible the deployment of the insights of everyone in the community in the interpretation and understanding of present realities and complexities in the dynamic search for solutions which conduce to human and cosmic flourishing.

The African palaver gave people in traditional society, especially those who were facing injustice and oppression (i.e., the poor, the marginalised), hope that their communities will fight for them through communal solidarity. Kasonga wa Kasonga proposes that in translating palaver to Christian practice, the centrality of hope must be emphasised: "Hope is a Christian virtue based not on human promises but rather on divine promises (…). Hope must be the main thread orienting the whole process of Christian palaver. It provides a theological foundation for healing from enslaving situations, granted that healing is one of hope's realisations."[57] This aspect of healing and hope is what is lacking in many recent synods where marginalised and invisible communities and voices in the Church are often drowned out by dominant perspectives and teachings. In many cases, some of the contested moral and social issues in the Church have been framed through a Western epistemological hegemony and debates that often mute the voices of the Global South.

Finally, the African palaver *rejects dogmatism, absolutisation of truths, fundamentalism, and dualism of left and right, traditionalists and progressives.* It opens wider the sacred space for religious freedom, cultural pluralism, interfaith, intercultural, interracial, and interethnic encounters and welcomes opposing world views and religious convictions as long as they do not harm human and cosmic flourishing.[58] Traditional Africans did not wage religious

---

57   Kasonga wa Kasonga, "African Christian Palaver: A Contemporary Way of Healing Communal Conflicts and Crises," in *The Church and Healing: Echoes from Africa,* eds. Daisy Nwachukwu, Emmanuel Yartekwei Lartey, and Kasonga wa Kasonga (New York: Peter Lang, 1994), 58.

58   Bujo, *Foundations of an African Ethic,* 162-163.

wars nor were their religious affinity sources for radicalisation and terrorism. In place of fundamentalism, extremism and polarisation, the palaver encourages the search for the Golden Mean.

This practice of looking at everything twice and looking at the other side of the coin is a principle of the African palaver that can be an effective method for the synodal process in the papacy of Francis. It is an approach that is capable of moving ecclesial dialogue beyond binary thinking, oppositional camps, and dualism. African traditional societies did not lock themselves in dualistic thinking and enslavement to traditions as Benezet Bujo asserts strongly, "the tradition does not prevent African ethics from being innovative."[59] This point is also attested to by Laurenti Magesa, when he noted that the traditional palaver offered a space for dialogue on ethical norms since traditional African society did not impose moral precepts on people except through a communal act of collective discernment and decision. "In the palaver," Magesa argues, "ancestral precedents are recalled in various ways, not, however as cut-and-dried principles, but as guidelines for the existential situation."[60]

The palaver rejects all forms of dogmatism and embraces the hermeneutics of duality (not dualism) and multiplicity. This openness to duality addresses in a healthy manner the complexities of faith and morality. The African mind rejects absolute claims. Expatiating on this, Elochukwu Uzukwu writes: "In West Africa, ambivalence, collaboration and the hermeneutic of suspicion, especially the suspicion of absolutes, are the rule for accessing reality. This allows room or liberty to always adopt or search for a 'second point of view' to practice 'looking at everything twice.' What is not relational, would be a degeneration and could

---

[59]   Bujo, *Foundations of an African Ethic*, 43.
[60]   Laurenti Magesa, *Anatomy of Inculturation: Transforming the Church in Africa* (Maryknoll, New York: Orbis Books, 2004), 161.

harden intolerance."[61] This openness of people in Africa to the possibility that things exist in complementary and participatory relationship leads to openness in exploring the relationships between seemingly contradictory realities; the ability to live with contraries and even ambiguities; and an admission that life is a shared relationship in which all things count. This stance leads to the acceptance of complementary duality. This approach to seeking a middle point and consensus is capable of thawing the theological rigidity and fundamentalism of our times characterised by a stubborn clinging to unchanging positions by both liberals and conservatives that has made it impossible for any theological progress to be made in recent synods under Pope Francis.[62]

Expanding the Space for Participation for the *Invisibles and Voiceless* through the Palaver

An ecclesial synodality developed along the patterns of the African palaver (*enkiguena, indaba* and *ịkpá ṅkàtá*) will open a sacred space for dialogue into which all are invited. It will lead to what Lieven Boeve proposes as the needed open-structure narrative practices which could help free theologians and pastors from theological fundamentalism or enslavement to "the contingent particularity of our own narrative" to "an open sensitivity towards otherness" and a recognition of our own boundaries and the boundary experiences of others.[63] In that space, everyone is involved in the search for common answers to common problems, each contributes as the Spirit gives him or her the grace of utterance.

---

[61] Elochukwu Uzukwu, *God, Spirit, and Human Wholeness* (Eugene, Oregon: Pickwick Publications, 2012), 13.

[62] Stan Chu Ilo, "Reform from the Margins: Pope Francis and the Renewal of Catholic Theology," in *All the Ends of the Earth: Challenge and Celebration of Global Catholicism*, eds. Jane E. Linahan and Cryil Orji (Maryknoll, New York: Orbis Books, 2020), 146.

[63] Lieven Boeve, *Interrupting Tradition: An Essay on Christian Faith in a Postmodern Context* (Louvain: Peeters Press, 2002), 94-96.

Vatican II when read in this context of the African palaver was the Church's first attempt in the modern era to celebrate an ecclesial variant of the African palaver. However, the palaver of Vatican II was incomplete because the voices of some people were not heard.[64] Those missing voices were those of Africa among other needed perspectives as well as the narratives of other Non-Western societies outside of the Northern hemisphere. Africa did not have a significant representation at Vatican II. Thus, the decisions made at that Council, even though they have shaped modern Catholicism in Africa, did not sufficiently represent Africa's concerns and the mission of God in Africa.[65] Can we say that the voices of those unrepresented voices, today in a post-Western Catholicism and a post-Christian Western society are now being heard in the Church? Who are those voiceless and invisible members of our faith communities whose voices are muted in the Church today? Who are those who are not under the palaver tree or around the Eucharistic table in our Church today? How can the Church reach out to them just as the Maasai people did in traditional *enkiguena* gathering, where women were also invited, and where failing to speak in the dialogue process will delay the final decision until every voice is heard? Why is there no place in our Churches where people can lament and where the tears of the broken and wounded among us and the rejected in our Churches and societies can give us the sources of wisdom, which is often lacking in gatherings dominated by power contestations and turf wars?[66]

---

[64] On Africa's limited participation at Vatican II, see Agbonkhianmeghe Orobator, "Look Back to the Future: Transformative Impulses of Vatican II for African Catholicism," *Concilium: International Journal of Theology* 2012/3 (2012), 97-102; See also Agbonkhianmeghe Orobator, ed., *The Church We Want: Foundations, Theology, and Mission of the Church in Africa: Conversations on Ecclesiology* (Nairobi: Paulines Publications Africa, 2015).

[65] The account of the efforts of Alioune Diop and African colleagues in making African voices present before, during and after the Council have been well documented in a recent book, Charles Becker, Jeanne Lopis-Sylla and Aloyse-Raymond Ndiaye, eds., *Présence Africaine: Revue Culturelle du Monde Noir, 50 ans après Vatican II* (Paris: Présence Africaine, 2019).

[66] One of the hermeneutics of ecclesial lamentation as a source for synodal pedagogy for

The Church must pay attention to the stories of everyone as the African ancestors once did. This African wisdom was captured so profoundly by African novelist, Chinua Achebe in these words: "It is the story, not others, that saves our progeny from blundering like blind beggars into the spikes of the cactus fence. The story is our escort; without it, we are blind…They are all we have…to fight off illness and death. You don't have anything if you don't have the stories."[67] In the story of everyone, in the stories of the cries of the earth and the cries of the poor, I can hear my own story. It is only by paying attention to how our human and cosmic stories are connected can we see how our stories can be redeemed by love. When we listen to the stories of others especially those who are hanging on the cross today, we can see how that unconditional manifestation of love on the Cross by the pain, suffering and death of the poor man of Galilee becomes a unique exemplarity of what happens every moment when the closed narrative of humanly designed structures and institutions meet their limit before the infinite and open narratives of divine love on Calvary which have no limits.

In doing this, it is important to take into consideration the power differentials within a group like a World Church where participation could be a new form of tyranny.[68] Sherry R. Arnstein in her influential essay, originally published in 1969 titled "A Ladder of Citizen Participation" offers some helpful insight for reflecting on the limitations of the participatory practices and processes which can apply in any global organisation like the Catholic Church. Although she was writing in the context of a liberal democracy, her insights are generalisable in conceptualising a more inclusive participation. She writes that "there is a critical difference between going through the empty ritual of partici-

---

a listening and discerning church see Bradford Hinze, *Prophetic Obedience: Ecclesiology for a Dialogical Church* (Maryknoll, New York: Orbis Books, 2016), 85-89.

67 Chinua Achebe, *Anthills of the Savannah* (New York: Anchor Books, 1998), 124.

68 Bill Cooke and Umah Kothari, eds., *Participation: The New Tyranny?* (London: Zed Books, 2001).

pation and having the real power needed to affect the outcome of the process."[69]

Arnstein makes a distinction between three kinds of participation and non-participation in her ladder of participation. The first, at the base of the ladder, is *manipulation and therapy* where participants are actually non-participants even though they may be present at a meeting. This is because the holders of power "educate" the participants in a way that makes them accept the existing structures of power relationships and why it is good for those on the lower rungs of the ladder. The holders of power are also interested in "curing" the participants of any tendencies to upstage the power arrangement through protests and opposition to the status quo. The second grid in this ladder of participation or non-participation is what she calls "degrees of tokenism" which involves *information, consultation, and placation.* Here, the voices of people may *be heard* by those who hold the levers of power, but the people "lack the power to ensure that their views will be *heeded* by the powerful."[70]

Tokenism gives the veneer that people are being consulted, that they are being informed, and that their needs are being addressed. Sadly, this is not always the case because the holders of institutional power retain the sole power of decision-taking. In addition, at the end of the consultation, there is no follow through by the rank and file to bring about any fundamental alteration of the power balance or the structural nature of the power differential in the group. The synodal process in the Catholic Church has stayed at these two levels because the fundamental episcopal, clerical, and male dominance of the institutions of the Church has remained intact and untouched. The centralisation of power in the papacy remains the same and carried out through the curia. In many instances, the laity are often manipulated to

---

[69]   Sherry Arnstein, "A Ladder of Citizen Participation," *Journal of the American Planning Association* 85/1 (2019), 24.

[70]   Arnstein, "A Ladder of Citizen Participation," 25.

bring about some predictable outcomes, while the "therapeutic approach" is applied in suppressing or muting the voices of those who are crying in the Church or who attempt to enact alternate ecclesial sites where their needs are addressed.

There is the need then to create both *a space for true representation and a space for speech and active participation in a dialogue in a synodal Church*. I am referring to how to overcome "presence without taking active part" (not speaking or being heard) or what Arnstein refers to as "participation as window dressing."[71] A participatory synodal Church should embrace *participatory power* where there is a respectful partnership between those in authority and the people so that they can together bring about real changes and reform in the Church. A participatory synodal Church must also embrace *delegated power* wherein there is a decentralisation and devolution of power and responsibility in recognition of the joint stakeholding ability of each person. A participatory synodal Church *must create rooms for mutual accountability, and transparency in the whole body* of the Church between the laity and the clergy for instance. It should also canonically create new structures that accords the laity a measure of control over the synodal process, governance in the Church through shared responsibilities based on charism, expertise, and the principle of subsidiarity.

Adopting the palaver method will require a more expansive and contextual engagement that should be done more at local and regional levels than the unwieldy synodal process and procedures that currently exists when representatives of regional episcopal conferences gather in Rome with few lay representatives. One must also consider the ecological and financial implications of bringing so many people to Rome for such synods in the future. What it means is that greater canonical recognition should be given to such synodal process in local Churches and regions. This is because the future may not be determined by unanimity

---

71   Arnstein, "A Ladder of Citizen Participation," 31-32.

of every region in all issues, but a negotiation and acceptance of our differences on some of these contested issues—women's place in the Church, the rights of LGBTQI+ people, clerical celibacy among others. Creating *a space for speech and active participation in a dialogue in the freedom of the Spirit*, is in my mind, what the African palaver method offers. Dialogue goes beyond formal structures of consultation in the Church through the hierarchy, to a commitment to listening to what the spirit is saying to and through the whole People of God and acceptance of participatory decision-making and decision-taking as fundamental to life of the Church at all levels.

Conclusion

One of the arguments against the African palaver which has been raised by a number of African theologians is that this cultural tradition seems to be more an academic, political, and theological conversation in Africa than a value, method and praxis being applied by political and church leaders in today's Africa. Many Africans and critics of such African claims like palaver ask about the validity of the much vaunted African spirit of community represented in the Nguni word, *ubuntu,* in the face of the Rwandan genocide, the pogrom in the Nigerian-Biafran war, the endless wars in the Congo and the atrocities in Sudan, South Sudan, Central African Republic, the xenophobia in South Africa, and the asymmetrical radical Islamic warfare by Nigeria's Boko Haram and the Ansar Dine in Mali.

In the same way, when one looks at the state of dialogue and communion in the Church in Africa and the abuse of power in African politics, the suppression of oppositions and the intimidations and persecution of minorities and religious groups in Africa, one will wonder if the African palaver just presented has any validity if it does not inform the political culture and political socialisation in the African polity, and synodality in the

African Church. Elochukwu Uzukwu, for instance, concluded that African leaders today "have failed to live under the gaze of the ancestors and God, in order to qualify to draw from the pool of that creative and healing Word which is 'too large' for the mouth of one individual, but which is so crucial for upbuilding the community."[72]

The truth is that the African palaver is an ideal to be pursued rather than a complete horizon of being and living which has ever been perfectly realised. The African palaver is not a magic wand, nor has it effectively been applied in Africa's social, political, and religious space. However, the African palaver is an ideal that I have tried to appropriate in this essay in order to propose what Jean and John Comaroff call some alternate "fertile staging grounds and laboratories" for new practices and knowledge that could help depolarise the theology and ecclesiology of modern Catholicism. There is the need to subvert this epistemic scaffolding cast around the contending narratives of modernity that holds the Catholic Church in perpetual unresolved tension and a misleading sense of unity.[73]

As a cultural and historical tradition, the African palaver also bears the wounds of human distortions both in the norming of ethics, in reconciling differences or maintaining justice. As Wilson Maina noted, in most cultural traditions in Africa, the palaver marginalises the voices of women in the decision-making process, as a result it should not be seen as a perfect participatory process.[74] While not devaluing the contributions of African societies and cultures in developing universalisable moral truth and ecclesial practices like synodality, Paulinus Odozor challenges African theologians and church leaders to a more critical attitude at the individual, communal and group levels, as to how we have

---

[72] Uzukwu, *A Listening Church: Autonomy and Communion in African Churches*, 129.

[73] Jean Comaroff and John Comaroff, *Theory from the South: Or, how Euro-America is Evolving Toward Africa*. (New York: Routledge), 2012, 7.

[74] Wilson Muoha Maina, *The Making of African Christian Ethics: Bénézet Bujo and the Roman Catholic Moral Tradition* (Eugene, Oregon: Pickwick Publications, 2016), 88.

betrayed who we are and who we wish to be in the current violation in Africa of those values which constituted us as a people.[75]

By way of conclusion, the goal of this article is to point out the need to pay closer attention to social processes, cultural traditions, and hidden wisdom in societies in Africa which can be inculturated in the search in Africa and in the World Church for a fruitful and workable synodal process at all levels of the life of the Church. My contention is that a value like the African palaver can help initiate a process for bridging the widening divisions in our Church today. I also argue that the African palaver is one of the many tools from outside the non-Western world that should be creatively explored and applied in the needed creative dialogue for birthing an effective process and praxis for synodality in the Church today.

The palaver has been applied successfully by African theologians in many of the convenings of African Church scholars which have taken place within the last ten years. The palaver method was employed during the Pan-African Catholic Congress on Theology, Society and Pastoral Life in 2019 to mark the 50th anniversary of the founding of the Symposium of the Episcopal Conferences of Africa and Madagascar. The application of the palaver method functioned as a means of creating a reverential space where all the contributors could meet in a friendly and supportive setting to engage in open, collaborative, participatory dialogue, and mutual learning from one another. The palaver was particularly presented in the adoption of the final statement by consensus rather than through voting. The palaver method is also being adopted by African dioceses like Awgu in Nigeria in the collaborative and dialogical search for inculturated pastoral practices for adult and prophetic faith.[76] The palaver method—

---

[75]   Paulinus Odozor, *Morality Truly Christian, Truly Africa: Foundational, Methodological, and Theological Considerations* (Notre Dame: University of Notre Dame Press, 2014), 160.

[76]   See Kingsley Anagolu, *The Relationship Hermeneutics in the Context of Pastoral and Catechesis – Locus for Dialogue with Culture in the Mission Ecclesiae. Towards a Subject Oriented Pastoral and Catechetical Planning in the Nigerian-Igbo Church with Focus on*

indaba—has functioned since its adoption by the Anglican Church in 2008 as a tool for negotiating and embracing differences which emerged with the ordination of openly gay priests and bishops, same-sex marriage, and ordination of women. The *indaba* method was credited as the tool that helped the delegates at COP17 and the 2015 UN Climate Change Conference to reach a landmark decision on the agreement on Climate Change signed by the countries of the world.[77]

The palaver method has also become a tool for theological research and conversation particularly in the narrative theology of Joseph Healey in the African Small Christian Communities, and among African women through the Circle of Concerned African Women Theologians.[78] However, the most developed form of the palaver as a theological method in Africa today is in the works of Emmanuel Katongole, who has reinvented the African palaver as a way of listening to the story of Africans as well as listening for those untold stories that are often drowned in silence, in tears, and in the drums of war.[79] The palaver is a tool for following the different stories that make up the story of our Church and our world. It should serve as a veritable tool for paying attention to the stories that have not been heard or told and for inviting the invisible and forgotten to the table of fellowship in a participatory synodal Church.

Awgu Catholic Diocese (Vienna: Lit Verlag GmbH & Co. KG, 2016), 112-113.

[77] See "The African Discussion Style 'Indaba' Thrived at Climate Talks," *Washington Post*, December 18, 2015, https://www.wsj.com/articles/the-african-discussion-style-indaba-thrived-at-climate-talks-1450456996. (accessed September 2, 2020).

[78] Joseph Healey and Donald Sybertz, *Towards an African Narrative Theology* (Maryknoll, New York: Orbis Books, 1999), 324-336. See also, Mercy Amba Oduyoye, "The Search for a Two-Winged Theology: Women's Participation in the Development of Theology in Africa," in *Talitha, Qumi! Proceedings of the Convocation of African Women Theologians, Trinity College, Legon, Accra, September 24-October 2, 1989*, eds. Mercy Amba Oduyoye and Musimbi R. A. Kanyoro (Ibadan: Daystar, 1990), 47.

[79] Emmanuel Katongole, *Born from Lament: The Theology and Politics of Hope in Africa* (Grand Rapids, Michigan: William B. Eerdmans Publishing Company, 2017), 37.

CHAPTER 5

Ubuntu and Synodality

Josée Ngalula

Three specific African elements of culture and ecclesial experience can be fruitful while reflecting on synodality: the African understanding of palaver, the African experience of Small Christian or Basic Christian Communities, and the Ubuntu spirituality. African Theology has drawn on the riches of African religions, proverbs, songs, folktales, the dialogical emphasis on palaver rooted in what is summed up in the African concept of Ubuntu, to express with African images and perceptions, the riches of Christian theology and spirituality. In this dynamic, in recent years we have been hearing about a Christian Ubuntu theology.[1] It would be interesting to discover the implications for the practice of synodality. This essay will focus on Ubuntu as a paradigm of deconstruction, firstly as an ideal of human relationships in African anthropology, secondly as a paradigm of deconstruction in individual relationships between Christians, and thirdly how this deconstruction also concerns the understanding of a synodal Church.

---

[1] As examples: Tobias Nhlanhla Mcunu, *The Dignity of the Human Person: A Contribution of the Theology of Ubuntu to Theological Anthropology* (Pretoria: University of South Africa, 2004). Kapya J. Kaoma, *God's Family, God's Earth: Christian Ecological Ethics of Ubuntu* (Malawi: Kachere Series, 2014). Elina Hankela, *Ubuntu, Migration and Ministry: Being Human in a Johannesburg Church* (Johannesbourg: Brill, 2014). Jaco Dreyer, Yolanda Dreyer, Edward Foley, Malan Nel, *Practicing Ubuntu: Practical Theological Perspectives on Injustice, Personhood and Human Dignity* (Münster: LIT Verlag, 2017). Nokukhanya Pearl Shabalala, *Truth and Reconciliation in Light of the Cross: Martin Luther's Theology of the Cross in Relationship to the Current Ubuntu Theology of Desmond Tutu* (Clayton: Concordia Seminary, 2019).

The Ideal of Ubuntu

In Africa, the concept of humanness is expressed in the notion of Ubuntu. The word Ubuntu comes from "ntu", a root word that is used to refer to the human being in sub-Saharan Africa languages; its variants are "ndu", "tu", "hu", "tho" and "to." Its abstract noun for saying "humanity" is then "Ubuntu/umuntu/bumuntu/ kimuntu/unundu/ngumuntu/ngabantu/unhu/botho/bomoto."[2] But the word Ubuntu and its variants do not only designate humanity as a category in creation, it is also a philosophical and ethical concept used in everyday life to highlight relationships that place an important value on being human. In Bantu languages, people who do not live in good relationships with others are spoken of pejoratively this way: "he/she is not at all a buntu/a muntu/a nundu!" The word Ubuntu has become popular worldwide as a concept from their application in political and spiritual context by two South African Nobel Laureates, Nelson Mandela and Desmond Tutu.

Ubuntu philosophy can be captured this way: *my humanness is dependent upon my relationship with others that are marked by the recognition of their human dignity as equal to mine, and as conditioning mine.* Human relationships are healthy where every person, regardless of his/her condition, location, and qualifications, is first and foremost considered and treated as a human being. That is humanity: I am human because all together we are equal human beings. To reject, hate or diminish another human being is to reject and diminish oneself, because the destiny of each human being is linked to the destiny of all human beings. Therefore, when I belittle and harm the humanity of my neighbour, I automatically

---

2   For Ubuntu see, for example: Mandivamba Rukuni, B*eing Afrikan: Rediscovering the Traditional Unhu-ubuntu-botho Pathways of Being Human* (San Rafael: Mandala Publishers, 2007). Michael J. Battle, *Ubuntu: I in You and You in Me* (Cape Town: Church Publishing, 2009). Jordan K. Ngubane, *Ubuntu: The Philosophy and Its Practice* (Durban: Mepho Publishers, 2015). Mungi Ngomane, *Ubuntu, Je suis car tu es* (New York: Happer Collins, 2019). Nompumelelo Mungi Ngomane, *Everyday Ubuntu: Living Better Together, the African Way* (New York: Random House, 2020).

degrade the humanity of both of us. The whole of existence must be imbued with this philosophy of Ubuntu, that is at the same time a spirituality. It does not mean that in everyday life, all Africans practice Ubuntu. Rather, it is an ethical imperative that is constantly recalled by adages and proverbs, because wherever human beings are, the violent negation of the humanity of one's neighbour is always a present risk in all spheres of life: in family, in society, in economic and political spheres, between individuals and between groups.

Ubuntu, as a philosophy and spirituality, is used in Africa as a paradigm of deconstruction of all kind of relationships between persons and groups that are based on a non-recognition of the equal humanity and dignity of all human beings. In everyday life, it is expressed through proverbs and sayings calling for a behaviour that engages in a reciprocity of recognition of human dignity that must be preserved and consolidated permanently at all levels of human relations. In the history of Africans (in Africa and Diaspora), Ubuntu has been the great source of the resilience of peoples faced with contempt for the black race institutionalised in the forms of slave trade, apartheid, racism, the degrading aspects of colonisation, or certain economic systems. The victims revolted and organised civil disobedience against the oppressors who despised their humanness, telling them the profound truth: *we are human beings and not machines to produce your prosperity; stop denying our humanity, let us walk in human fraternity in an inclusive society that recognises the dignity of all without exception, because this is the condition for us to live together in peace.*[3]

Because it affirms humanity as humanity, the Ubuntu philosophy, with its spiritual and ethical aspects is simply universal. In any country, culture and civilisation, every human

---

[3] See for example: Samuel A. Paul, *The Ubuntu God: Deconstructing a South African Narrative of Oppression* (Oregon: Wipf and Stock Publishers, 2009). Mark Mathabane, *The Lessons of Ubuntu: How an African Philosophy Can Inspire Racial Healing in America* (New York: Skyhorse, 2018). Henri Mova Sakanyi, *Ubuntu et résilience des peuples africains* (Paris: L'Harmattan, 2021).

being can recognise himself/herself in this anthropological imperative that deconstructs all options of violent relationships between persons and groups.

Ubuntu as a Paradigm of Deconstruction of Interpersonal Christian Relationships

Ubuntu spirituality is above all an ethical imperative that calls for an "art of living" going in the direction of a communion between human beings based on the recognition of the intrinsic dignity of every human being. It is not surprising that Christian theological circles have recognised in it some elements of Christian spirituality.

In Ubuntu spirituality, being humane is regarded as the supreme virtue. That is why it highlights a relational ethic of mutual love and compassion. It has been used to present Christian ethics based on God's love as the cornerstone for developing a spirituality of justice and liberation in human communities. In order to enjoy life and happiness, no one can tolerate the suffering of others.[4] Ubuntu invites people to embrace positive behaviour in the human community. To harm another human being in anyway means that one lacks the spirit of Ubuntu. As a paradigm, Ubuntu has been used to present in African words and images a theological anthropology grounded in Christian Scriptures, to denounce negative behaviours that have taken root in African Christianity about the way we understand community,[5] and pastoral care,[6] amidst the oppressive cultural practices and beliefs

---

[4]   Example: Jaco Dreyer, Yolanda Dreyer, Edward Foley, Malan Nel, *Practicing Ubuntu: Practical Theological Perspectives on Injustice, Personhood and Human Dignity* (Münster: LIT Verlag, 2017).

[5]   Example: James Ogude, *Ubuntu and the Reconstitution of Community* (Indiana: University Press, 2019).

[6]   Tapiwa N. Mucherera and Emmanuel Y. Lartey, *Pastoral Care, Health, Healing, and Wholeness in African Contexts: Methodology, Context, and Issues* (Oregon: Wipf and Stock Publishers, 2017).

against women, children, and other categories of people often excluded from recognition of their human dignity in African societies.[7] In the Black Theology of South Africa, the Ubuntu spirituality was used in connection with the biblical notion of "shalom" and the Christian belief of every human being as created in the image of God, to prevent the building of a post-apartheid society based on hatred and vengeance: humanism integrating ethic of Ubuntu and a restorative forgiveness must be the basis for this new society.[8]

In Ubuntu anthropology, the human person is not isolated but always related and linked to other persons and institutions, generally in the context of extended family. But Ubuntu adds an ethical imperative. Living in relationship to other human beings, the basis must be positive behaviour based on a solidarity and fraternity grounded in the respect of the humanity of all human creatures; to be "human" with all human beings is a communal and ethical imperative. Unfortunately, many complex situations rooted in the consequences of modernity in Africa have produced a kind of belonging that is against the Ubuntu ethic, because belonging to an extended family has concretely become synonymous with hatred and violence towards people. Violent hostility, which deny the humanity of others because of differences of clan, tribe, race, nation, and religions is replacing the Ubuntu ethics in Africa. The ecclesiological option of using the image of the Church as the Family of God as a model of evangelisation aims to revive the Ubuntu bond of life, not only at family or city/village level, but at a global level, in order to establish a wholesome African society where every human person is considered in his/her human dignity, and is at home irrespective of family orientation or tribal background.[9]

---

[7]   See, for example: Jacquineau Azetsop, *HIV & AIDS In Africa: Christian Reflection, Public Health, Social Transformation* (New York: Orbis Books, 2016).

[8]   Michael J. Battle, *Reconciliation: The Ubuntu Theology of Desmond Tutu* (Cleveland, OH: The Pilgrims Press, 1997).

[9]   Gerald K. Tanye, *The Church-as-family and Ethnocentrism in Sub-Saharan Africa*

Revitalisation of Ubuntu Through Small Christian Communities

The option of Basic Christian Communities (BCCs)/Small Christian Communities (SCCs) is a deconstructive paradigm at the service of revitalisation of Ubuntu, that joins the will of God as expressed in *Lumen Gentium*: "God, however, does not make men holy and save them merely as individuals, without bond or link between one another. Rather has it pleased Him to bring men together as one people, a people which acknowledges Him in truth and serves Him in holiness" (*LG*, 9). No Christian should live in isolation.

The 1994 Synod of Bishops in Africa recognised the importance of the Basic Christian Communities (BCCs)/Small Christian Communities (SCCs) already existing in Africa for more than 30 years, as an experience of building the church from the grassroots, by listening to God who is speaking to all humanity through Holy Scripture. That is exactly where the People of God, the faithful of Christ learn and experience from the grassroots the true spirit of the extended family of God, a sense of family that excludes racism, tribalism, ethnocentrism, and all other exclusive senses of belonging that generate violence in the societies.[10]

Ubuntu as a Paradigm that can Deconstruct Bad Understandings of Synodal Church

To speak of the synodal Church is to invite us to "walk together." However, not all ways of "walking together" are truly

---

(Münster: LIT Verlag, 2010).

[10]   The first Synod of Bishops, "Ecclesia in Africa", 89. See also Joseph Healy, *Building the Church as Family of God: Evaluation of Small Christian Communities in Eastern Africa* (Nairobi: CUEA, 2012). Maximian Khisi, *The Church as the Family of God and the Care for Creation* (Malawi: Mzuni Press, 2019). Donatus Oluwa Chukwu, *The Church as the Extended Family of God: Toward a New Direction for African Ecclesiology* (Indiana: Xlibris Corporation, 2011).

synodal. The Bible contains many accounts of violence that reflect the non-recognition of the equal humanity of the other, within the same family and the same people. Our life together on earth is both a chance to grow together in humanity, and a risk of harming each other and thus destroying our common humanity. We also experience it wherever there are human beings living together in the world. We can walk together side by side without the desire or practice of fraternal communion. We can walk together, one behind the other with a mentality of hierarchising human beings, to the point that those who are in the lead believe that the humanity of those behind them is less. We can be together by sitting in a circle around a meal, but with a mentality of mutual rivalry and jealousy, we can also be together face to face, in a search for a destructive fusion of the otherness of the other.

African Christians hear in *Fratelli Tutti*, the words of Pope Francis talking about the spirituality of Ubuntu, when he writes: "Each of us is fully a person when we are part of a people; at the same time, there are no peoples without respect for the individuality of each one" (*FT*, 182). In 2001, Pope John Paul II already alerted the world on the striking resonance of the understanding of Church as Communion, by inviting us to a "spirituality of communion," in words that sounds to African ears as Ubuntu spirituality:

> To make the Church the home and the school of communion, that is the great challenge facing us in the millennium which is now beginning (…). A spirituality of communion indicates above all the heart's contemplation of the mystery of the Trinity dwelling in us, and whose light we must also be able to see shining on the face of the brothers and sisters around us. A spirituality of communion also means an ability to think of our brothers and sisters in faith within the profound unity of the Mystical Body, and therefore as "those who are a part of me." This makes us able to share their joys and sufferings, to sense their desires and attend to their needs, to offer them deep and genuine friendship. A spirituality of communion implies also the ability to see what is positive in others, to welcome it and prize it as a gift from God: not only as a gift for the brother or sister who has received it directly, but also

as a "gift for me." A spirituality of communion means, finally, to know how to "make room" for our brothers and sisters, bearing "one another's burdens" (*Gal* 6:2) and resisting the selfish temptations which constantly beset us and provoke competition, careerism, distrust and jealousy. Let us have no illusions: unless we follow this spiritual path, external structures of communion will serve very little purpose. They would become mechanisms without a soul, "masks" of communion rather than its means of expression and growth (*Novo Millenio Inuente,* 43).

Ubuntu is like a symbolic matrix that fertilises Christianity by provoking it to specify its originality with regard to the concrete institutional implications of the nature of the Church as communion, with the dynamism of a spirituality of communion. The proper nuance that Ubuntu philosophy brings to the Christian practices is the ethical imperative that invites human beings to live with each other in true humanity. The Ubuntu philosophy encourages African Christians to say this: the human being is not only created "in the image of God" (cf. *Gn* 1), but more precisely in the image of the Triune God, who is relational by nature. However, this relationship is of such that it is respectful of otherness and open to the other without any violence or domineering tendency, leading to the mutual valorisation between the Father, the Son and the Holy Spirit. In this perspective, the Catholic Church must not invite the People of God to the synodal path without being mindful of the possible minefield in the practices of this synodality, and especially the ethical imperatives and habits required for all who are journeying together.

With this in mind, I would like to address some urgent challenges, namely, deconstruction of clericalism and of the complex of superiority of some local Churches.

Deconstructing Clericalism

Pope Francis draws our attention to the pervasiveness of clericalism in the Church when he writes: "There is that spirit of clericalism in the Church, that we feel: clerics feel superior; clerics distance themselves from the people. Clerics always say: 'this should be done like this, like this, like this, and you – go away!'" It happens "when the cleric doesn't have time to listen to those who are suffering, the poor, the sick, the imprisoned: the evil of clericalism is a really awful thing; it is a new edition of this ancient evil". But "the victim is the same: the poor and humble people, who await the Lord."[11] Priests who have clericalist mentality understand their role as spiritual leaders and spiritual "fathers" as a "power" granted to them by the sacrament of Holy Orders upon lay people. Because of that, there are regular tensions in some dioceses and parishes between clergy and laity, because clericalist priests are afraid that the laity will take their place and power. So, they do not think in terms of communion and working hand in hand with laity in the mission of the Church. They think that the Church belongs to them, and the laity has been called to help them as servants. They think of the Church as a place of relationships based on power, and not on fraternity based on the recognition of equal dignity in humanity and in salvation. In Ubuntu spirituality, such a mentality and consequently behaviour is called "inhumane," "non-Ubuntu" because the human being called "layperson" is not looked at from his/her human dignity first, that is, a human being created in the image of God and the brother/sister "for whom Christ died" (1 *Cor* 8:11).

Despite their training in theology, many priests have forgotten the definition of the word "faithful" and think that only the laity are the "faithful" in the Church. Canon 204 §1 says: "The Christian faithful are those who, inasmuch as they have been incorporated in Christ through baptism, have been constituted as the People of God. For this reason, made sharers in their own way in Christ's priestly, prophetic, and royal function, they are called

---

11   Pope Francis, "Homily in Casa Santa Marta", December 13, 2016, https://www.vatican.va/content/francesco/en/cotidie/2016/documents/papa-francesco-cotidie_20161213_people-discarded.html (accessed 3 January 2023).

to exercise the mission which God has entrusted to the Church to fulfil in the world, in accord with the condition proper to each." And Canon 207 §1 adds: "By divine institution, there are among the Christian faithful in the Church sacred ministers who in law are also called clerics; the other members of the Christian faithful are called lay persons."

Many things will positively change in relationships in the direction of Spirituality of communion and Ubuntu within pastoral structures in the Catholic Church, if all Bishops, priests and deacons remember that they belong to the "faithful" in the Church. That means, according to Canon 208, that "From their rebirth in Christ, there exists among all the Christian faithful a true equality regarding dignity and action by which they all cooperate in the building up of the Body of Christ according to each one's own condition and function." The recommended "human" behaviour which fits best to the human nature that is created in the image of the Triune God is communion, the Ubuntu, as expressed by the Canon Law: "The Christian faithful, even in their own manner of acting, are always obliged to maintain communion with the Church" (Canon 209 §1). Consequently, in the Catholic Church the ministerial priesthood is not a power to be exercised over another faithful. The Church is not at all a property of the clergy in which the laity would also be welcomed by favour. Giving a voice to the laity in the Catholic Church is not a favour, a supplement, but an inescapable necessity, a duty for those having authority in the Church.

In the organisation of the seven sacraments in the Catholic Church, there are three sacraments of Christian initiation, two sacraments of healing, and two sacraments of service. The sacrament of Holy Orders is classified as service. According to the definition of Jesus Christ himself, to be called "Lord" means concretely to wash the feet of others. None of the seven sacraments is classified as power. In the Catholic Church today, how many priests are proud to display in their offices, albums and Facebook accounts the photo of Holy Thursday where the Catholic

Church forces them to wash the feet of the faithful? Do they do so reluctantly, or with the joy of expressing that this is the fundamental meaning of the sacrament of Holy Orders?

It would be a great help for a truly synodal act, that is, fully human (Ubuntu) experience in relations between clerics and laity in the Catholic Church, if the next synod takes one moment to look at the articles of Canon Law that contain ambiguities that induce clerics to understand their ministry of service in terms of the hierarchical power and privilege over the Christian faithful that would give them a certain domination over the laity, unlike the spirituality of communion. Ubuntu spirituality and ethics asks this question to the Catholic Church as we undertake this synodal journey on synodality: for example, is it possible to imagine the Church deciding that to be a sacristan in a parish, one must have received the sacrament of Holy Orders, because it is a true service, but that does not imply at all a state of authority over any other faithful in the Church?

Deconstructing the Superiority Complex of Some Local Churches Over Other Churches

For centuries, the Christian mission and, therefore, the relations between the Churches initiating evangelisation and the Churches founded as a result of this evangelisation have been marked by the values of the capitalist world. Capitalism has produced a kind of cultural narcissism that has taken hold within the Church of God itself, there are Christian individuals who always look at others from above, and there are also local Churches that always look at other local Churches from above. Even in the relations between the local Churches, this mentality has existed in history and continues in some circles until today. The hand that gives is considered above the hand that receives; the one who has more material means decides that it is the one who has the right of decision, and the word of the weak has no weight. The strong considers itself a "benefactor" over all that the weak possess, and takes from the weak what is best for itself, including the way the weak think and should act. Ubuntu tells us that this state of affairs is not normal, because it does not correspond to the quality of humanness; because it is a system that devalues, and even denies the dignity of the other. The Church of Jesus Christ is by nature a family founded on fraternity: no one or any particular Church can consider itself either above another, or below, not in the centre, nor on the periphery. The local Churches are sisters to each other.

Let me draw from an important moment during the Council to make this point. October 21, 1963, at the Second Vatican Council, Bishop Raimundus Tchidimbo, Archbishop of Conakry in Guinea, already expressed this absence of Ubuntu in relations between local Churches in these terms:

"There is therefore no inequality in Christ and in the Church as to nationality, social condition, sex, etc. ... St Paul proposed and defended this, as a precondition (...). Therefore, to speak explicitly, we say this: 1. International Organisations, because of their financial aid, for which we are thankful and is obvious in favour of the Third World, must not believe that they were sent by God to show us how the apostolate is to be organised in the country that is foreign to them. One must have the utmost respect for the particular characteristics of each nation and their civil institutions transmitted by their elders, and be wary of any project of domination.... May Europe give us the grace to seek its services first. We believe that the first specialist of the diocese is the bishop, the shepherd of his people. He was sent to answer alone before God and before Peter for his apostolate in his Church."[12]

---

[12]   Raimundus Tchidimbo, "Intervention in Congregatio generalis LII 21 October 1963." *In Acta Synodalia sacrosanti concilii oecumenici Vaticani Secundi. Volumen II. Pars III.* 150-152. [translated by myself]. The original text in Latin is: EXC. MUS P. D. RAIMUNDUS TCHIDIMBO, Archiepiscopus Konakriensis "(…) *Nulla igitur Christo et in Ecclesia insequalitas spectata nation, condicione sociali, sexu, etc. ....S. Paulus, ut praeviam condicionem sine qua non (…) Quapropter, ut explicite loquamur, sequentia dicimus: 1.- Internationales Organisationes, quia pecuniac carum adiumentum, pro quo gratias agimus, in*

Many years later, Jean-Marc Ela said that the communities of Jesus' disciples in Africa "do not need to be antennas of the rich Churches."[13] Some local Churches have proclaimed themselves "mother" churches that expect others to behave towards them as their "daughters", because they have been initiators of certain evangelising activities and have more financial means; they grant themselves the right of interference in these "daughter churches" in perpetual situations of obedient minors. In this 21st century, this goes as far as exploiting the economic fragility of the Churches of the South by the Churches of the North, who take unfair advantage of pastoral staff in the Churches of the South. A local Church in the South invests in the formation of its seminarians and young priests, and when the fruit is ripe, it is the rich dioceses that benefit from it, without having first asked permission or dialogued with the local Churches concerned.

Will the next synod on synodality have the courage to address the situation of suffering of the Bishops of poor countries who see the Bishops of rich countries stripping them of priests trained for the growth of the local Churches of the South in great need of apostolic staff, in the total absence of dialogue with the Bishops of the poor countries concerned? For here it is the synodal dimension of episcopal collegiality that is at stake, and which is flouted when the fellow Bishop is ignored in his episcopal and human dignity because of the "poverty" status of his country and his diocese. It is the same when the members of the Roman Curia treat the Bishops of poor countries as beggars who deserve no respect, while the goods offered to their dioceses are the property of the universal Church and not of the Roman Curia. Where is Ubuntu? Where is the ecclesiology of communion? Where is episcopal collegiality?

---

favore Tertii Mundi evidens est, non credant se simul a Deo missas esse ut nobis ostenderent quomodo apostolatus ordinari deberet in terra nobis nota sed eis aliena.(…) Opinamur primum specialistam in dioecesi episcopum esse, pastorem populi sui. Ipse missus est, ut solus coram Deo et Petro, de apostolatu in Ecclesia sua respondeat."

13 Jean-Marc Ela, *Repenser la théologie africaine: Le Dieu qui libère* (Paris: Karthala, 2003), 173.

Conclusion

The ecclesiology of the Church family of God/Fraternity does not concern only the internal life of the Churches of Africa. It is the whole Church of Christ in its universal and local aspects, which is a family in which Ubuntu must reign, that is, the mutual respect and promotion of the human dignity of the other. In relations between local Churches, some must not believe that they are superior to others in dignity, because they have more material means or other assets.

For Ubuntu philosophy and spirituality, considering that the other is no less human than me, and building interpersonal relationships on this basis, is a matter of ethical honesty. Living in the dynamics of true synodality, that is, imbued with Ubuntu, is ultimately a matter of honesty before God, who has revealed his Trinitarian dimension so that we may discover how to live truly as humans and embark on the path of spirituality of communion. And this, at the individual and institutional levels.

CHAPTER 6

Chinua Achebe's *Arrow of God*:[1]
A Postcolonial Theological Critique of Clericalism

Ikenna U. Okafor

With his gospel of mercy and his appeal to priests to become shepherds with the smell of the sheep, Pope Francis has without doubt demonstrated his desire for a Church that is rid of clericalism. His concern for the voices from the peripheries also inspires his imagination of a model or pilgrim path that God expects of the Church today, one that will require changes on how we conceive our pastoral mission as Church in the present world. That imagination is what is summarised in the word "synodality," which is the new focus of Pope Francis's pontificate. This new focus is informed by the fact that the way we do things determines the quality and outcome of our performance. With this in mind, this chapter throws light on the theological content of the postcolonial narrative of Chinua Achebe, using it as a hermeneutic tool to interrogate how clericalist attitudes obscure the emergence of a synodal church in Africa; how it works as a toxin that has the potential of poisoning evangelical progress and of actually destroying, or harming both the priesthood and the Christian religion. This chapter adopts an inter-

---

[1]   *Arrow of God* is a novel written by Chinua Achebe. The edition used in citations in this paper is the second edition Chinua Achebe, *Arrow of God* (London: Penguin Books, 1974). I have decided to include the chapters in my citations so as to help the reader locate the references easily in other editions of the novel.

disciplinary hermeneutic which uses African literature as authentic tools for theological interpretation in the African context.

According to Kwaku Larbi Korang, "in Achebe's delimitation of the modern literary author-function as African, we might see a post-imperial gesture of restoration wherein the representative African author reaches for the authority to restore (a) the human to Africa and (b) to give Africa back to the world in literary-humanist measure and form."[2] This is so evident in his two books, *Things Fall Apart* where Achebe challenges the arrogance as well as unmasking the naivety of the colonial narrative of imperialism while also exposing the weakness of the traditional African spirituality in its neglect of the ethic of care and compassion/fraternity; and in *Arrow of God*, which dwells on the excesses of the priestly power and authority. The conflicts that result from the confrontation with cultural modernity[3] form part of the basis of the narrative in Achebe's *Arrow of God*. For the insolent standoff with Captain Winterbottom over the offer of warrant-chieftaincy, served as catalyst to the communal crisis that doomed the chief priest and his people.[4] As the internal divisions, disagreements, and confusions of the community of Umuaro become exacerbated in and by the British colonial presence we see *Arrow of God* thematising the vagaries and ruptures that come with such a modern "transition and assimilating these to the consciousness of Ezeulu in ways that register the novel as a supreme example of existentialist literature."[5] Interpreted from the point of view of Christian theology, one sees that incidentally, perhaps providentially too, Achebe uses the narrative in *Arrow of God* to warn us about the consequences of a failure of synodality.

---

[2] Kwaku Larbi Korang, "Homage to a Modern Literary Father" in *Project Muse*, Research in African Literatures, Vol. 42, No. 2, Summer (Indiana University Press, 2011), xi.

[3] With cultural modernity, I mean the repercussions of colonial intrusion. For, Ezeulu's loggerhead with his community was precipitated by the effects of colonial presence, which caused his incarceration by the District Commissioner for allegedly insulting the Whiteman.

[4] Achebe, *Arrow of God*, 150.

[5] Korang, "Homage to a Modern Literary Father", xii.

One can translate the general thrust of Achebe's works of literature or cultural anthropology into theology particularly when read in the context of post-colonial theology that seeks to retrieve, rehabilitate, and reclaim African voices through the insertion or rather reinvention of the Church in Africa by an appeal to some of the wisdom that we find in the work of Achebe. This wisdom will be projected as vital for the emergence of a strong synodal culture in the African Church. A hybrid reading of *Arrow of God*, a work that has been described as "the richest and most suggestive of Achebe's novels, which is to say one of the richest and most suggestive novels of the twentieth century,"[6] helps us in appreciating the fact that synodality is more about attitude than it is about doctrine. It teaches that the best way of understanding and appreciating synodality is in acknowledging what must be avoided in order to achieve the synodal goal. Synodality shuns excessive preoccupation with self, hence, its primary challenge to the Church is to find ways of curbing the excesses of both clericalism and anti-clericalism.

For, if Achebe's novels are read as an illumination of the present, then the gesture toward their own forms and language become a part of that illumination, an assertion of who we are, not who we were. In the rest of this discourse, situated in the present, therefore, I will explore theologically the novel *Arrow of God* and how it unravels the perils of allowing human hubris to jeopardise the wellbeing of a community. I develop my discourse thus: First, I will give a brief summary of what synodality is in general. Second, I will give a synopsis of *Arrow of God* and the meaning of synodality in the African context. And third, I will appropriate with a theological commentary three important symbolic themes of the novel to shed some light on the relevance of the narrative to the theme of synodality in the mission of the Church today.

---

6   Korang, "Homage to a Modern Literary Father", xiv.

Synodality in the Church: Meaning and Implications in Light of *Arrow of God*

The most common meaning of the term synodality is derived from the ancient Greek word, synod, which is composed of a preposition συν (with) and the noun ὁδός (path), and indicates the path along which the People of God walk together.[7] It is a particular way of understanding the relationships between the Pope, the Bishops, and the rest of the baptised. It was an essential mark of the early Church and is key to the missionary impulse that the Church needs. It has been defined as the "mutual collaborative listening, guided by the Holy Spirit, in which all of the faithful have something to learn from each other, in order to know what God is saying to the Church."[8] The ecclesiology of Vatican II, the "People of God" stresses the common dignity and mission of all the baptised in exercising the diversity and interwoven richness of their charisms, their vocations, and their ministries.[9] For Pope Francis, there is a new form of ecclesiality which is best captured in the term synodality. Vatican II's concept of communion expresses the profound substance of the mystery and mission of the Church,

---

[7]   ITC, *Synodality In The Life And Mission Of The Church*, 3: accessed online 06.08.2022.

[8]   Pope Francis, 50th Anniversary of the Institution of the Synod of Bishops "Address of His Holiness Pope Francis" (17 October 2015) accessed online 13.12.2021 http://www.vatican.va/content/francesco/en/speeches/2015/october/documents/papa-francesco_20151017_50-anniversario-sinodo.html.

[9]   International Theological Commission, "*Sensus Fidei* in the Life of the Church" (2014).: accessed online 13.12.2021. Cardinal Walter Kasper has been very helpful in illuminating the understanding of this common dignity, which derives from the one baptism and gift of the Holy Spirit to all believers (1 *Jn* 2:20-27). The vocation, mission, and co-responsibility of every baptised person in the church arise from this gift of the Spirit (1 *Cor* 7:7) on the basis of a common priesthood of all the baptised (1 *Pt* 2:9; *Rv* 1:6; 5:10) (*LG*, 11). Since the one Holy Spirit is given to all, the People of God and the pastors of the Church are no longer opposed to one another like government and parliament. In the one Holy Spirit, the Church is the people united with the pastors, in which a "remarkable harmony (*conspiratio*) reigns between the Bishops and the faithful" (*DV*, 10). Therefore, not only should the believers listen to their shepherds; the shepherds must also listen to what the Spirit is saying to the churches (*Rv* 2:7, etc.). The saying: "Do not quench the Spirit of God!" (1 *Thes* 5:19) applies to everyone. See "Kirche ist Synode. 50 Jahre Limburger Synodalordnung" accessed online 18.01.2022: https://bistumlimburg.de/fileadmin/user_upload/Festvortrag_Kasper.pdf.

whose source and summit is the Eucharistic synaxis. Synodality expresses the specific *modus vivendi et operandi* of the Church, the People of God, which reveals and gives substance to her being as communion when all her members journey together, gather in assembly and take an active part in her evangelising mission.[10] As Pope Francis puts it, a synodal Church is a Church which listens, a Church which realises that listening is more than simply hearing. It is a mutual listening in which everyone has something to learn. The faithful, the college of Bishops, the Bishop of Rome: all listening to each other, and all listening to the Holy Spirit, the "Spirit of truth" (*Jn* 14:17), in order to know what he "says to the Churches" (*Rv* 2:7).[11]

The success of the first and second African synods which were Africa's reception of the Second Vatican Council, has enriched the evangelical resources of Africa for the Church in the modern world. The gift of the ecclesiology of the Church as family of God, for example, whose rich academic theology has not yet been exhaustively explored, and the vocation to reconciliation and peace, which are fruits of the two African synods respectively, are signs of the theological and pastoral profundity, creativity, and fecundity that characterise African Christian palaver or reverential dialogue (*shikome*), *ụka*, or *indaba*.

Arrow of God: A Synopsis

Arrow of God tells the story of Ezeulu, chief priest of the god Ulu, who was rigidly dogmatic and opposed to his kinsmen, Umuaro, who depended on his sighting of the new moon and eating of the sacred yams in order for them to harvest their new yams. Intent on punishing his people for not coming to his aid when he was detained by the colonial authorities at Okperi, Ezeulu is in no

---

10   International Theological Commission, *Synodality In the Life And Mission of the Church*, 43 (accessed online 06.08.2022).

11   Pope Francis, "50th Anniversary of the Institution of the Synod of Bishops."

hurry to call the date of the New Yam Festival, and as long as he did not call the date, the villagers could not harvest their new yams. Despite the looming disaster, Ezeulu refused to listen to the elders who suggested a change in custom and were even willing to bear the responsibility for any consequences such a change might unleash from the god. He remained recalcitrant in his rigid interpretation of the ritual of the yam festival. "Intoxicated" with the thought of himself as an "arrow in the bow"[12] or a "whip"[13] in the hand of the god, his conceit and vain clutching to his sacerdotal ego could not allow him to distinguish between himself and the god he was serving as chief priest. When eventually his favourite son, Obika, dies he suffers madness believing that Ulu, the god he has served so well, has deserted him at his moment of need. But the people's verdict is different. To Umuaro, Ezeulu ventured into war against his clan, and expectedly had lost. "Their god had taken sides with them against his headstrong and ambitious priest and thus upheld the wisdom of their ancestors – that no man however great was greater than his people."[14] Undoubtedly, a priest can still be respected as the "arrow of God" today. The question, however, is whether he is a healing arrow or a chastising one; a friendly protective arrow or a hostile one. In Ezeulu's case, the people's unsympathetic interpretation of his misfortune underscores the significance of a harmonious "walking together" between the priest and the people.

Remarkably, Achebe begins this story with Ezeulu musing about a great discursive technique;

> ... the immensity of his power over the year and the crops and, therefore, over the people [that] he wondered if it was real. It was true he named the day for the feast of the Pumpkin Leaves and for the New Yam feast; but he did not choose it. He was merely a watchman. His power was no more than the power of a child over a goat that was said to be his. As long

---

[12]   Achebe, *Arrow of God*, 193.

[13]   Achebe, *Arrow of God*, 210.

[14]   Achebe, *Arrow of God*, 232.

as the goat was alive it could be his; he would find it food and take care of it. But the day it was slaughtered he would know soon enough who the real owner was. No! the Chief Priest of Ulu was more than that, must be more than that. If he should refuse to name the day, there would be no festival—no planting and no reaping. But could he refuse? No Chief Priest had ever refused. So it could not be done. He would not dare.

Ezeulu was stung to anger by this as though his enemy had spoken it. "Take away that word 'dare'" he replied to this enemy. "Yes I say take it away. No man in all Umuaro can stand up and say that I dare not. The woman who will bear the man who will say it has not been born yet."[15]

This introduction to the story elucidates the internal conflict that plagues the mind of Ezeulu, the chief priest, a conflict that invariably obscures the communal promenade of the whole community. It is a conflict that revolves around the nature and extent of the clerical power and authority, a power that is as important and undeniable as it can be pernicious. One hears Ezeulu asking himself: "What kind of power was it if it would never be used? Better to say that it was not there, that it was no more than the power in the anus of the proud dog who sought to put out a furnace with his puny fart."[16] Achebe underscores the significance of the sacerdotal powers as demonstrated in the benedictions[17] which Ezeulu usually invokes upon the whole community each time he announces the advent of the new moon. Unfortunately, these priestly benedictions fail to compensate a "smouldering anger" which the chief priest nurses against some perceived enemies of his in the community,[18] an anger that will fester and eventually consume the priest, the people, and the deity.

The anxiety over the relevance or otherwise of the priestly power awakens in Ezeulu the temptation to abuse the power for revenge rather than to exercise it in a compassionate pastoral

---

15   Achebe, *Arrow of God*, 3.

16   Achebe, *Arrow of God*, 3-4.

17   Achebe, *Arrow of God*, 6.

18   Achebe, *Arrow of God*, 6.

service of his people. Maureen Warner Lewis aptly observes that having seen his significance as arbiter of both political and religious opinion successfully challenged, Ezeulu believes that "in order to exercise power in any positive way, that is, in order for the clan to feel the weight of his power, he would need to withhold, negate, his services."[19] But before I delve into a theological excursus, I will take a brief look at synodality in the African context.

Synodality in the African Context

In the current synodal process on synodality, Achebe's postcolonial critique is an important vehicle for transmitting the African voice on new ways of looking at the issues in question. Synodality, understood as a practice of listening to one another, is not alien to Africa. It has been practised by our ancestors in many African communities and has survived in forms known today as palaver, or *shikome* among the Sukuma people of Tanzania, *indaba* in South Africa, and *ụka* among the Igbo of eastern Nigeria. In Igboland, this practice of palaver became so intimately associated with the Church from earliest missionary times that Christians, perhaps due to the frequency of their meeting together (weekly), were named '*ndị ụka*' (the palaver people). Christianity thus came to mean, for the Igbo, the religion of weekly palaver. Far from being a long unproductive talk, palaver is a political and social exercise of respect for individual freedom of participation in finding communal consensus as a solution to collective problems. It is the acknowledgement of the right of every person in the society to make his or her voice count in decisions that affect the community. It is a kind of family tête-à-tête on the community level. And this chapter focuses on the knowledge brought to us

---

19   Maureen Warner-Lewis, "Ezeulu and His God: An Analysis of Chinua Achebe's Arrow of God" in *Black world*, Journal 24/2, 71-87 (Chicago: Johnson Publication, December 1974), 75. Available online at: https://books.google.at/books?id=sbIDAAAAMBA-J&printsec=frontcover&source=gbs_ge_summary_r&cad=0#v=onepage&q&f=false (accessed 07.01.2023).

about this practice or model of social engineering through the postcolonial literature of Chinua Achebe in his cultural classic, *Arrow of God*. Occasions of palaver are frequent in the novel, but the most remarkable is where the elders of Umuaro gathered at the house of their chief priest to ask him to eat the sacred yams and avert an impending crisis.

> The news of Ezeulu's refusal to call the New Yam Feast spread through Umuaro as rapidly as if it had been beaten out on the *ikolo* [the wooden gong]. At first people were completely stunned by it; they only began to grasp its full meaning slowly because its like had never happened before.[20]

The intervention of the elders failed to influence the priest in any positive way to exercise his pastoral prudence. Instead, he thinks of himself as a "whip with which Ulu flogs Umuaro."[21] Anichebe Udeozo's speech in the eighteenth chapter sums the people's desperation:

> Yes, we are Umuaro. Therefore, listen to what I am going to say. Umuaro is now asking you to go and eat those remaining yams today and name the day of the next harvest. Do you hear me well? I said, go and eat those yams today, not tomorrow; and if Ulu says we have committed an abomination, let it be on the heads of the ten of us here. You will be free....[22]

What was in the narrative akin to a synod (like the first council of Jerusalem in Acts of the Apostles 15) failed to yield positive fruits due to the intransigence of the priest and his lust for revenge against his people. Also at stake is the question of whose authority supersedes the other: the priest's or the people's? The priest's inability to listen and his failure to see the priesthood not as his own possession but as a sacred office in the service of the people doomed him, his god, and his religion. As a result, Christianity emerged as the beneficiary of the crisis. For, as Achebe concludes,

---

20   Achebe, *Arrow of God*, 207.

21   Achebe, *Arrow of God*, 211.

22   Achebe, *Arrow of God*, 210.

"many a man sent his son with a yam or two to offer to the new religion and to bring back the promised immunity. Thereafter, any yam harvested in his fields was harvested in the name of the son."[23]

From the point of view of Chinua Achebe's narrative in *Arrow of God*, a parallel exists in the praxis of synodality between the African traditional religious dispensation, which Achebe's narrative illuminates, and its Christian religious counterpart. This parallel hinges on the nature of the relationship between the people, the priest, and the deity in any given faith community.[24] Hence, within the context of the faith pilgrimage of a people, synodality could be understood as the communal praxis which ensures that a healthy balance of mutual respect is maintained in such a way that religious institutions function as true channels of grace and guarantors of fraternity and abundant life.

Whenever undue arbitrary power is usurped by any of the parties in the faith community, either by the priest or the people, the ecclesial balance is tilted, and the community loses equilibrium. *Arrow of God* is a perfect example of a postcolonial narrative that discloses the loss of such equilibrium and its consequences for the people, the priest, and the deity at the same time. Even though we cannot delve into details about the postcolonial thrust of the narrative, suffice it to say that Achebe underscores the erasure of colonial binary when he exonerates the Whiteman from any blame for the local crisis of Umuaro. In chapter 12 of the novel, Ezeulu is heard telling his friend Akuebue:

> We went to war against Okperi, who are our blood brothers over a piece of land which did not belong to us, and you blame the white man for stepping in. Have you not heard that when two brothers fight, a stranger reaps the harvest? How many white men went in their party that destroyed Abame? Do you know? Five. (…) Now have you ever heard

---

23   Achebe, *Arrow of God*, 232.

24   This assertion is already portrayed in Ezeulu's musing about the nature and extent of his priestly power. The story indicates a test of the communal ability to listen to each other in mutual respect and good will.

that five people – even if their heads reached the sky – could overrun a whole clan? Impossible.[25]

However, oblivious to the priest, he is one of the chief architects of the crisis that will engulf his community. At the end of the story, we see a pathetic image of a deranged chief priest, a local deity who by destroying his own priesthood "had also brought disaster on himself," and a people defecting to a new religion as they bring their offering to a more humane God.[26] This image adroitly discloses a synodal path gone awry due to the intransigence and refusal to listen on the part of a priestly class that has become over-conscious of its own powers. What became evident is that theistic humanism is the soul of religion. Synodality in Africa will be an empty platitude if it does not lead us to demonstrate the ability to recognise and treat each other not as rivals, but as sisters and brothers.

The document of the International Theological Commission (ITC) on "Synodality in the Life and Mission of the Church" makes clear that "synodality is not simply a working procedure, but the particular form in which the Church lives and operates."[27] This presupposes a dynamic process in which such a form of living and operating as a Church is always impacted positively or negatively by various external and internal factors. Achebe's critique of synodality, therefore, is about an implicit warning against such factors that could obscure the synodal path from bearing the desired fruits. In this case, clericalism. For, as Ogbuefi Ofoka sums it in the novel, "a priest like Ezeulu leads a god to ruin himself."[28]

Achebe's critique can also be seen as an exposition of the traditional society's confrontation with and response to cultural

---

[25] Achebe, *Arrow of God*, 132.

[26] Achebe, *Arrow of God*, 232.

[27] International Theological Commission, *Synodality in the Life and Mission of the Church*, 42.

[28] Achebe, *Arrow of God*, 215.

modernity. The African world Achebe inhabits and proffers in representation is, in the words of Kwaku Larbi Korang, modern. For Korang, "modern time is when, as a consequence of the unleashing of the dynamic, revolutionary, alienating, and all-conquering forces of capitalism and colonialism, 'all that is solid melts into the air'. It is a time when the solidity of communal pasts, the continuity of traditions, the stability of cultural norms, and assured visions of a common social future—said to be characteristic of premodern and precolonial worlds—give way before contingency, contradiction, and fragmentation."[29] It is a time of interrogation, understood as critical listening to one another and to the spirit of the time, which is precisely mirrored in the idea of synodality. Hence, Korang appropriating the titles of Achebe's first two novels would say that "*things fall apart* with the onset of modern time, and humanity's existential condition is to be *no longer at ease.*"[30] At such times of transition, it is neither the office nor administrative structure, but rather the character and attitude of (not only) the priest which play a crucial role in guiding the religious community. How adequate Ezeulu is in the possession of the requisite character and what lessons to be gathered therefrom will be shown in the following theological excursus. I have identified three major points of challenge which Achebe establishes at the beginning of his story, and whose theological import I want to unpack in this discourse, namely:

- the short-sightedness of the chief priest and his anxiety about relying on others to fulfil his function.
- his egotistic preoccupation with the powers of his office.
- the ominous future that looms in the horizon.

My theological excursus will, therefore, be restricted to these three points as I try to show how the narrative relates to the discourse on Synodality.

---

29   Korang, "Homage to a Modern Literary Father", xi.
30   Korang, "Homage to a Modern Literary Father", xi.

Theological Excursus on Arrow of God

The first point is about pastoral/doctrinal myopia versus foresight. The second is what I will call "sacerdotal megalomania." The third is the consequences of one and two. A closer look at the above three points will reveal the allegorical character of the narrative and throw more light on its significance in the present theological and pastoral reflections on the synodal path of the Church in the modern world.

The Short-Sightedness of the Chief Priest and his Anxiety about Relying on Others to Fulfil his Function

The first point of challenge is short-sightedness. I call it pastoral and doctrinal myopia versus foresight. Achebe intentionally creates an intrinsic connection between the priestly function and the visionary ability of the priest. In order to function well, the priest must be a visionary with a far-reaching goal or foresight. Even in his community, Ezeulu does not lose sight of his visionary role. He boasts to his friend about his ability to see the future.[31] Onyemauche Ejesu, hence, casts Ezeulu as a promethean figure with conscious intellect and foresight. He argues that Ezeulu's promethean aptitude explains his pragmatism in sending his son to learn the white man's culture and religion.[32]

In fact, Achebe's role for Ezeulu involves the ability to see and announce to the people the advent of the new moon. The moon which is, so to say, the target of the priest's vision symbolises the eye of the god and the extra-terrestrial dimension of the religious

---

[31]   Speaking to his friend Akuebue in chapter 12, Ezeulu said: "I can see things where other men are blind. That is why I am Known and at the same time I am Unknowable. (…) I can see tomorrow; that is why I can tell Umuaro: *come out from this because there is death there* or *do this because there is profit in it*. If they listen to me, o-o; if they refuse to listen, o-o." Achebe, *Arrow of God*, 133.

[32]   Onyemauche Anele Ejesu, "Achebe's Arrow of God, the Anti-Promethean Figure and the Lukacs's Sociological Approach to Tragedy" in *Okike An African Journal of New Writing*, 52, 1, (November 2014), 257-270.

pilgrimage at which the priest leads his community. Hence, at the beginning of the novel, the gradual onset of myopia, a visual impediment, in Ezeulu already casts a shadow and spells out the challenges that are about to obscure the effectiveness of the priestly authority which Ezeulu exercises. The priest's reluctance to accept the inevitability of his impairing vision, which is a reminder of his finitude and the limits of his powers, is arguably a metaphor of the delusion and arrogance of clericalism in any modern religion. And that arrogance is a repudiation of Ezeulu's foresight. Ezeulu's physical short-sightedness can be interpreted as a metaphor of the functional myopia caused by an over-bloated ego. He simply lacked the requisite foresight to see beyond his own egotism.

Foresight is the virtue that can help the *clerus* in the art of listening, in order to overcome the distractions that come from myriads of disruptive voices that rob the priest of attention and thus prevent him from listening to the voice of the Spirit. Such distractions took the form of the sad, measured monotone of the bell of Oduche's people[33] [the church] saying, "leave your yam, leave your cocoyam and come to church," which Ezeulu interpreted as "the song of extermination."[34] Here is a new religion that is summoning the people to abandon their means of livelihood to adopt an alien tradition. The distraction of the church bell hindered the chief priest himself from paying attention to a crucial message of the oracle. Similarly, as voices from mainstream media, social media, secular culture, women who are demanding equality in evangelical ministry, and all other dissenting voices that feel marginalised ring bells of reform of the prevalent system of pastoral administration in the Church, it has become a test of character for the Church leadership today to respond in a true spirit of synodality. These are disruptive voices, which question traditions and doctrines, and often evoke

---

[33]   Achebe, *Arrow of God*, 212.

[34]   Achebe, *Arrow of God*, 44.

anxieties in the Church, especially but not exclusively among the clergy.[35]

The Church leadership requires foresight to be able to resolve positively and astutely the conflict between the new disruptive voices and the voice of doctrinal conservatism, in order to hear and discern well the message of the Spirit. This is true also about the Church's reliance on cultural knowledge. Excessive reliance on Western theological hermeneutic may also lead to pastoral and doctrinal myopia in the Church. If Eurocentric theological hubris and patriarchal conservatism is allowed to obscure the vision of the Church, the faithful may well be singing and dancing to an "evil moon." The Holy See, but also all ecclesiastical authorities must, therefore, demonstrate the ability to *see* the light on the horizon for the Church and have an integrated vision of the Church's missionary goal and her pastoral destination in the twenty-first century. For me, nothing represents that vision better than what Pope Francis calls "universal fraternity."

Pope Francis has again and again reiterated his intention to avoid the pitfall of dancing to an "evil moon" and hence emphasised his vision of a synodality that is grounded on a true spirit of fraternity which cuts across religious, cultural, and class divides.[36] Therefore, synodality is all about having the extensive and all-encompassing gaze of a shepherd who is close to the sheep. It is about having the necessary prudence, understanding, patience, and docility to the Spirit to protect the sheep from wolves who would scatter the flock.[37] The leadership of the Church needs to see beyond ideological divides and prejudices, to acknowledge its limitations, and appreciate the human capital in the laity, through which God chooses to assist as well as admonish the

---

[35] One remembers, for example, the controversial document *Syllabus of Errors* with which Pope Pius IX reacted to the disruptive forces of modernity in his time.

[36] Andrea Tornielli, "Francis to Mexico's Bishops," https://www.lastampa.it/vatican-insider/en/2016/02/13/news/francis-to-mexico-s-bishops-do-not-underestimate-challenge-drug-trade-represents-1.36564001 (accessed 31 January 2022).

[37] Pope Francis, *Evangelii Gaudium,* 171.

clergy. It must also be able to communicate and implement this vision in all levels of the Church's pastoral administration. The laity, on the other hand, must acknowledge that the priesthood is a gift which requires the joyful appreciation of the whole community.

Egotistic Preoccupation with the Powers of Office

The second point of challenge is the priest's personality which Achebe paints in *Arrow of God*. The chief priest of Ulu sees himself as a king per se, and indeed one whose authority no one "dares" to challenge.[38] The priest Achebe creates in Ezeulu, in spite of his wonderful charisms in ritual performance and pragmatism, is more of an autocrat than a shepherd. He is the type that destroys religion rather than promotes it. Analogically, even though priests are ordained to govern, the politics of unquestionable authority which some priests desire to arrogate to themselves, either as diocesan Bishops or as parish priests or rectors, destroys the Church and undermines the many wonderful services rendered by priests to their fellow Christian brothers and sisters.

Some cases of protracted crisis associated with appointments of Bishops in local Churches—crises that hinge on mundane, vainglorious understanding of the episcopal office, lead to the conclusion that the notion of the bishopric or sacerdotal power among some Christians today is flawed. Such crises call for interrogation and ecclesial review in the light of synodality, for the arrogance of one proud priest or Bishop could cause damage that may take many years to remedy. A Church yoked by what I would call 'sacerdotal megalomania' will most certainly fail or falter in providing the pastoral accompaniment that could ameliorate the grief of her members and offer succour in times

---

38   Achebe, *Arrow of God*, 3.

of adversity.[39] A correct understanding of synodality helps the Church in imbibing the right attitude to the exercise of power and authority, without which it will definitely suffer avoidable self-inflicted wounds.

The Vatican II Council's Decree on the Training of Priests, *Optatam Totius*, acknowledges that "the desired renewal of the whole Church depends in great part upon a priestly ministry animated by the spirit of Christ, and it solemnly affirms the critical importance of priestly training."[40] It then enjoins priests to foster priestly vocations "by the example of their humble, hardworking and happy lives, as well as by their mutual charity and fraternal cooperation."[41] The Code of Canon Law also aptly describes clerics as "stewards of the mysteries of God in the service of His people."[42] Therefore, understanding that ecclesiastical governance is in the first place a divine mystery prepares one to approach this mystery with humility and awe. This is paramount to genuine synodality.

Kurt Appel offers a good analysis of Antonio Rosmini's (1797–1855) work on "the five wounds of the Church" that is helpful in elucidating the points I am making here. The first of these five wounds—the separation of the people from the clergy in the public cult (*Divisione del popolo dal clero nel pubblico culto*)—according to Appel, does not only separate God's people from an important source of its spiritual existence, but also transforms the clergy into administrators of sacral power, which becomes

---

39 In February 2022, for example, the famous Nigerian writer, Chimamanda Ngozi Adichie, bemoaned publicly how the clericalist attitude of her parish priest contributed to magnifying her family's grief as she and her siblings mourned their deceased parents. See Chimamanda Adichie, "I Am Not Strong In The Face Of Grief" https://youtu.be/NZ--DQvMUIE (accessed online 16.02.2022).

40 Second Vatican Council, "Decree on the Training of Priests, *Optatam Totius*", (28 October 1965) Introduction, in Austin Flannery, ed., *Vatican Council II, volume 1, The Conciliar and Post Conciliar Documents*, (Northport, New York: Dominican Publications, 1998), 707.

41 Second Vatican Council, "*Optatam Totius*", 2, in Flannery, ed, *Vatican Council II*, 708.

42 *The Code of Canon Law*, Can. 276 §1, (Bangalore: Collins, 1983) 47.

their possession.[43] This appropriation of sacral power is indeed affirmed by Pope Pius XI in his 1935 encyclical, *Pastor Bonus*, which states that "wherever there is religion, wherever altars are erected, there is also a priesthood surrounded with special gestures of respect and reverence."[44] This made Pope Pius XI argue that even if the weaknesses of some unworthy priests are so deplorable and painful, they are not able to obscure the splendour of such a high dignity, and the unworthiness of the bearer in no way invalidates the exercise of the office.[45] The truth, however, is that the inadequacies of clerics can and have sometimes indeed jeopardised the integrity of the religion itself.

Nonetheless, the major problem is not that sacral power is given to the clergy, but that some clerics actually believe that it is their possession. Herein lies one of the major hurdles to synodality. "When the agency – which has the task to keep the Church's space open to the encounter with Christ, and to represent him (not itself) in its divine highness (which manifests in kenosis and in abandoning oneself) – begins to glorify its own power, it perverts the holiness of the Church."[46] In what he identifies as "the five new wounds of the Church," Appel bemoans a new clericalist orientation of the Catholic Church since the 1980s, whereby largely only those Bishops whose seminaries were crowded and who produced many priests made a successful career. It was of little importance whether this came along with an enduring evangelisation, and whether the new clergy showed any pastoral, social or spiritual competence.[47] In *Arrow of God*, Chinua Achebe allegorises this problem in the

---

[43]   Kurt Appel, "Reform and Renewal in Local Churches" in Stan Chu Ilo et al. (eds.), *Faith in Action, vol. 1, Reform, Mission and Pastoral Renewal in African Catholicism Since Vatican II*, (Lagos: Paulines Africa, 2020), 81.

[44]   Pope Pius XI, *Pastor Bonus, Ad Catholici Sacerdotii*, Encyclical (Rome: Vatican, December 20, 1935; Wien: Priesterbruderschaft St Petrus, 2011) [my translation from German], 10.

[45]   Pope Pius XI, *Pastor Bonus*, 21.

[46]   Appel, "Reform and Renewal in Local Churches," 81.

[47]   Appel, "Reform and Renewal in Local Churches," 85-86.

functional inadequacies which Ezeulu personifies as a priest who lacks not only genuine foresight but also the requisite pastoral humility and empathy to perform well at the crossroad of encounter with cultural modernity.

Achebe and Rosmini appear to share the same prophetic message, albeit in different literary genres and in different worlds. The separation of the people and the priest is even more pronounced in *Arrow of God*. Achebe accentuates this cultic separation in his description of the liturgical regalia and actions of the priest at the festival of the Pumpkin Leaves:

> The left half of [Ezeulu's] body – from forehead to toes – was painted with white chalk. [indicating half spirit, half human] (…) he ran forward… as though he had seen a comrade in the vacant air; he stretched his arm and waved his staff to the right and to the left. And those who were near enough heard the knocking together of Ezeulu's staff and another which no one saw. At this, many fled in terror before the priest and the unseen presence around him.[48]

It must be noted, however, that the underlying motif for the mystification of the priest and his being indulged with sacral power is that he expiates[49] the sins of the community, since sacral power is invested for the purpose of atonement and benediction, not to dominate, subjugate, or victimise anyone. Maureen Warner Lewis is of the opinion that

> Only when we examine the practical and spiritual significance of Umuaro's great festivals—of the Pumpkin Leaves and the New Yam—do we appreciate the central role which the priest of Ulu plays in the social context. The festival of the Pumpkin Leaves has a function akin to … Good Friday and Easter of Christianity. It signifies the cleansing of evil from the people and the renewal of benevolent spiritual forces.[50]

---

[48]   Achebe, *Arrow of God*, 72.

[49]   It is to be noted that the festival of the Pumpkin Leaves as described by Achebe in *Arrow of God* was for the expiation of the sins of the community. It is akin to the paschal feast.

[50]   Lewis, "Ezeulu and His God", 75.

This is precisely why any abuse of sacral power is tantamount to a deathblow to synodality. As Kurt Appel, says, "clericalism shows its full absurdity and virtuality when, simply as a display of power, newly-created bishops and priests randomly erase forms of spirituality and structures which had been patiently built (often by lay men and women)."[51] In Africa, such usurpation of sacral power beyond the confines of sacramental succour is not only absurd but also very destructive and must be curbed by the Church. It is a manifestation of sacerdotal megalomania which Christianity repudiates (cf. *Mk* 10:45; *Mt* 20:28).

The Ominous Future that Looms in the Horizon

The two points of challenge mentioned above—pastoral cum doctrinal myopia and sacerdotal megalomania—work together to conjure inevitably a doomed future for true synodality. In a premonition that anticipates the consequences of the failure to "walk together" between the people and their priest, Achebe's narrative identifies the new moon whose advent Ezeulu had announced at the beginning of the novel as "an evil moon."[52] Achebe thus anticipates the direction to which Ezeulu's short-sightedness and egomania will be leading the community, namely, to a disaster. The crisis that will eventually engulf the clan of Umuaro is an allegorical warning about how clericalism jeopardises the future of any religion. For, it initiates a regime of strife between the priest and the people.

A Synod on Synodality indicates Pope Francis's under-standing of the urgent need to forestall a gloomy future for the universal Church. The synod has been interpreted as a call to change our ways of doing things, in order to become more of who we truly are as a Church, walking together, as one human

---

51   Appel, "Reform and Renewal in Local Churches", 86.

52   Achebe, *Arrow of God*, 2. Ezeulu's younger wife Ugoye makes this observation, likening the moon to an evil moon.

family that is guided by the Holy Spirit. Pope Francis has stated that this collaborative, inclusive approach of synodality is precisely "the path that God expects of the Church in the third millennium."[53] But what are those ways of doing things which need to be changed, and what could happen if they are not changed? This chapter cannot provide a definitive answer to this question, but I have so far identified one of the pernicious obstacles to synodality, namely, clericalism. This chapter's interdisciplinary hermeneutic sees in Chinua Achebe's *Arrow of God* a perfect allegory of synodality (*via negativa*). It shows the dangers of a failure to walk together as a family of God, as well as underscores the importance of the clergy and their role in meeting the challenges of a fruitful synodality.

Achebe's allegory demonstrates that the possible logical conclusion and climax of, and or a metaphor for, any form of episcopal or sacerdotal megalomania is insanity. It also shows that the call to walk together and listen to each other as a community of faith is more about cultivating the attitude of respect to each other as equal members of a family of God than it is about creating a perfect structure of ecclesial administration. Whatever structure or system may be created, one thing is certain: the ministerial priesthood will arguably always remain indispensable in the life of the Church. Therefore, the pertinent question is what kind of priest or Bishop, and what understanding of the sacerdotal office is required to guarantee a fruitful synodality? In *Arrow of God* Ezeulu refuses to take advice from anyone and, therefore, needed to be reminded that "The man who carries a deity is not a king."[54] Ogbuefi Ofoka is convinced that "a priest like Ezeulu leads a god to ruin himself."[55] Likewise, the Church may ruin itself if pastoral governance is not exercised in the spirit of fraternal charity. It may also be ruined if the priestly function is undermined by the

---

53   International Theological Commission, *Synodality in the Life and Mission of the Church*.

54   Achebe, *Arrow of God*, 27.

55   Achebe, *Arrow of God*, 215.

laity that fails to overcome rancour in its dealing with the priest's shortcomings.

Conclusion

On 11 February 2013, Pope Benedict XVI taught the Church that the ability to acknowledge the boundaries of one's power is not a sign of weakness but of strength and character of a good pastor when he renounced the Petrine ministry and announced his resignation to the world on account of his aging and waning physical strength. Many, including his most vociferous critics lauded that bold action as a courageous and exemplary legacy for which he will for a long time be remembered. In Africa, where leadership at all levels seems to have been confiscated in many instances by octogenarians, the Church must not fail to be a model of the type of servant-leadership that acknowledges shortcomings and creates room for synodal participation. Some text-critics of *Arrow of God* have given us illuminating analyses of the conflict that pervades the narrative. David Cook observes that the novel "searches into the limits of individual power in a system controlled by tradition,"[56] something that makes it precisely a suitable hermeneutic tool for the discourse on synodality, since the Church itself is guided by tradition. For Cook, therefore, the structure of *Arrow of God* necessarily leads to the climactic point of the priest's self-destruction. Thus, when Ezeulu "is destroyed, the community sees this as a judgment on the man who opposes the spirit of the group."[57] Maureen Warner-Lewis sees the conflict that pervades the narrative in terms of an undeclared war between the priest and his clan, each claiming to be the repository of knowledge and authority for the common good. Lewis argues that Ezeulu is piqued by the limitations on his own power.[58]

---

[56]   David Cook, *African Literature. A Critical View* (Bristol: Longman, 1977) 18.

[57]   Cook, *African Literature*, 19.

[58]   Lewis, "Ezeulu and His God", 75.

Beyond these criticisms which focus more on the cultural anthropological perspective, this chapter demonstrates that another kind of interpretation of this novel is possible, one that is theological and ecclesiological. As the Church continually listens to the voice of the Spirit in history, may it learn not to overlook what the same Spirit is saying to us in African literature. May we learn to see literature as authentic channels of revelation. In the culture of palaver, *indaba, ụka,* or *shikome,* which Achebe copiously depicts in *Arrow of God* we have shown how important synodality is, not only to the Catholic Church, but to all religions. We have also seen that the failure of synodality attracts unpleasant consequences, whose avoidance demands from the clergy a great deal of responsibility.

CHAPTER 7

The Social Dimension of Ecclesial Synodality in Africa: A Call to Walk in Communion with the Laity in Doing Theology

Nicholaus Segeja

Introduction

The awareness of the specific role of the laity in the Church and society has apparently continued to increase especially since the Second Vatican Council (Vatican II).[1] It is now clear that in the spirit of communion, the laity because of the secular character of their life and Christian vocation[2] are uniquely assigned to the apostolate by the Christ.[3] Thus, together with

---

[1]   Cf. Second Vatican Council, The Dogmatic Constitution on the Church, *Lumen Gentium*, (November 21, 1964); Vatican II, The Pastoral Constitution on the Church in the Modern World, *Gaudium et Spes* (December 7, 1965; and Vatican II, The Decree on the Apostolate of the Laity, *Apostolicam Actuositatem* (November 18, 1965). In the same line of thought John Paul II, after the 1987 Synod of Bishops on the topic "Vocation and Mission of the lay Faithful in the Church and in the world" issued the Post-synodal Apostolic Exhortation, Vocation and Mission of the Lay Faithful, *Christifideles Laici* (December 30, 1988).

[2]   Cf. Second Vatican Council, *Gaudium et Spes*, nos. 1-2. See also John Paul II, The Church in Africa, *Ecclesia in Africa* (September 14, 1995) no. 16; Benedict XVI, The Church in Africa on Reconciliation, Justice and Peace, *Africae Munus* (November 19, 2021) no. 17; Catechism of the Catholic Church, (Vatican City: Libreria Editrice Vaticana, 1993), nos. 899 – 900.

[3]   Cf. Second Vatican Council, *Apostolicam Auctositatem,* no. 3. See also 1 Pt 2:4-10. John Paul II, *Christifideles Laici*, no. 15.

all other Christian faithful, the laity share a *sensus fidei* because of the Holy Spirit working in them. Consequently, the role and duty of the laity is more pressing especially in situations where it is only through them that people can hear the Gospel. In such situations, therefore, there is an urgent need for the laity to seek understanding of the faith for new evangelisation. Since doing theology is vital, especially in the processes of discernment and decision-making, the involvement of the laity becomes inevitable particularly due to the social dimension of ecclesial synodality.[4] The Church-Family journeying in solidarity and synodality with the world to fulfilment in the *Parousia*, therefore, requires promotion of the laity in doing theology. Subsequently, we intend to demonstrate how the involvement of the laity in doing theology can promote synodality for new evangelisation especially in Africa today. With cited but not limited case studies from the Church in AMECEA[5] region, I wish to argue that besides a concerted critical and creative theological reflection on the contemporary world, there is need to adopt a paradigmatic shift, both in doing theology and engaging the laity in it for new evangelisation. I further argue that articulation of the social dimension of ecclesial synodality subsisting in the practice of reverential dialogue activates conversion to a renewed way of evangelisation in Africa and beyond.

---

[4] Social dimension of ecclesial synodality in the light of the Second Vatican Council has at least two implications. On the one hand, it embraces the basic pastoral activities geared for the growth of the Church in concrete situations; namely, catechesis, spirituality of the faithful, liturgy and sacramental life. On the other hand, the social dimension ecclesial synodality is at encompasses the missionary nature of the Church and therefore is at the service of evangelisation in all its expressions like proclamation; witness; ecumenism; interreligious or interfaith dialogue; reverential dialogue (*shikome, baraza, indaba, palaver*); integral/holistic development; reconciliation, justice and peace; inculturation; deeper and new evangelisation. For more discussion, Cf. Nicholaus Segeja, "Social Dimension of Ecclesial Synodality: A Pastoral Reflection" *African Christian Studies*, 32, no.2, (June 2016), 50-74.

[5] AMECEA, an abbreviation for Association of Member Episcopal Conferences of Eastern Africa is a regional grouping of Episcopal Conferences of at least eight countries, namely, Sudan and South Sudan, Ethiopia, Eritrea, Uganda, Kenya, Tanzania, Malawi and Zambia. Rwanda and Burundi are associate members.

Popular Understanding, Challenges and Opportunities

In our case study, we sampled informants - clergy, religious and lay people, from Tanzania and Kenya respectively.[6] The focus was on their general understanding of doing theology, challenges and opportunities in the local Church and beyond. What we share here is a summary of what appeared common in our interactions with them as our basis for further discussion. Generally, and according to our informants from Tanzania and Kenya, doing theology is viewed as a professional activity undertaken mostly by the clergy. People often talk about theology when referring to people in the formation to priesthood, major seminarians in particular, or teachers in theological institutions. Our informants from Tanzania reported to knowing no lay theologian, except professionals in other areas involved in Church related issues. Kenya has a number of lay theologians, some of whom teach in centres of higher learning. In either case, lay theologians form no structures that bring them together at any level. Of course, the informants also acknowledged other ways of doing theology by the laity, though not in a professional way like engagement in catechesis, planned seminars and workshops, Small Christian Communities (SCCs), marriage and family life, parish forums of leadership, movements and associations. Informants also observed a way of doing theology where the laity take part in the structural administration and celebration of both diocesan synods and the synods of Bishops. Nevertheless, although all these engagements are important, doing theology apparently appears a business for few, like a *cult,* especially for the clergy.

---

6   The study used qualitative research design. The sample size targeted up to 100 laypersons and at least 20 clergy and religious from 4 universities in Kenya and Tanzania. Focus groups were chosen because it is widely employed as a qualitative strategy to understand social issues in detail. Instead of using a statistically representative sample of a larger population, the strategy seeks to collect data from a deliberately chosen group of people - informants. There were ten focus groups made of about ten lay people including priests and religious – six in Kenya and four in Tanzania, working in Catholic universities.

There are positive and negative effects. On the one hand, one may single out the respect and trust generally given to the priests by lay faithful as confirmed by almost all our informants. Priests, having done theology, are better positioned to expound matters related to faith. The laity, however, would always approach priests as knowledgeable pastoral leaders. In most cases, unless proved otherwise by the standards of the laity, theology by priests is a source of confidence, hope and encouragement among the faithful. On the other hand, confining professional theology to the domain of the clergy and teachers in theological institutions has unpleasant effects. The majority of lay faithful with their Christian experience are apparently and practically excluded in the communal praxis of doing theology. In fact, because of such a situation, doing theology then is considered as not part of the vocation of the laity except few who are perhaps engaged in teaching theology. This leads to quite a number of challenges. Priests who may have not acquired the chance to do further studies in theology, at least some of them, do not feel part of the *"body-theologic."*[7] The parish work, therefore, does not necessarily need further theological training besides that which takes place in the seminary. Perhaps this explains why most of our theological institutions, though considered centres of research are not necessarily linked to pastoral ministry in the local Churches. Research related to the life and mission of the Church is mostly done by researchers as a requirement to obtain their respective diplomas. Consequently, doing theology, which apparently features as a *cult,* meaning that it is a responsibility of few people, becomes redundant. Speculative study then becomes the focus of doing theology. Thus, the experiences of the laity in living their faith fail to be integrated as part of the basis of doing theology.

It was also observed that although it appears like a *cult,* that is, an elite exercise, the majority of the informants wished that

---

[7]   *Body-theologic* here simply means those who consider themselves as having the duty and responsibility to do theology.

the laity were fully involved in doing theology at the professional level. In our analysis, we argue that upholding doing theology as a *cult* eventually poses the danger of obscuring the theological task and makes it less capable of transforming reality and making faith and life intelligible. It also narrows the theological craft to an exclusive domain of a few sundering it from its true purpose and mission. In this case, theology could become something to be understood rather than something that we do. Truth and faith are not conceived as praxis originated by reality and oriented to change. In most cases, the concern of doing theology is detached from the lived experience of faith by many, especially the laity, in situations where only through their secular character, the Gospel message can be effectively realised.[8] Pope Benedict identifies such situations as key areas of apostolate today, like *new worlds* to be evangelised.[9] Pope Francis also reiterates the importance of society to be faith imbued by capitalising on the social dimension of evangelisation. Thus, he affirms that: "If this [social] dimension of evangelisation is not properly brought out, there is a constant risk of distorting the authentic and integral meaning of the mission of evangelisation."[10] Consequently, the Church can effectively become part of the history in which the Christ event yields salvation through the Holy Spirit by the involvement of the laity not only in living the faith but also in doing theology. In this way, the Church will also focus and look out to the world in solidarity by being a divine instrument of unity and salvation.[11]

Involving the laity in doing theology is not only in line with advancing their apostolate but also an expression of *synodality* in light of the Church-family especially in Africa. Though it may require new approaches and paradigms, involving the laity in

---

8   Cf. Second Vatican Council, *Lumen Gentium*, nos. 31-32.

9   Cf. Benedict XVI, *Africae Munus*, nos. 132-146.

10   Francis, Apostolic Exhortation, The Proclamation of the Gospel in Today's World, *Evangelii Gaudium* (November 24, 2013), no. 176.

11   Cf. Second Vatican Council, *Gaudium et Spes, nos.* 1 and 4.

doing theology in Africa seems to be a clear sign of our times. In fact, the practice that apparently prevails today seems to suggest the need of its realisation. The laity in AMECEA region and beyond, for example, show much interest and concern to take part in the structural administration and celebration of both diocesan synods and the synods of the Bishops. This also has been the experience during the first phase of the preparation of the synod on synodality, which emphasised more on consultation, and involvement of all as an expression of Ecclesial synodality. Thus, the concern of the laity in all this is not only to express their *sensus fidei* but also to seek to understand and appreciate who they are as Christians amidst the dynamics of both the Church and society. One can also add here that since the formation of Small Christian Communities as a way of being Church today is largely managed by the laity, especially in the AMECEA region, their praxis is an expression of "communal faith seeking understanding" and celebration of synodality. Thus, while doing theology could be informed by the human experience of life in SCCs, it is also challenged to transform the praxis of SCCs – make tangible effects on the very fabric of daily life in favour of the Church's mission.

Biblical and Theological Insights of Social Dimension of Synodality

The need to engage the laity for the mission of the Church in light of synodality is an Ecclesial concern. As Donald Wuerl rightly says: "It is increasingly clear that the New Evangelisation is not one specific action or activity of the Church, but rather a way of seeing a whole range of activities carried on by the Church to spread the Good News of Jesus Christ."[12] This comprehensive approach to the Church's activities is vital not only as a sign of the times but also because of the biblical and theological insights.

---

[12]   Donald Wuerl, *New Evangelization: Passing on the Catholic Faith Today*, (Indiana: Our Sunday Visitor, Inc., 2013), 14.

Scriptures, especially the Old Testament, reveals the People of God as called to a promised land – to heaven, hence, it is always in a way, synodality, to perfection and holiness. Besides considering it as the Body of Christ and the Temple of the Holy Spirit (cf. 1 *Cor* 12:13f; *Rom* 12. See also *Acts* 2:42-47; 4:32-37), the New Testament shows this people as newly constituted by God the Father through Christ: "But you are 'a chosen race, a royal priesthood, a holy nation ... Once you were 'no people' but now you are God's people'" (1 *Pt* 2:9-10. See also *Heb* 8:13, 9:15, 10:9, 12:24; 1 *Cor* 1:30; *Eph* 2:11-22). Building on this and other biblical texts, Vatican II affirms that God the Father, through Christ has made a new people for himself, not according to the flesh, but in the Spirit.[13] Engagement of the laity in doing theology is not only an expression of synodality but is also demanded by it.

Perhaps, the conversion of the Ethiopian eunuch in the Bible can give us some insights (*Acts* 8:26-27). Philip, the evangelist, plays the role of a theologian in a concrete situation as he encounters the Ethiopian eunuch reading the book of Isaiah (specifically *Is* 53:7-8). In fact, the Ethiopian eunuch confessed saying "How would I understand unless I have a teacher to teach me?" (*Acts* 8:31). Philip explained the text to him in a way that made value to his life and he asked to be baptised (*Acts* 8:37). One sees here a connection between theology and evangelisation. So, Vatican II further teaches that by virtue of baptism all People of God are consecrated and share the holy priesthood and prophetic mission of Jesus Christ, through the anointing of the Holy Spirit.[14] Consequently, because the Church, the communion, the People of God, is missionary in nature, and because of her sacramental structure and the Holy Spirit given to all, then all Christians, equally without distinction are called to do theology.[15]

---

13   Cf. Second Vatican Council, *Lumen Gentium,* nos. 9–10.

14   Second Vatican Council, *Lumen Gentium,* nos. 10-17. See also James O'Halloram, SDB, *Small Christian Communities: A Pastoral Companion,* (Bangalore: Claretian Publications, 1997), 13–16.

15   Cf. John Paul II, *Ecclesia in Africa,* nos. 51, 53-54, 63, and 181. See also Benedict XVI,

Synodality in different forms and ways, like diocesan synods and synods of the Bishops, for the Church-Family has become a dynamic impetus for today in the Church's mission in the world as she seeks to understand the concrete challenges affecting her life and mission. Perhaps the etymology of the word *synodality* may prove to be inspirational. From ancient Greek the word *súnodos* (σύνοδος) means assembly or meeting.[16] It originates from the word σύν (*sún* in English *syn-*) meaning "with" and ὁδός (*hodós*) meaning "way". *Synodality*, therefore, embraces at least two concepts, namely, the coming together of people for a purpose, and the reality of moving or being on the way together. It is both the going and the way. Because of their social and secular character, the laity in doing theology, therefore, are integral to Ecclesial *synodality*. This implies at least two related realities. In the first place, doing theology is an Ecclesial duty invested in the custodianship of the *Magisterium* specifically focusing on the Christian teaching or doctrine. The second reality derives from the significance of context in doing theology. Truth is always revealed in a given context. Hence, it should embrace different styles of living the Christian faith.

Some christological and ecclesiological insights especially from Vatican II also offer useful guidelines.[17] The laity too are incorporated into Christ. They are sent to witness to him in the secular sphere. Subsequently, as the decree on the lay apostolate illustrates:

> The laity must take on the renewal of the temporal order as their own special obligation. Led by the light of the Gospel and the mind of the Church, and motivated by Christian love, let them act directly and

---

Africae Munus nos. 128-131; International Theological Commission, *Synodality in the Life and Mission of the Church*, (March 2, 2018), nos. 6-9, 54-57, 64, 103-105, 118-119. And Second Vatican Council, *Lumen Gentium*, nos. 9-10.

[16]   Note also that the *synodos* in Greek like *synodus* in Latin points to a reality of assembly or meeting - a coming together.

[17]   Cf. Second Vatican Council, *Lumen Gentium*, no. 30-38. See also Francis Arinze, *The Lay Person's Distinctive Role*, (San Francisco: Ignatius Press, 2013), 33-50.

definitely in the temporal sphere. As citizens, they must cooperate with other citizens, using their own particular skills and acting on their own responsibility.[18]

The apostolate of the laity, therefore, takes on a specific character in that it is carried out in the ordinary surroundings underscoring especially the social dimension of ecclesial synodality. Thus, intrinsic to its realisation is the awareness of God's presence with us.[19] In this case, the two realities, namely, Ecclesial nature and context requiring the secular character of the laity, should go together in doing theology lest it fails to serve and originate from the Church as communion where realities of participation and collaboration emerge as its expressions. This brings us to the idea of the theology of the local Church in relation to the diocese. The theology of the local Church describes the diocese as: "a section of the People of God entrusted to a bishop to be guided by him with the assistance of his clergy so that, by adhering to its pastor and formed by him into one community in the Holy Spirit through the Gospel and the Eucharist, it constitutes one particular Church in which the one, holy, catholic and apostolic Church of Christ is truly present and active."[20] The laity, therefore, participate in this community – the People of God.[21] By implication, one can also say that in their own way they do theology in communion with the other Christian faithful.

This description embraces at least two implications to doing theology. On the one hand, like the other faithful, the laity are called to actualise the mission of the Church, hence, should

---

[18]　Second Vatican Council, *Apostolicam Actuositatem*, no. 7. See Arinze, *The Lay Person's Distinctive Role*, 41.

[19]　Cf. Wuerl, *New Evangelization*, 81. See also Second Vatican Council, *Apostolicam Actuositatem*, no. 7; Catechism of the Catholic Church, no. 1060.

[20]　Second Vatican Council, Decree on the Pastoral Office of the Bishops in the Church, *Christus Dominus* (28 October, 1965), no. 11.

[21]　Cf. Vatican II, *Lumen Gentium* no. 31. See also John Martin "Participation of the Laity in the Teaching Function of the Church" *African Christian Studies*, 26, no. 3 (September 2010), 50. The author discusses concrete activities the laity can do in the Church by virtue of their baptism.

participate in doing theology. On the other hand, the laity, due to their secular character have a special vocation to realise the mission of the Church in the world. Consequently, the effectiveness of the laity in doing theology will depend on the exploration of the orientations and dynamics of the contexts - the world in particular, in the light of the Christ's event.[22] Pope Francis, after illuminating the social dimension of evangelisation, and therefore of ecclesial synodality goes further to explain its spirit responding to the deepest yearning of the heart, and "a sense of mystery" in the ordinary.[23] Like at Pentecost, the Spirit gave to the Apostles the courage and ability to reverentially dialogue with the world – to speak with respect and reverence the language understood by all even when opposition was certain. The involvement of the laity, therefore, should contribute towards a theology capable of speaking to each person in his or her own language in the Church as Family, and in the *new worlds* of education, health care, information technology and communication.[24]

Towards *Synodality* in Doing Theology

Since doing theology with laity is inevitable today in the service of synodality, there is need to explore and determine the orientation and dynamics of working together. Key to all this is both the secular character of the laity and the pilgrim nature of the Church-Family as a communion. Recapturing the broad understanding and motive for doing theology gives it a general new orientation and approach. Faith seeking understanding – is essentially an act of both the mind and the will. Therefore, in the first place, it should invest on and foster the ability to think and understand. In this respect, promotion of critical and creative

---

[22]   Cf. Nicholaus Segeja, "Pastoral Theology as a Hermeneutical Activity: A Contextualized Approach" *African Christian Studies*, 29, no. 4 (December 2013), 28-49.

[23]   Cf. Francis, *Evangelii Gaudium*, nos. 176-258; the author spends time to explain the social dimension of evangelisation. And in nos. 259-288, the author discusses, though briefly, the new spirit of the new evangelisation.

[24]   Francis, *Evangelii Gaudium*, no. 260.

thinking, which encourages growth in moral values as Pope Francis suggests is vital.[25] Thus, centres of learning at all levels, as they contribute towards personal and communal growth in knowledge are crucial, requiring a paradigm shift. They should be able to accompany all calibre of students in recalling ideas, and principles in light of the truth of faith. This is more than just teaching religion or catechesis in schools, even doing chaplaincy ministry, teaching theology, although these are not excluded. It would also require it to appeal and make sense at the level of comprehension and application of knowledge. The process of comprehension should reflect the idea of discernment.

Nevertheless, we must add a precautionary note here. Although it is certain that human sciences, especially the need for genuine anthropology and social analysis, may serve as a starting point of doing theology, one should avoid embracing the ideologies behind them, which are more often than not incongruent with the gospel values. Thus, doing theology must itself critically distil this analysis and respective sciences within a theological and ecclesial perspective.[26] Since discernment involves an aspect of decision, it is precisely related to the will of the human person. This is when the human person, even in very ordinary daily undertakings, continually exercises his or her freedom and makes judgments that affect personal and communal life. In the process, all this does not only form a *theological locus* but also becomes a source of discernment in the process of faith seeking understanding to be brought forth in reverential dialogue with the other sources, namely, the Bible and the tradition of the Church.

It is good to note that, as characterised by the process of discernment, the involvement of the laity in doing theology should

---

[25]   Cf. Pope Francis, Message broadcasted by Radio Vatican 7/2/2015. See also Vatican II, *Gaudium et Spes*, nos. 4 and 62. The Church explicitly recommends the use of human sciences in theological research.

[26]   Cf. Wijsen, F. Henriot, P., et al., eds. *The Pastoral Circle Revisited*. (Nairobi: Pauline Publications Africa, 2006). See also Segeja, Nicholaus, *Pastoral Theology: New Understanding and Orientations*, (Eldoret: AMECEA GABA Publications, 2020), 70-72. 75-104.

promote a deepening of theology and praxis. In fact, fostered by reverential dialogical praxis, it should enhance *synodality* and Catholicity. Doing theology that is sensitive to the secular character of the laity and that takes the dynamics of the world seriously, therefore, should be inclusive. It is a theology, which is open to all People of God, in the manner proper to their respective modes of apostolate in a communal event of faith seeking understanding. In this respect, there are at least two features, which influence the *modus operandi* and approach of doing theology, namely, plurality on the one hand, and *ordinarity* of life on the other. It is becoming increasingly common to have people from different sociocultural contexts coming together in life especially in areas of apostolate, like *new worlds* to be evangelised which include education, health care, communication and information technology.[27]

What then do plurality of culture and different sociocultural contexts say about doing theology? At least two aspects are apparently clear. All cultures have the ability to interact. The other aspect is the power of the *new worlds* to influence the sociopolitical and economic life of the people. In all this, doing theology should be open to different sociocultural contexts, hence requiring a reverential dialogical approach. On the one hand, this approach will broaden the scope or focus of different ways of doing theology. In the context of plurality of culture, the theology of inculturation, for example, will have to eventually open up to interculturation in favour of the new evangelisation. Likewise, contextual theology[28] (or theologies) to be relevant in a cultural

---

[27]   Cf. Benedict XVI, *Africae Munus*, nos. 132-146.

[28]   What makes contextual theology precisely *contextual* is the recognition of the validity of present human experience as another *locus theologicum*. In other words, contextual theology realises that culture, history, and contemporary thought forms are to be considered, along with scripture and tradition, as valid sources for theological expression. For further reading Cf. Stephen B. Bevans, *Models of Contextual Theology: Faith and Culture*, (Maryknoll, New York: Orbis Books, 2002). The author discusses six models of contextual theology, namely transcendental, anthropological, praxis, synthetic, translation and countercultural models, respectively. See also Victor, I. Ezigbo, *The Art of Contextual Theology: Doing Theology in the Era of World Christianity*, (Eugene, Oregon: Cascade Books, 2021). The author discusses the role of theology in the imagination and articulation of Christianity's inherent multiculturalism and multi-

pluralistic situation has to graduate to intercontextual theology. One can even think of *interlocal* theology, interdeconstruction and interconstruction theology and others. Transcending cultural and situational boundaries is precisely one of the features of doing theology that is sensitive to the secular character of the laity and the world. In fact, it is theology emanating from the fundamental truth that creation is integral. On the other hand, plurality of culture and contexts interwoven requires a way of doing theology that does not only embrace differences but fosters an *interdisciplinary* approach and relationship among them in favour of the new evangelisation.

Another feature that describes the uniqueness of the apostolate of the laity as related to their secular condition is *ordinarity*.[29] Concretely, this would require doing theology by listening with reverence to ordinary things as they happen. Surely, this feature entails a number of challenges, which require a hermeneutical approach. This approach will enable this kind of theology to talk about the concepts embraced in the history of salvation in an ordinary way – like on Pentecost (cf. *Acts* 2:5-11; 9:2; 19:9; 22:4; 23; 24:14, 22). It requires imploring the Holy Spirit to renew the Church, stir and impel her to go forth boldly to evangelise all peoples. It is a theology which brings to the surface the *diaconal* dimension of faith and translates the mystical notions into tangible activities. This is a theology with personal and communal spirituality bringing into reverential dialogue substantive moments of prayerful life and charisms or services. It embraces the deepest needs, yearnings, of the human person. In this way, one can develop a spiritual taste for being close to people's lives and to discover that this is in itself a source of doing theology as it fosters "a sense of mystery."[30] Consequently, theology has to bring on board all those who entrust themselves to God in love and

---

vernacularity by exploring the nature and practice of contextual theology.

29   Cf. Second Vatican Council, *Lumen Gentium*, no. 35.
30   Cf. Francis, *Evangelii Gaudium*, nos. 265, 267, 279.

be open to all acts of charity, generous efforts and endurance in doing what is good.

Conclusion

The involvement of the laity in doing theology is certainly a sign of our times for the missionary conversion required for evangelisation today. Thus, the laity should be engaged in doing theology. This is more than confirming the anthropological nature of theology.[31] Besides being an appreciation of *chronos*, secular time like an opportunity, the involvement of the laity in doing theology appears to us as the *kairos* for doing theology.[32] Hence, orientation and focus in doing theology that is sensitive to the secular character of the laity and the world should accommodate as its *theological locus* especially the key areas of apostolate today, the *new worlds* to be evangelised, namely, life of the Church, education, health care and information and technological communication. However, in a synodal way we still need to explore how doing theology by the laity and with them will address these key areas. Special attention should be given to the use of the temporal goods – stewardship and leadership in society, and environmental issues. Furthermore, besides being inclusive, pluralistic, and ordinary in its approach, doing theology should incorporate discernment or rather hermeneutics as its integral activity. Subsequently, one of the implications would be to rethink the ministry of discernment so as to embrace not only the role of the clergy, but also both the vocation of the laity– especially due to their secular character – and the practice of the social dimension of ecclesial synodality.

---

[31]   Clement Majawa "Theology in the Catholic Church" in John Kyule, et. al., eds, *A Guide to Research Work and University Studies for the Faculty of Theology*, (Nairobi: CUEA Press, 2013), 16.

[32]   Cf. James Sweeney, "Catholic Theology and Practice Today" in James Sweeney et al., eds, *Keeping Faith in Practice*, (London: SCM Press, 2010), 15. See also Segeja, "Pastoral Theology as a Hermeneutical Activity, 47.

CHAPTER 8

Contested Moral Questions in Africa
Inspirations for Moral Discernment
in a Synodal Church[1]

Raymond Aina, MSP

What exactly do we mean by moral disputes in Africa? We refer to continuing arguments over moral convictions and points of view. The Roman Catholic Church today is divided on many important moral questions. I read a piece about the next significant magisterial stance that Pope Francis might hold. The projected encyclical will centre on moral theology, like Pope John Paul II's encyclicals *Veritatis Splendor* and *Evangelium Vitae*, which concentrate on moral theology and contemporary ethical issues. From 30 October to 1 November of 2021, the Pontifical Academy for Life held an interdisciplinary seminar in Rome. This anticipated encyclical is expected to tie together the palaver-like discussions that took place there. According to Gerard O'Connell,

> . . . the participants addressed such fundamental issues as "the relation between nature and culture," "the understanding of conscience in relation to law and discernment," "the use of an approach to the characteristics of phenomena through the various disciplines," "the inseparable link of theology and pastoral experience," "the understanding of history

---

[1] Some sections of this chapter are redactions from and further elucidations of a commissioned paper I delivered at the 2022 Annual Conference of the Catholic Theological Association of Nigeria in Lagos on April 21, 2022.

in the elaboration of moral theology" and "the relativity of all language—since it cannot pretend to fix forever the understanding of the faith."[2]

Catholics continue to disagree with these fundamental issues' moral implications. Africans are not left out. I am a member of the Catholic Archdiocese of Abuja's Theological Commission. Shortly before his retirement, the emeritus Archbishop, Cardinal John Onaiyekan, challenged the Commission to facilitate an archdiocesan conversation about specific moral issues that everyday lay believers are currently facing. He notably brought up the rising use of ARTs (Assisted Reproductive Technology) in the Federal Capital Territory, as well as the ethical dilemmas associated with divorce and lawful remarriage. The Commission accepted the challenge. It sparked a discussion about IVF (In vitro fertilisation) and other ARTs at the archdiocesan level, and the results of the decentralised conversations were brought together in an archdiocesan gathering.

Contested moral issues are not just about sexual ethics and bioethics. There are contested moral issues about social morals: corruption and transparency in the Church and society; politics—between involvement and neutrality. These contestations centre on tensions. We have the tension between sin and conscience—between objective good and lesser evil arguments; between pragmatism (what works) and normativity or doctrine (what's given); or the hermeneutical clash on given doctrinal position. In exploring these tensions, some key questions drive this chapter. When we passionately disagree on moral grounds or issues, how do we find our way together in an atmosphere of toxic emotions? Why is it difficult for Catholics to have in-house conversations with one another? I want to suggest and pursue three factors—psychological, formative, and lack of skills. However, some marginal voices on synodality in the Church

---

2   Gerard O'Connell, "Birth control, IVF, euthanasia: The Vatican encouraged dialogue on polarising life issues. Is a papal encyclical next?" *America—The Jesuit Review*, July 11, 2022, https://www.americamagazine.org/faith/2022/07/11/moral-theology-vatican-pope-francis-bioethics-243337 (accessed 11 July 2022).

have informed some sensitivity in this chapter. These are children from an orphanage and students of a major seminary on the *Vademecum* for the Synod on Synodality; and insights from a non-Catholic text on moral discernment at the service of building *communio*.

Synodality and "Apostolate of the Ear"

Synodality as a way of life appears appealing and peaceful when we are considering the beauty and grandeur of our faith that we are reflecting upon in the world as a Church of spirit-filled evangelisers, to use Pope Francis's language in *Evangelium Gaudium*. Synodality challenges the People of God to embrace the "Apostolate of the Ear" towards "building communion amid disagreement."[3] The option for open dialogical processes at all levels follows the path of Pope Francis's disposition to "the role of conflict and honest speech (*parrhesia*) in the life of the Church..."[4] He reiterates this in *Fratelli Tutti*.[5] Authentic reconciliation involves a paradox, according to Pope Francis's teaching. This is because true reconciliation is "achieved *in* conflict, resolving it through dialogue and open, honest and patient negotiation."[6] Without honest discussion of differences anchored on justice, trust cannot be rebuilt—which is reconciliation. Reconciliation leads to unity that does not absorb differences or create a "syncretism."[7]

---

3   Francis, *Apostolic Exhortation Evangelii Gaudium to the Bishops, Clergy, Consecrated Persons and the Lay Faithful on the Proclamation of the Gospel in Today's World* (Vatican City: Vatican Press, 2013), no. 228.

4   Bradford Hinze, "Can We Find A Way Together? The Challenge of Synodality in a Wounded and Wounding Church," *Irish Theological Quarterly* 85, no. 3 (2020): 215-29, at 17, https://doi.org/10.1177/0021140020926595.

5   Francis, *Encyclical Letter Fratelli Tutti of the Holy Father on Fraternity and Social Friendship* (Vatican City: Vatican Press, 2020).

6   Francis, *Fratelli Tutti*, no. 244 [italics original].

7   Francis, *Fratelli Tutti*, no. 245.

If moral theology will help pastors and leaders of the Church to recover from her internal crises, a top-down approach cannot work. We must embrace the inverse pyramid of Pope Francis's synodal Church. This does not mean a synodal Church is jettisoning the idea of a teaching Church. Listening to the voice of the people sends the strong message that in a synodal Church, we complement a strong teaching Church with a passionate listening Church—to the People of God, the Clergy, the Magisterium, and the Holy Spirit. All in the Body of Christ are committed to listening to themselves and listening to the Holy Spirit. This is called total listening. A synodal Church listens first and foremost to the Spirit. This calls for embracing what the Auxiliary Bishop of Abuja Archdiocese, Most Rev Dr Anselm Umoren, MSP, termed the "Apostolate of the Ear," or hearing with "the ear of the heart."[8] This entails feeling the pulse of the People of God. In a synodal Church, everyone, especially those in command and governance positions, must always strive to live and walk with the people as shepherds with large ears of the rabbit.

Marginal Voices from Nigeria on Synodality in the Church

As we move on in the synodal conversations, the ancient wisdom of the *Rule of St Benedict* reminds us: "by the Lord's inspiration, it is often a younger person who knows what is best."[9] This informed the deliberate turn to two marginal voices in the Catholic Church, in particular in the Catholic Archdiocese of Abuja—Holy Family Sisters of the Needy Orphanage and Home for Destitute, and The National Missionary Seminary of

---

8   Most Rev Dr Anselm Umoren expressed these words during his lecture at the Synodal assembly organised by the National Association of Catholic Theology Students (NACATHS), NAMISEM Gwagwalada—Abuja Chapter on March 26, 2022. The theme of the Assembly was: "Synodality and the Catholic Church in Nigeria: Listening to the Voice of the People".

9   Congregation for Institutes of Consecrated Life and Societies of Apostolic Life, *New Wine in new Wineskins: The Consecrated Life and its Ongoing Challenges since Vatican II*, Trans. Christina Cooley (Vatican City: Libreria Editrice Vaticana, 2017), no. 20.

St Paul, both in Gwagwalada, Abuja. I chose these two groups because of their proximity and easy accessibility.

A. Methodology for the Focus Group Conversations

In this section, I employ a descriptive and explanatory approach to transmit the findings from the two focus groups. Descriptive research offers explanations for certain patterns of behaviour or relationships and delivers a clear image or description of a certain scenario.[10] This strategy is appropriate for the two case studies, whose participants might not be extremely knowledgeable about all aspects of synodality. However, this strategy aids the theologian in creating what Bernard Lonergan refers to as precritical histories of case study participants. A precritical history, according to Lonergan is a method in Theology, which is narratively linear and characterised by "organised recital of events."[11] Precritical history is concerned with people, time, reasons, and outcomes. Nevertheless, it fulfils a useful purpose. It provides a means of (collective) identity development to be devoted to a purpose, survival, and growth. Precritical history is therefore neither a simple presentation nor a simple fabrication of facts. Lonergan lists the following characteristics of precritical history:

i)   It is artistic in that it chooses, arranges, and recounts events in a way that will inspire or encourage the reader.

ii)   It is ethical in that it does not merely recount the past. It places blame (on the other) and gives credit (to those who make the focus group's life better).

iii) Explanatory: It is a genealogy because it provides explanations for why certain things are the way they are and different from other areas.

---

10   Lawrence Neuman, *Social Research Methods: Qualitative and Quantitative Approaches* (Boston: Allyn and Bacon, 1997), 19-21.

11   Bernard Lonergan, *Method in Theology*, Hardcover ed. (London: Darton, Longman & Todd, 1971), 185.

iv) Apologetic: It debunks contrary claims from outsiders concerning actions of one's people's past. It contests narratives of "calumny" against the group.

v) Prophetic: It joins how the past was with how the future will be.[12]

My research's two targeted groups had a similar, albeit not identical, trajectory. For instance, the children of Maryland Orphanage[13] started their synodal conversations with a prep talk from me. Of their volition, some of the children spontaneously brought out their phones to do voice recording of the conversation. This gesture was a lesson, that giving an accurate account of a teaching moment means being committed to the whole truth and the transmission of truth by communicating what one hears as accurately as possible. For, according to the children, the voice recording of my prep talk would be an arbiter whenever conflicts arise later in their conversations about the interpretation of what I asked them to do or the plan/trajectory of action. It was instructive to see that these children took the process seriously. They broke into three small groups of diverse backgrounds. They always began conversations with one of the scriptural references I provided. To ensure that no one was left out, they split up into smaller groups to allow for everyone's participation. At the conclusion of their discussions, they chose a team of redactors to create a synthesis of their discussions, which they formally submitted at a Sunday Mass after providing an overview of the results of their discussions with the congregation.

On the other hand, the synodal conversations among the students of the National Missionary Seminary of St Paul,[14] took

---

[12]   Lonergan, *Method in Theology*, 185.

[13]   The Holy Family Sisters of the Needy Orphanage and Home for the Destitute, Gwagwalada, Abuja accommodates about eighty children ranging from newborns to fresh university graduates yet to find gainful employment or accommodation to begin their independent lives.

[14]   The National Missionary Seminary of St Paul (henceforth, NAMISEM) belongs to the Missionary Society of St Paul of Nigeria, the first indigenous missionary congregation in Africa. During the 2021/2022 academic year, the seminary had a student population

place in the first quarter of 2022. The Seminary's Director of Apostolate, Fr Idara Otu, MSP, had a general conference with students, giving an overview of the synodal process, from the perspective of the *Vademecum*, and the intended conversations. The students had an opportunity during the Question and Answer (Q&A) sessions to deepen their understanding of the process and the task. The students broke into groups along their class lines. Each class had two sets of questions. The first set focused on the general question of their varied experiences of synodality in their local Church. All six groups had this question. The second set of questions for the six small groups consisted of two questions each from the ten Questions for Discussions in the Synod on Synodality's *Vademecum*. Most of the questions focused on managing differences and conflict resolution. Each group synthesised their conversations, which the respective class representatives handed over to the Seminary's Director of Apostolate.

B. Findings from the Focus Groups

1. Most Significant Optimistic Experiences of Synodality in the Local Church

For the children of Maryland Orphanage, the most significant, which cut across the three groups, is "the ability of individuals and groups to work together in harmony in the consultation."[15] Also, they recognise the need for fair and equal opportunity for the reception of the sacraments, education, and in assigning responsibilities.[16] For them, the reception of the sacraments is significant, given that this is an orphanage and home for the destitute. All have equal opportunities to receive the sacraments.

---

of eighty-six, divided into Philosophy and Theology departments, from various parts of Nigeria. The students belong to various congregations.

[15] Maryland Orphanage, "General Report," 1.

[16] Maryland Orphanage, "General Report," 2.

It is faith and right dispositions that matter. They note some attitudinal dispositions that were pointedly present during their synodal conversation and discernment. These dispositions include not giving up on anyone, co-operation, and organisation of ongoing formation programmes especially on facilitating synodality.

On the other hand, for the NAMISEM students, some significant experiences of synodality as a fact of life in the local Church among philosophy students include home visitation to the homebound. For the participants, this underscores the reality that no one is left alone in the Church, regardless of one's moments of vulnerability. Another significant experience is communal accompaniment, with particular emphasis on the material dimension. This point emphasises that *'communio'* ecclesiology costs money, but a Church of communion does not mind. Faith formation at various levels in the local Church is another experience of synodality. This ensures that people grow into, and are formed into a *communio* mindset and discernment. Summarily, *communio* brings joy among the People of God; and this is demonstrated in various ways like effective liturgy, with people experiencing healing within the 'Church-at-Prayer'. People experience the joy of synodality with their sense of belonging, mutual respect, and understanding among individual members and various sodalities—even within the seminary community.

2. Most Significant Negative Experiences of Synodality in the Local Church

Beginning with their synodal conversations, the children of the Maryland Orphanage admitted that despite the readiness and willingness to speak out, they experienced "disagreement and tension in the listening process."[17] On their experience of synodality as a way of life in the local Church, they offer that notwithstanding "myriads of human, monetary, and material

---

[17]   Maryland Orphanage, "General Report," 1.

resources capable of sustaining her in her journey," they experience "desolation" in the Church, with the increasing rate of disaffiliation and laxation "due to the conventional style of the Church."[18] They also note that some appointment processes have not been transparent; were undemocratic, characterised by low collaboration and "selective and preferential assignment of" some responsibilities. For instance, they singled a practice in the Home—serving at Mass. The conversation addressed the reality of abuse of power and privilege by "the bigger boys" who assign themselves to assist at Mass on special occasions—episcopal Mass, and other "big occasions." The younger boys and all the girls are relegated to "Morning Masses and the usual Sunday Masses."[19] They also observed another example of abuse of power concerning ecclesial conflicts. The participants note that in a neighbouring parish, parishioners are denied Holy Communion on the ground that they did not participate in the parish sanitation exercise. According to the participants, this is morally outrageous.

NAMISEM students also acknowledged that despite their optimism in synodality as a fact of life in the local Church, there are some difficulties facing deepened synodal way of life. Even in places where the local Church tries to resemble a synodal Church through some commitment to communal discernment, people experience a sense of "a 'bracketing' of discussion."[20] When the local Church gathers for listening in communal discernment, the scope is limited and discussions are tailored toward some ends, and some concerns even forced to be discussed are left un-attended to due to "a dogmatic approach to issues sometimes without viewing (sic) from the parishioner's (sic) perspective first ...."[21] At other times, when the People of God come together in

---

[18] Maryland Orphanage, "General Report," 1.

[19] Maryland Orphanage, "General Report," 2.

[20] 400L students of the National Missionary Seminary of St Paul, "Responses to Questionnaire 'For a Synodal Church: Communion, Participation and Mission'" (unpublished, Abuja, n.d.), 1-2, at 2.

[21] 400L students of NAMISEM, "Responses to Questionnaire," 2.

dialogue on some contested ecclesial issues, they end up arguing sentimentally. Thus, the subjective factors driving the sentimentality override the objective interest at stake.[22] This reveals a crucial point, namely, we are poor or unskilled in interactive conflict resolution, especially on how we can deconstruct constructively the narratives of "incompatibility and indivisibility"[23] to discover the objective interests and subjective factors regarding contested ecclesial issues. This unskillfulness creates a communication gap and apathy in the Church, which eventually leads to some dropping out of the Church in frustration.[24]

C. *Dreams about a Synodal Church: Summing Up Synodal Conversations*

The constructed 'precritical history', Lonergan notes, contain meagre wisdom.[25] Hence, one must move beyond the descriptive 'precritical history'. To a large extent, I agree with Lonergan's understanding of research method. It is not a checklist, or a set of constant prescriptions. On the contrary, a research method, even in theology, is *a normative pattern of recurrent and related operations yielding cumulative and progressive results*. The research method Lonergan has in mind has the following characteristics: i) Ongoing inquiry; ii) Accuracy in observations and understanding; iii) Formulated hypotheses derived from insights; iv) Deductive – in relation to hypotheses and experience; and v] Progressive and cumulative results.[26] In the light of this, I tease out the following

---

22   Theology 2 students of the National Missionary Seminary of St Paul, "Responses to Questionnaire 'For a Synodal Church: Communion, Participation and Mission'" (unpublished, Abuja, n.d.), 1-4, at 3.

23   The term "incompatibility" suggests that problems resulting from radically construed identities cannot be sufficiently compromised to allow them to coexist. On the other hand, indivisibility suggests that the issues at hand are viewed as a single unit and cannot be divided into smaller parts as required in negotiated peace agreements.

24   400L students of NAMISEM, "Responses to Questionnaire," 1.

25   Lonergan, *Method in Theology*, 185.

26   Cf. Lonergan, *Method in Theology*, 4-5, quotation on 5, italics in the original.

as a cumulative of the sense the children of Maryland Orphanage and NAMISEM students make of synodality in the Church in their synodal conversations. For these communities of very young (and vulnerable) members of the Body of Christ, what are their dreams of a synodal Church that they will grow up in, and possibly minister to? If they will not drift away from the Mother-Church that allowed them to be alive and on the way to becoming somebody in life, what is the vision of the Church that will remain attractive and persuasive enough to keep them? They have two dreams:

i) *Journeying Together as a Necessity*: They dream of a Church that preaches and demonstrates that a deeper sense and reality of interconnectedness is indispensable for evangelisation. No one is saved alone. No one evangelises alone. Hence, networking and division of labour must become more realities in the Church. Just as they have experienced in their lives in the orphanage and during their synodal conversations, no one is useless in the work of evangelisation: "Some provide financial support; others moral support, and yet others their presence, time, etc to realise. . .help to those in need."[27]

ii) *Views from Below*: To improve and foster journeying together the Church must never forget the poor and all at the margins. Sometimes encountering these voices from below can be both a *kairos* and a theophany. Hence, the fruits of all the synodal conversations and consultations should be adapted by the local Church, diocese, and the Church at large, as *this is the essence of the synod*. The essence of the whole discussion on synodality in the Church comes down to the equitable mix of "affective" and "effective" consultations. This is authentic synodality, as opposed to apparent consultation.

---

[27] Maryland Orphanage, "General Report," 5.

Moral Disputations, Synodality and Insights from the World Council of Churches

The lessons I highlighted above from the synodal conversations at the Maryland Orphanage and NAMISEM offer insights on what to expect when we take seriously our moral disputations in the Church. Following the apostolic exhortation of Pope Francis on how to handle conflict and opposition in an atmosphere of unity and solidarity,[28] how do we do this in practice? Archbishop Vincenzo Paglia, the president of the Pontifical Academy for Life, describes a contemporary response:

> We did this not only in an atmosphere of *parrhesia* [a bold and courageous freedom of speech] that stimulates and empowers theologians, academics and scholars. But also with a procedure similar to the *quaestiones disputatae:* to pose a thesis and open it up to debate. The *quaestiones disputatae* is a medieval method of philosophical and theological discussion to dispute issues pertinent to society, where one scholar presents a thesis and another responds in dispute.[29]

The *quaestiones disputatae* model appears to have yielded desired results from the review of the proceedings of the expert seminar referred to in the introduction to this chapter. According to Roberto Dell'Oro and M. Therese Lysaught, in the review essay on the published proceedings,[30] the drive for transcendence is rooted in an anthropological approach to religion, and *Etica Teologica della Vita* demonstrates how theological research completes this drive. *Etica teologica della vita* shows that even if

---

28   Francis, *Evangelii Gaudium*, nos. 226, 28.

29   "Archbishop Paglia on Pope's teaching on 'Theological Ethics of Life,'" *Vatican News*, June 30, 2022, https://www.vaticannews.va/en/vatican-city/news/2022-06/archbishop-vincenzo-paglia-pope-francis-interview-theological-et.html (accessed 10 August 2022).

30   *Etica Teologica Della Vita: Scrittura, Tradizione, Sfide Pratiche* (*Theological Ethics of Life: Scripture, Tradition, Practical Challenges*) (Libreria Editrice Vaticana, 2022) exists as of now only in Italian. For a succinct introduction and summary, see Pontifical Academy for Life, "Theological Ethics of Life: Scripture, tradition, practical challenges," https://www.academyforlife.va/content/pav/en/news/2022/theological-ethics-of-life.html (accessed 12 August 2022).

moral interlocutors have "a multiplicity of approaches," they can have "an uncanny unanimity of method."[31] As we embrace the *quaestiones disputatae* model for our contested moral issues, we can learn a few things from the analytical framework for moral disputations the World Council of Churches developed.

WCC started this effort to help churches deal with moral disputes by offering approaches to comprehending the other side's perspective. Its framework might be useful in overcoming the toxic emotions, especially animosity, distrust, and aggression, which sometimes develop between and within churches when there is a moral dispute.[32] To move from passionate moral disagreements to reconciliation, we must renew our understanding of communal discernment. Communal discernment, anchored on faith, the holiness of life and active ecclesial participation, helps to discover the truth of the faith or the authentic path regarding any knotty issue on faith and morals. Given this perspective about moral conversations on contested issues, then our spiritual conversation over moral disagreements, according to the WCC study, should always begin from a point of commonality—the dual charity of God and neighbour (cf. *Mt* 22:34-40).

D. WCC's Tool for Moral Discernment in the Church

The WCC study opines that we must provide our people with an analytical and conversational tool on moral conflicts that will present their values (similar moral languages or expressions), the factors that cause moral disagreements and the

---

[31] Roberto Dell'Oro and M. Therese Lysaught, "Review Essay—Theological Ethics of Life: A New Volume by the Pontifical Academy for Life," *Journal of Moral Theology* 11/2, 65-77 (2022), 75.

[32] World Council of Churches, *Churches and Moral Discernment—Volume 3: Facilitating Dialogue to Build Koinonia*, Faith and Order Paper, (Geneva: WCC Publications, 2021), no. 23.

elements of moral norms and traditions that cannot change.[33] Consequently, the study offers a good tool that I find plausible.[34]

TOOL FOR MORAL DISCERNMENT

Elements	More Stable	←→	More Contingent		
Moral Norms	Fundamental Norms	Intermediate Norms	Concrete Material Norms	Plau-sibility	Context: Church-state/ Civil Relations
Ecclesial Understanding of Authority and Purpose of Discourse	Doctrinal/ Whole Church	Mid-Level Authority e.g. Synodal, Local Church	Pastoral/ Individual Christian		
Ecclesial conception of Salvation history	Transcendent	←→	Immanent		
Ecclesial Identity and disposition to change	Unchanging	←→	Constantly reforming		

Mode of Moral Reasoning
Intentions; Actions; Fruition

Circumstances: Aggravating, Mitigating, Justifying

E. **Figure 1: Adapted from WCC,** *Facilitating Dialogue to Build Koinonia,* **52, Figure 8.**

This tool captures the "conscience of the Church" at work each time there is a need for moral discernment. It depicts the elements where conflicts occur (moral norms, ecclesial understanding

---

33   World Council of Churches, *Churches and Moral Discernment*, nos. 71, 73, and 76.

34   World Council of Churches, *Churches and Moral Discernment*, 52, Figure 8.

of authority, goal of moral discourse, Church understanding of salvation history, and attitude to change).[35] The Plausibility Tool is a tool for the Church to give an account of the reasonability of its moral truth and norms. The stable and contingent aspects clash with the method of moral reasoning, which consists of intentions, the act, and the products of the will when moral processing occurs.[36] The contingency of moral norms and permitted acts depends largely on where the Church draws the line between the more stable and more contingent norms. This is where mid-level authority (the Petrine Office, episcopal conferences, Local Ordinaries) becomes very important. This mid-level authority can help to make clearer where a moral conflict is located.

MSP Ethical Disposition for Moral Disputations in a Synodal Church: A Proposal

Our Roman Catholic moral tradition is rooted in the nuanced moral discernment of Thomas Aquinas and Alphonsus Liguori. Because of inadequate moral tradition building, our people fight and engender toxic emotions in one another. We need to assist our people in acquiring the Church's attitude towards moral judgement. Hence, I make some specific recommendations for how we might provide our people with this traditionally Roman Catholic moral reasoning, albeit with a modern twist by referring to the MSP ethical framework. Ian Markham, who wrote about religious ethics in a pluralist society, coined the acronym MSP, which stands for "Morally Serious Person(s)".[37] The MSP framework has seven components: Citizenship, Tolerance, Informed, Interiority, Contextual, Moral Imagination, and Moral

---

[35]   World Council of Churches, *Churches and Moral Discernment*, no. 87.

[36]   World Council of Churches, *Churches and Moral Discernment*, nos. 81-85.

[37]   Ian Markham, *Do Morals Matter?: A Guide to Contemporary Religious Ethics* (Malden; Oxford; Victoria: Blackwell, 2007).

Conversation. For want of space, I will focus on the commitment to moral conversation.

F. Commitment to Moral Conversation

Interaction—even conflict—between two or more competing value systems leads to moral development or growth. The search perspective is crucial for MSP as a result. The morally serious individual is open to discourse with partners from many religious traditions as well as from the secular world in their pursuit of viewpoints and a larger understanding of ethically contentious matters. The ethical *trifecta* of pluralism—the reality of difference, tolerance—allowing for points of disagreement—and conversation—exchanging opposing viewpoints in public—are also given specific consideration by MSP.[38] The main takeaway is that a discussion partner using the MSP framework will engage in four essential processes when debating moral problems.

1. Step One—Parties Identify the Issue

Naming the issue to be considered ethically is crucial. All the parties should ensure that they agree at least regarding the facts about the identity of the moral issue, and the stakeholders. What individuals and groups have an important stake in the outcome? Are some concerns more important? Why?

2. Step Two—Research the Issue

Parties do not just jump into a conversation about contested moral issues. They will strive to be abreast with the current state of the disputations. What are the relevant facts of the case? What facts are not known? Can we learn more about the situation? Do we know enough to make a decision? This is why doing some research on the *status quaestionis* and *status disputatae* are inevitable.

---

[38]   Markham, *Do Morals Matter?*, 193-194.

3. Step Three—Ethical Deliberations on Options for Moral Decision and Action

As previously stated, MSP is dedicated to the ethical trinity of plurality, toleration, and discourse. There are numerous solutions and answers for every contentious moral issue. Parties that desire morally righteous outcomes will be receptive to these and related inquiries: Which option will produce the best and do the least harm? (Utilitarian); what does the Law say? What are my obligations? (Deontology); which option best respects the rights of all who have a stake? (Rights); which option treats people equally or proportionately? (Justice); which option best serves the community as a whole, not just some members? (Common Good); which option leads parties to act as the sort of persons they wish to be? (Virtue ethic). Have all the relevant persons and groups been consulted? If the parties told those they respect—or told a television audience—the option they chose, what would they say?

4. Step Four—Decision-making and Anticipated Outcomes

The moral disputations will occasionally turn towards resolution. MSP will make sure that the decision is executed with the utmost care and respect to the concerns of all stakeholders in light of the decision and viewpoint. They will plan for the consequences of their choices. What have people taken away from this particular ethical situation? The parties must choose what is best to do after carefully considering each of these factors.[39]

MSP acknowledges the need to base ethical decisions in part—but not entirely—on scientific data. Assumptions, hearsay, and biased reporting are all rejected. A morally responsible person does not confine themselves to a limited selection of media or ideological cocoons. With attention and a critical eye, s/he reads and listens. This component also considers temporal judgements,

---

[39]   Markham, *Do Morals Matter?*, 41-42.

which are assessments and viewpoints that represent judgments made by people in historical circumstances.[40]

Since the ethical truth from an initial doctrinal event is not disclosed once and for all, we can see why MSP's commitment to moral discourse is crucial for moral disputes. Over time, it comes into view. To support the work of an ever-expanding hermeneutics of comprehension and experience, theological conversation within the Church is crucial. The notion that *"normative determinations* are kept in motion by a more original process of *determining"*[41] inspires us to embrace the challenging, but always beneficial, exchange of theological views. Pope Francis reminds us that "truth, in fact, is *logos* which creates *dia-logos*, and hence communication and communion."[42] If we must capture the depth of what the Spirit is saying to the universal Church and local Churches today, our moral conversations must be "argumentative and narrative, theoretical and sapiential, phenomenological and interpretative."[43] This is the true spirit of African ethical discourse, which accepts the plurality of moral arguments and calls for conversation partners to ethically deliberate through perplexing experiences to reach an ethical conclusion regarding the choices that are best for humans as a whole within a community.[44] Palaver satisfies the need to offer a critical interpretation of the applicable legislation and the current circumstance by providing a continual *dia-logos* and communion regarding ethical concerns impacting a community. Community discernment is significant

---

[40]   Markham, *Do Morals Matter?*, 185-187.

[41]   Dell'Oro and Lysaught, "Review Essay—Theological Ethics of Life," 76, italics original.

[42]   Francis, *Evangelii Gaudium*, no. 4.

[43]   Archbishop Vincenzo Paglia, "Introduction," in *Etica Teologica Della Vita: Scrittura, Tradizione, Sfide Pratiche* (Vatican City: Libreria Editrice Vaticana, 2022), 7-12, at 8; https://www.academyforlife.va/content/dam/pav/documenti%20pdf/2022/Etica%20 Teologica/PAGLIA_INTRODUZIONE_ENG_.pdf (accessed 12 August 2022).

[44]   Wilson Muoha Maina, "African Communitarian Ethics in the Theological Work of Bénézet Bujo," *Pacifica* 21, no. 2 (June 2008): 192-209, at 193, https://doi. org/10.1177/1030570X0802100205; Paulinus Odozor, *Morality Truly Christian, Truly African: Foundational, Methodological, and Theological Considerations* (Notre Dame, Indiana: Notre Dame University Press, 2014), 154-55.

for African moral discourse in the service of life.[45] We understand that traditionally moral findings are reached through a "tradition of inquiry" that is mostly inductive or improved deduction. This procedure goes beyond a simple deductive analysis of natural law and metaphysics. Norms are created inside a particular society and tradition, albeit in the case of dispute, as Bénézet Bujo contends, they have to defend their legitimacy in the palaver.[46]

Conversion to a More Synodal Church and Moral Contestations

Back to the synodal discussions of the Maryland Orphanage. They argue in their reflections on synodality and conversion that for a more deeply synodal Church, the Church must bridge the gap between faith and life.[47] Also, the Church should keep up its commitment from an imperial (excessively hierarchical overtly clericalist) system to an increasing "democratic governance system", i.e. more participatory system. It must show an irreversible openness to wide consultation in decision-making to "enable effective participation of members."[48] As a result, while discussing intra-ecclesial disagreements, the Church must accept more diversity and objectivity. By doing this, the faithful can get over their lack of concern for the intentions of hierarchy whenever a synod is called. This calls for conversion from the Church, which shows up as a commitment and ability to "walk together." This phrase describes a synodal Church that is willing to create dialogical processes that support daring and straight-forward honesty at all levels of the Church. Reconciliation (rebuilt trust) cannot happen unless there is an open discussion

---

[45] Cf. Bénézet Bujo, *Foundations of an African Ethic: Beyond the Universal Claims of Western Morality*, Trans. Brian McNeil (Nairobi: Paulines Publications Africa, 2003), 21-25.

[46] Bénézet Bujo, *The Ethical Dimension of Community: The African Model and the Dialogue between North and South*, Trans. Cecilia Nganda (Nairobi: Paulines, 1998), preface, n.p.

[47] Maryland Orphanage, "General Report," 3.

[48] Maryland Orphanage, "General Report," 4.

about disagreements that are based on fairness.[49] As a result, a powerful teaching Church needs to be accompanied by a passionate listening Church that honours people's moral responsibility and conscience. A truly synodal Church will be dedicated to shaping people's consciences rather than assuming control of them. The Church will devote time and resources to helping its members develop the moral discernment abilities that are indicative of moral maturity befitting a pilgrim people because it respects the moral agency of its members.

If the pastors of the People of God ensure adherence to the ground rules of interactive dispute resolution procedures in the Church, the conversion to the synodal manner will be fruitful. This conversion may provide the People of God with a chance to adopt St Thomas Aquinas' more traditional Roman Catholic method of moral reflection. It is the dialectical process in which disputants present reasons in support of an accurate hermeneutics of a theological proposition with calmness and sincerity.[50] Engaging in a continual discourse of this nature would be a sheer joy of life and faith.[51] In the synodal Church, this paradigm must serve as a framework for both thought and action. This concept is incompatible with a highly hierarchical and centralised Church. Any other paradigm would be out of sync in a synodal Church.

The adoption of the synodal manner will ideally take place when a spiritual formation process that can foster synodal dialogue is present. We can recognise our unity thanks to this formation, even when we are at odds. Members of the Church at all levels who are anchored in the Spirit will be dedicated to total listening to preserve this unity in conflict. We all have the best of

---

[49]   Francis, *Fratelli Tutti*, nos. 244-245.

[50]   Pierangelo Sequeri, "An Exemplary Case of an Authentic Synodal Exercise," *Avvenire* (July 2022). https://www.academyforlife.va/content/dam/pav/documenti%20pdf/2022/Etica%20Teologica/Sequeri%209%20luglio%20ITA%20ENG%20ESP%20POR/SEQUERI_ENG_Avvenire_An%20exemplary%20case%20of%20an%20authentic%20synodal%20exercise.pdf (accessed 15 December 2022).

[51]   Sequeri, "An Exemplary Case".

intentions when it comes to the welfare of the ecclesial community, thus there is no brusqueness. The People of God will develop new viewpoints based on the virtues of love, respect, caution, and trust as a result of this spirituality. Additionally, this spiritual training will cultivate in us genuine community discernment concerning moral disagreements. The General Secretariat for the Synod of Bishops offers us a handy resource that can help this spiritual formation. It is a four-paged text on a spiritual conversation. This text offers that spiritual discourse is an act of attentive character that involves embracing, respecting, and being kind to individuals in their current circumstances. Spiritual dialogue takes the inner thoughts of the participants seriously. Throughout the conversation, one must be conscious of their own and the other's spiritual growth.[52] We better understand communal discernment as a double contemplation of the Word of God and the people of the Word when we have a strong foundation in the spirituality of communal discernment.[53] Communicative discernment is not spontaneous; it is deliberate, systematic, and planned. Acts 15 shows how this notion of collective discernment was put to use in the early Church. We affirm once more that authentic collective decision-making by the Church is deliberate and the product of genuine discernment.

We should all share a fundamental notion of moral behaviour to respond to the synodal approach of "walking together" as one People of God. Fundamentally, love is the moral minimum of human existence. Contemporary African Moral theology and the broader Christian Ethics agree about the centrality of love in morality. For instance, Bénézet Bujo, a pioneer in African Moral Theology, makes a strong case for the relationship between

---

52   Synod of Bishops, "Spiritual Conversation," 1, n.d. https://www.synod.va/content/dam/synod/common/phases/en/EN_Step_6_Spiritual-Conversation.pdf (accessed 13 August 2022).

53   International Theological Commission, *Synodality in the Life and Mission of the Church* (March 2, 2018), no. 114, https://www.vatican.va/roman_curia/congregations/cfaith/cti_documents/rc_cti_20180302_sinodalita_en.html.

African anthropology—of relatedness and fellowship, historical memory (anamnesis), and narrativity—and African ethical reasoning. Accordingly, in African palaver ethics, material and secondary moral standards must be rooted in the first commandment—Life (or "vital force").[54] The fundamental moral foundation will, admittedly, be concretely presented and contextually functional.[55] Of course, this acceptance of pluralism in moral argumentation & normative formulation leads to divergent forms of praxis at the service of life.[56] This is not a tragedy to be avoided. Life is complex and demands responses and praxis that will further this life in context. Similar to this, Dell'Oro and Lysaught assert that a "love for life"[57] has an impact on the primacy of moral normativity, the applicability of ethical principles, and ultimately the development of praxis from a broader Christian ethical perspective. Additionally, this primacy establishes our fundamental perspective on the difficulties associated with life-shaping procedures, including those in the field of sexual and bioethics. An *Action Theory of Love for Life* at the service of a Christian virtue ethic is supported by theology for several reasons, including its recognition of the importance of the good, the relevance of morally noble personhood, its roots in the community, and the need to specify standards for what constitutes right behaviour in the context of comprehensive accounts of human fulfilment and flourishing. This Action Theory underscores virtue ethics' teleological direction "with a more original"[58] belief in the history of the good. The pursuit of a final good is grounded by the benefit provided by the gift of life.[59]

---

54   Bujo, *Ethical Dimension of Community*, 31, 44.

55   Bujo, *Ethical Dimension of Community*, 44.

56   Bujo, *Ethical Dimension of Community*, 41.

57   Bujo, *Ethical Dimension of Community*, 76.

58   Bujo, *Ethical Dimension of Community*, 76.

59   Bujo, *Ethical Dimension of Community*, 76.

Conclusion

This chapter has argued that discussions regarding contentious moral issues in Africa must always be located within the framework of the supremacy of love in the spirit of the demand for a synodal manner of being Church. This chapter was inspired by the enduring moral principles in African palaver as a method. Nonetheless, this ethical methodological approach may not be seen as an invitation for "anything goes" ethics, where "everything is negotiable, everything is open to bargaining."[60] Therefore, I have argued that moral debates on contentious topics, even in Africa, have to be anchored in a foundational theory of moral action—love for life. This is supported by the enormous contributions of the voices from Abuja margins on synodality and the Protestant world. Therefore, love as the centre of the Christian life, which has a preferential option for the poor and vulnerable, regardless of ethnicity, gender, or religion, must be included as an imperative in an African Christian moral discourse anchored in African theological anthropology. This is what can protect against the potential demonic aspect of the moral discourse found in African palaver. If not subordinated to a universal ethic, the narrative moral discourse can subvert justice and sacrifice the poor and vulnerable as "a willing holocaust."[61] Ultimately, a synodal Church especially in Africa has to be relentlessly open to intercultural and self-critical dialogue in the world of morality.

---

[60]   Odozor, *Morality Truly Christian*, 162.
[61]   Odozor, *Morality Truly Christian*, 160-162, quotation on 162.

CHAPTER 9

African Palaver and Interpretation of the Word of God with and for the People of God: A Case for the Dialogical Construction of the Homily in the Small Christian Communities in Africa

Ignace Ndongala Maduku

"The concern for the field and the fundamental reflection of men and the dimensions of social life must open us to the demands of a hermeneutics of speech." J.-M. Ela[1]

The Eucharistic liturgy of the Catholic Church gives an important place to the homily. The General Presentation of the Roman Missal in its number 9 presents the homily as a living presentation which increases the effectiveness of Sacred Scripture. In number 41, the document says, "it is necessary to nourish the Christian life [...] It must explain an aspect of the scriptural readings, or else of another text of the Ordinary or the Proper of the Mass of the day, in taking into account either the mystery being celebrated or the particular needs of the listeners." Numbers 31 and 33 of the Directory on the homily insist that the homily takes into account the particular requirements and expectations of the listeners.

---

[1] Jean-Marc Ela, *Repenser la théologie africaine: Le Dieu qui libère,* (Paris, Karthala, 2003), 14.

This contribution is based on lessons from an empirical experience highlighting the consideration of listeners in the process of elaboration of homilies. By reporting on the experiment carried out in 1999 at the parish of Sainte-Trinité in the diocese of Kinshasa (DR Congo), this chapter is interested in assessing the participation of the listeners to the development of the message in the course of the transmission of the homily. Our contribution proposes the preparation of the homily within the framework of a Basic Ecclesial Community (BEC) meeting. It finds its roots in the quest for a persuasive aim by taking into account the particular situation, the aspirations, the specific expectations and the pre-understanding of the listeners, in this case the members of the CEBs (BCC, Basis Christian Communities). The concern of this contribution is, therefore, to put into perspective, on the one hand, the emergence of a Church which joins the recipients of the Good News in their own universes, with their joys and problems, successes and failures, impasses and challenges, and meets human beings with their concerns where they live, and on the other hand, the construction of a communication device which makes the assembly pass from the status of listener to that of co-author in/of the production of the homily. In short, this project intends to open a path towards synodality from the homiletic interlocution.

We first present some elements of the method and then the conceptual framework. We will then return to the experience of the parish of Sainte-Trinité before identifying some perspectives for a synodal Church.

Methodological Framework

The research is based on a unique case. It makes it possible to initiate a reflection on the feedback of experience in the sense of a work that reflects on what was accomplished and observed in the past and how it can affect the development of future action. As such, it is based on the account of our own experience, supplemented, on the one hand, by six semi-structured interviews of half an hour each with four members of the Basic Ecclesial Community of the site under study. On the other hand, the work is also enriched with data from the content analysis of our field notes and our homily preparations of 20 years ago. Although the methodological framework has been revised downwards, it nevertheless allowed us to position ourselves at the confluence of two methodological approaches: ethnography and praxeology.

From a Homily for the People of God to a Homily with the People of God: Conceptual Framework

The theoretical framework of this contribution is based on the decolonisation of theological knowledge. With this expression, we intend to question the ways of doing things that have imposed themselves in time and space, leading to the depreciation of non-European conceptions of knowledge in favour of intellectual colonisation against the backdrop of the hegemony of Western episteme. This Eurocentric approach which consecrates epistemic coloniality in the sense understood by W. Mignolo requires the valorisation of other places of emerging epistemologies in consonance with other places of enunciation,[2] Indeed, the interpretation of the Word of God by the attendants of "the house of absolute knowledge,"[3] the place par excellence of orthodoxy, cenacle of any authorised and official instance of interpretation of the Word of God (exegesis as a discipline, Congregation for the Doctrine of the Faith as an institution, Bishops as guardians of the faith) does not escape a subtle form of coloniality. Given that the enunciation space of this house is occupied by consecra-

---

[2]   Walter Mignolo, "Géopolitique de la sensibilité et du savoir. (Dé) colonialité, pensée frontalière et désobéissance épistémologique", *Mouvements* 73, 2013/1, 181-190.

[3]   Walter Mignolo, *La désobéissance épistémique: Rhétorique de la modernité, logique de la colonialité et grammaire de la décolonialité* (Bruxelles: Peter Lang, 2015), 121.

ted ministers, the laity stay in the vestibule. Also, in a privileged and exclusive way, the space of enunciation interprets in an exemplary way the Word of God, authenticates, validates and evaluates other interpretations. It is also that same space of enunciation that, with regard to the homily, debases the interpretation of the base in the margins as a subordinate knowledge whose rationality and epistemic status are devalued.

These perspectives show that the coloniality of knowledge makes the difference between priests and lay people visible and inscribes it in liturgy, prayer and the relationship with God. It assigns a particular status to the laity. Canon 767 reserves the homily for priests and deacons, which is what the instruction *Ecclesiae de mysterio*, on certain questions concerning the collaboration of the faithful in the ministry of priests (1997) confirms in article 3. It is in the same line as the instruction *Redemptionis sacramentum*, on certain things to observe and avoid concerning the most holy Eucharist (64-66) and the Directory on the homily.[4] In addition to a difference in nature, conditions and status (ordained minister and non-ordained faithful), the homily will therefore have to put up with scholarly and dominant ways of interpreting the Word of God. It is based on power relations grounded in the superiority of the knowledge system erected by the space of enunciation (exegesis). It evolves in the coloniality of surviving power in the epistemic and cultural realm. Faced with this situation, we envisage a process of rearrangement, of ecclesial meshing, namely the reorganisation of the order of weaving of the mat of the Word. We mean by this to give voice back to obliterated experiences, to marginalised words and to make the proclaimed Word Good News which, in addition to making God desirable, illuminates the fields of experience and the horizons of expectation of the listeners, from of their place

---

[4]   Congrégation pour le culte divin et la discipline des sacrements, Directoire sur l'homélie, Cité du Vatican, 2014. Microsoft Word - riformattato direttorio omilettico traduzione francese.doc (catholique.fr).

and environment.[5] It is an exit from the assimilationist epistemic framework to legitimise readings and interpretations articulated around the experience of the community rather than based solely on the knowledge of individuals. Hence, the option for the construction of the homily by conjunction rather than by disjunction. It is a question of arriving at the co-construction of the homily.

We borrow the concept of co-construction from M. Foudriat and understand it in the sense of a process by which the different actors confront their points of view, commit to a transformation of these through exchange, through deliberation and agree on the translations, i.e. transform their point of view.[6] It is important to note that this process of co-construction, in addition to the expression of each other, promotes confrontation and leads to a consensus which generates new, even unprecedented knowledge. It goes without saying that the deployment of the interlocution constitutive of the homily is here carried by a collaborative research based on mutual understanding and companionship. It corresponds to the pastoral care of engendering[7] with as perspectives, "the gift of life, the complementarity of the masculine and the feminine, the reciprocity of exchanges, the birth of a new identity; an attitude of welcome and giving, of pleasure, joy, suffering too, by accepting mourning, crossing the unknown, surprise in the face of the unpredictable in life."[8]

---

5   See, for example, Stanley, J. Samartha, "Scripture and Scriptures," in R. S. Sugirtharajah, ed., *Voices from the Margin: Interpreting the Bible in the Third World,* 2nd ed., (London: SPCK, 1995), 11–36.

6   Michel Foudriat, *La co-construction: Une alternative managériale,* (Paris: Presses de l'EHESP, 2019).

7   Philippe Bacq and Christoph Theobald, éd., *Une nouvelle chance pour l'évangile. Vers une pastorale d'engendrement,* Bruxelles/Montréal/Paris, Lumen Vitae/ Novalis/Les éditions de l'atelier, 2004. Philippe Bacq, P. and Christoph Theobald, éd., *Passeurs d'Évangile. Autour d'une pastorale d'engendrement,* (Bruxelles/Montréal/Ivry-sur-Seine, Lumen Vitae/Novalis/Les éditions de l'atelier, 2008).

8   Philippe Bacq, "Vers une pastorale d'engendrement", in Bacq, et Theobald, éd., *Une nouvelle chance pour l'évangile,*17.

Back to the empirical observations of the parish of Sainte-Trinité [9]

An anecdote to situate the origin of the research project. It is a priest from the Archdiocese of Kinshasa who tells the story with great detachment, simplicity and humour. His Sunday sermons in French were punctuated by agitation on the side of the choir: smiles, laughter, whispers accompanied his speech. Convinced that it was a form of approval on the part of the choristers, he added to it and provoked an outbidding in the reaction of the choristers. One Sunday, as he was about to return to the sacristy with the feeling of a job well done, a choir member approached him and said to him: "Son, if you have difficulty preparing the homily, you can ask for help. Among us there are many ex-seminarians willing to help you."

This story came back to our mind after seven years of absence from the diocese. Our first Sunday sermon in Lingala (the liturgical language of the diocese of Kinshasa) met with fraternal criticism from the vicar. When we returned from Europe, our reading of the Word of God was based on a grammar whose roots were not always rooted in African lands. The reality had changed and the style of preaching had evolved. To be honest, we were out of step with our audience's expectations. We were nevertheless in a posture inscribed in a dualistic, Manichean typology which, by hierarchising readers and listeners, assigned us the beautiful place, that inhabited by the epistemology of academics, exegetical interpretation, in short, the authority of those who know and teach. This overvaluation and overdetermination of our interpretation of the Word of God came to a halt, because although it was decked out in exemplarity, it hardly fulfilled the expectations of the People of God. This awareness of our limits opened our eyes to the contradictions of the particular mode of appropriation of

---

[9]   Parish of the Saint Alphonse deanery, Sainte-Trinité is located in the Debonhomme district in the City Hall of Matete.

the Word of God that we had privileged until then, a mode that accommodated the subordination of the native reading and the obliteration of the original interpretation of the margins.

A monological genre whose preparation and materialisation mobilise an individual, presumed to be a specialist in the Word of God, the interpretation of the latter is based on a model of enunciation fixed by the Magisterium. The latter, with rare exceptions, recognises as agents of preaching only priests and deacons trained and conditioned according to a Western-centric approach, a Western rationality and conceptuality that carry the swelling of a "logic of coloniality."[10] Faced with the difficulty of making sense of a homily deemed too intellectual by some, disconnected from reality by others, speculative by still others, we remembered the anecdote of our colleague. She suggested that we solve the difficulty of being in tune with the parishioners by involving them in the preparation of the homily.

This solution did not take us away from the Presentation of the Liturgy of the Mass in the Zairian Rite. Indeed, she insists on the contribution of African oral styles to the celebration. Number 98 states that by virtue of its particular value, African speech "cuts monologue short. It arouses enthusiasm and promotes the participation of the people in community action."[11] It is certainly true that the Congolese Eucharistic celebrations include the participation of the whole assembly. In line with the oral tradition, this participation is felt in the homily in various ways: acclamations, applause, generous laughter, whistles, marks of approval or disapproval, marks of support, songs, bravos, slogans, prolonged hilarity, murmurs, sighs, cries, youyous, kinesic or

---

[10]   Anibal Quijano, "Colonialité du Pouvoir et Démocratie en Amérique Latine", in J. Cohen, H. Hirata et L. Gómez, dir., *Amérique Latine: Démocratie et Exclusion,* (Paris: L'Harmattan, 1994), 93-100.

[11]   CONFÉRENCE ÉPISCOPALE DU ZAÏRE, *Présentation de la liturgie de la messe. Supplément au Missel Romain pour les diocèses du Zaïre,* (Kinshasa: Éditions du Secrétariat Général de la CEZ, 1989), 18.

tactile behaviours, etc.[12] The interaction between the preacher and his audience is thought out within the limits of the reactions of the audience to the preacher's speech. Thinking about this interaction in line with a possible structuring, a possible production and co-production of the homily was the experience undertaken at the parish of Sainte-Trinité.

While the practice consecrated in Kinshasa makes the priest play the role of helper with a double competence supposedly experiential and doctrinal, against the background of a pre-eminence granted to the individuality of the preacher and the singular, we have resolved to privilege the mediation of the collective. Breaking with a procedure that is associated with a pastoral essentially articulated around the parish and the priest, a pastoral which empowers the priest, we have chosen to place the homily, on the one hand, in an African cultural context, and on the other hand, in line with a pastoral centered around the image of the Church-family of God and the Church-fraternity. With these two options, we have postulated the existence of a discursive and interpretative ecclesial community that includes priests and faithful in a companionship in tune with the culture of palaver. This allowed us to go beyond the usual binary oppositions (priests and lay people; those who know and those who do not know; scholarly knowledge and naive, inferior knowledge; exegesis and popular interpretation) and to open up the monological interpretation of the Word of God as a polyphonic device in tune with the culture of coextensive fraternal dialogue at the BCCs. One of the meetings of the BCCs was therefore devoted to the preparation of the Sunday homily. It was attended by members of the BCCs and other persons interested in the common preparation of the homily. It was done as simply as possible. We were welcomed by the head of the BCC who, after the opening prayer and the exchange of news, gave the floor

---

12   Ignace Ndongala Maduku and Job Mwana-Kitata, *Mots sur les maux du Congo: Le discours sociopolitique de Laurent Cardinal Monsengwo Pasinya*, (Paris: L'Harmattan, 2020), 70.

to the priest to introduce the practice of *kodongola liloba*.[13] After the reading of the Word of God, the Word circulated under the moderation of the priest. This did not seek to "translate" into theological knowledge the stammerings of the margins, but welcomed them as they were. The sharing of the Word ended with common prayer and the conclusion by the head of the BCC. It then remained for the priest responsible for the Sunday sermon to order the shared Word and to structure it into a homiletic-type sermon that made sense.

For the first time, we were learning to unlearn our book knowledge. We learned from the knowledge of our communities, our thinking being nourished by questions and interrogations, answers and certainties, aspirations, silences and doubts of the members of the communities who over the course of the meetings became our pedagogues. From the community, we received the words to speak of God in the light of his Word and with regard to the experience of his people. On the strength of the achievements of this exchange, the shared Word was innervated by the life lived and entered into consonance with the existence of the listeners. It resonated with the daily banality of the audience. He found in his story traces of the presence and action of a God who reveals himself as writing history by and with him. The experience gave rise to a hermeneutics of existence making the homily as familiar as it is existential, embodied as it is alive. She made us discover alleys of suggestive and new meanings that have renewed both our approach to the Word of God and our conception of priestly ministry.

---

[13] The term is used for the cassava leaves that are separated from the inedible stems. Applied to the Word of God, the operation which requires attention and dexterity can be assimilated to the dissecting of the word.

Towards the Horizons of Synodality: The Weaving of the Mat of the Word of God in the Church

The common preparation of the homily by the priest and the faithful within the framework of the meetings of the BCCs at the parish of Sainte-Trinité is in line with the ecclesiology in force in the churches of Africa. The ecclesiology from which we should start again in a synodal perspective is that which values baptismal grace and the *munus docendi* (duty to teach) of the faithful in a differentiated way.[14] Participating in the *munus docendi* of Christ, the faithful can take an active part in the liturgical work by preparing the homily. Being part of this dynamic is a way of getting started, of walking with each other in a process of listening that particularises the reception of the Word of God and contextualises its interpretation. With some contextual adaptations, the experience of Sainte-Trinité can be recommended as a generalisable pastoral practice. Indeed, the experience that founds this communication is seen as a process of learning a collaborative way of interpreting the Word of God. Recognising the priest's role as preacher and combining his competence with that of the members of the BCCs, the process of production, better still of co-production, of the homily is based on the *sensus fidei* (*LG*, 12). Made witnesses to the Gospel message by baptism and confirmation (can. 759), endowed with doctrinal discernment and endowed with an instinct for the truth of the Gospel, the baptised members of BCCs have the duty to exercise their prophetic vocation and to inscribe their *sensus fidei* in the *sensus fidelium*. It is here that, in line with the International Theological Commission, "the faithful are not only the passive recipients of what the hierarchy teaches and what theologians make explicit; on the contrary, they are living and active subjects

---

[14]   See Dominique Le Tourneau, "La prédication de la parole de Dieu et la participation des laïcs au '*munus docendi*': fondements scripturaires et codification", *Ius Ecclesiae* 2 (1990), 101-125.

within the Church."[15] The BCC becomes this place of listening and sharing where the priest learns from the faithful and the faithful learn from the priest in a pooling of knowledge and experiences that builds faith and deepens revelation.[16] This way of involving the BCC in the elaboration of the homily anchors it to listening to God in real and concrete situations, and the sowing of the Word from the margins. The interlocution of the homily brings about an interrelation between the Word of God and the experience of the community convened as God's elective audience. It establishes it as a discursive and interpretative community. Thus emerges an understanding of the Word of God founded and legitimised by the participation of all (Sunday assembly), under the aegis of a few (members of a BCC) and the coordination of one (ordained minister).

The priest's homily is now enriched by the grammar and syntax of the margins, and remains anchored in the concern for the field and backed by the dimensions of social life. It covers the mother tongue evoked by Pope Francis: "Christian preaching, therefore, finds in the heart of the culture of the people a source of living water, both to know what to say and to find the appropriate way to say it. Just as we like to be spoken to in our mother tongue, so too, in faith, we like to be spoken to with the terms of the 'mother culture,' with the terms of the mother dialect (cf. 2 *Mc* 7:21, 27), and the heart is disposed to listen better. This language is a tone that transmits courage, breath, strength and impulse" (*EG*, 139).

We join here the perspective opened by the theology under the tree of Jean-Marc Ela on three levels. First, that of welcoming the

---

15   Commission Théologique Internationale, *Le "sensus fidei" dans la vie de l'Église*, (Paris: Cerf, 2014), 56.

      Voir   Vatican.va/roman_curia/congregations/cfaith/cti_documents/rc_cti_20140610_ cerf-sensus-fidei_fr.html#:~:text=Dans%20la%20pensée%20du%20pape%20 François%2C%20comme%20d'ailleurs,tradition%20apostolique%2C%20mais%20 il%20aussi%20une%20valeur%20prospective.

16   Fortin-Melkevik, A., "L'interprétation croyante de l'existence", in G. Routhier, dir, *Évangélisation. Réflexions à l'occasion d'un synode*, (Ottawa: Novalis, 1993), 105.

banality of the existence of margins,[17] then that of the dialogical approach to the Word,[18] and finally, that of the elaboration of a discourse that is the hermeneutics of existence. It is important to note here that the movement inscribed in the preparation of the homily is also felt in the way of giving the homily. This no longer feeds on the solipsism of the preacher, a connoisseur of the Word of God who comments on it for a group from which he stands out, but on the willingness to welcome the cognitive and epistemic contribution of the margins. The auctorial positioning of the preacher undergoes a readjustment and goes from the "I" mode to the "we" mode. With this passage, it is the shift from monotony to polyphony of voices, from the monological genre to the dialogic genre that is essential. From this plurality of voices, new paths open up that renew oratorical practices that have become increasingly collaborative. Thus the feeling of being part of a community is consolidated, in a logic of complementarity which allows the priest not to speak "in the name of" nor to "represent" the experiences of the margins, but to hear what the Spirit is saying to his own, to speak the mumbled inexpressible, to bring out the inarticulate Word, to give an echo to the meaning that circulates in its communities and to create conditions of audibility and say-ability of these words which proclaim God in the margins.

This way of taking the preacher out of the presbytery in a logic of complementarity allows the priest to speak of God in a relevant and efficient way, not alone but with others, not from a unilateral and unequivocal point of view, but according to a shared and concerted approach which integrates the spontaneous theology of the margins. There is here what we call an intertwining between the preacher and the BCC which makes the members of the BCC discover their potentialities to say and to do God. It follows that the homily becomes an interactive enunciation

---

17   Ela, *Repenser la théologie africaine*, 34.

18   Ela, *Repenser la théologie africaine*, 36.

in resonance, in echo, whose place of hatching is the life of the margins. It is the weaving of the mat of the Word of God by combining colourful threads made of myths, stories, rites, aphorisms, songs, symbols, maxims, proverbs and experiences that circulate as alternative knowledge in African communities.[19] Making the echo of the Word resound, making it resonate with the experience of one's people gathered around the palaver tree, in these places of emergence that are the basic ecclesial communities is an approach that can be taken up from a synodal perspective. In this respect, the preparation of the homily becomes a journey which constitutes a people on the move in the diversity of its charisms, in a fraternal dialogue which puts one and the other attuned to what the Spirit is saying to the Churches, and all together listening to each other.

It is suggestive to put oneself in the school of Pope Francis: To dream of a different future, we must choose as an organising principle fraternity rather than individualism. Fraternity, this feeling of belonging to the other and to the whole, is the ability to come together and work together on a common horizon of possibilities. It follows that the Church "which journeys together to read reality with the eyes of faith and with the heart of God" can include doing so together in the appropriation and interpretation of the Word of God. This journey, which involves lay people, pastors, the Bishop of Rome and believers all listening to the sense of the faithful "generates a synodal Church listening to what the Spirit of truth (*Jn* 14:17) is saying to the Churches (*Rv* 27)."[20]

Applied to the BCC, the synodal Church requires the willing-ness to learn from others and especially from the margins, to

---

[19]   See the article of Ignace Ndongala Maduku, "Résonances. Pour une approche décoloniale de la Parole de Dieu", in A. Ngengi Mundele, E. Wabanhu, J.-C. Loba Moke, dir., *Bible and Orality in Africa: Interdisciplinary Approaches*, (Nairobi: Bicam-Cebam Publications), 343-360.

[20]   Ndongala, "Résonances. Pour une approche décoloniale de la Parole de Dieu", 343-360.

get rid of one's ideas and to debate them with others. The emergence of a listening Church requires dialogical fraternity, open to subsidiarity and respect for the delegation of powers. More than an informal meeting of the members of the BCC, the preparatory meeting for the homily is a dialogical device open to complementarity, sharing, mutual enrichment combined with living together. However, it is not a panacea, because it requires continuous learning and acquisition of various skills; in the tradition of the palaver, we lean on the principles of inclusion, equality, solidarity, equivalence, freedom of speech and mutual recognition. In this way, in an endogenous process of transformation, the BCCs become an inclusive space and an enabling environment open to the co-construction of the Sunday liturgy. Their involvement in the preparation of the liturgy should not be limited to collecting the offerings and preparing the bowl for the poor. It should extend to the homily and could also concern universal prayer. From a celebration for a community, we thus move, thanks to a shared approach, to a celebration with and by the community. That this passage becomes, in a formal and institutional way, a synodal experience remains the task of our BCCs of tomorrow.

Conclusion

As part of the general issue of synodality, this contribution revisited an experience of preparation of the Sunday homily by the priest and the members of a BCC. The theoretical positioning of this research is close to works on decoloniality and co-construction. On the theological level, this research joins the questions on the principle of fundamental equality of the faithful and the participation in the prophetic *munus* of Christ. During this review of a first experience of pooling the popular reading of the Word of God with exegetical reading, the empirical study was articulated around observations in the field. Although provisional, the results of the research show the heuristic dimension of the process of co-construction of the homily. This process of homiletic interlocution nourishes the capacity of a community to walk together by appropriating and interpreting the Word of God by consensus. It goes without saying that the necessity, the usefulness and the pastoral fruitfulness of this process are relevant to a Church-Family and on every act of fraternity of the children of God. The interpretation of the Word of God with and by the People of God opens a path towards synodality whose avenues remain to be traveled.

CHAPTER 10

Five Key Lessons of Synodality for the Church-Family of God in Africa

Francis Appiah-Kubi

T he Synod on Synodality has become a *kairos, a moment of grace* for the Church in Africa to critically re-examine itself and its internal mechanisms. This chapter which is a contribution to building a synodal Church in Africa, oscillates around five major selected key lessons. It examines, first the theological formation of her agents of evangelisation, especially the priests and catechists. Second, it draws attention to the role of hierarchical or ecclesial authority which in a synodal Church should be all inclusive and render service to all. Third, it tries to emphasise the correct nature and responsibility of the lay faithful in a synodal Church. Fourth, the chapter tries to conjugate, from the perspective of the theology of Church as Family of God, the relational networks to underscore unity and diversity as major resources for ecclesial communion in a synodal Church. That is, seeing synodality as an ecumenical learning process. Then fifth, it elaborates the dangerous dichotomy of orthodoxy and orthopraxy as contrary to a synodal Church. It insists on listening to dialogue, listening to discern and listening to harmonise doctrine with praxis. In conclusion, the chapter affirms strongly that if we are ontologically the Church, then all are participants, and no one is spectator; all are sent on mission and all are builders of the Church. With this understanding, therefore, the formation of all agents of evangelisation is crucial to a fruitful synodal process in the Church.

The Formation of Agents of Evangelisation

All formation takes place within a context and the formation of the agents of evangelisation is not exempted. In *Pastores dabo vobis*, Pope John Paul II highlights the importance of context when he writes, "God always calls his priests from specific human and ecclesial contexts, which inevitably influence them; and to these same contexts the priest is sent for the service of Christ's Gospel."[1] In fact, poverty of leadership, an effect of the kind of formation received has been identified as a major factor standing in the way of the Church's witness as a credible institution for social change in Africa.

For a synodal Church, priests, catechists, all agents of evangelisation must be formed in a way that is distinctively African, yet absolutely and truly Christian in its doctrine and at the same time open to the challenges of our time. David Bosch once insisted that we need a theology that will afford our people to worship God as Africans in a way which is compatible with our spiritual temperament, of singing to the glory of God in our own way, of praying to God and hearing His Holy Word in idiom which is clearly intelligible to the African sensitivity.[2]

The agents of evangelisation such as priests, catechists, leaders of various societies need and deserve the formation of high standards, with effective methods, and comprehensive goals. A synodal Church is expected, therefore, to provide a thorough and ongoing formation considering the four areas of formation, namely, human, spiritual, intellectual, and pastoral, as a framework for the formation of agents of evangelisation. Such

---

[1]   John Paul II, Apostolic Exhortation, *Pastores dabo vobis*, (Roma: Libreria Editrice Vaticana, 1992), 5.

[2]   J.D. Bosch, "Currents and Cross Currents in South African Black Theology", *Journal of Religion in Africa*, 6 (1974), 10.

formation should prioritise inculcating human qualities critical to forming wholesome and healthy relationships, necessary to be apt instruments of God's love and compassion. Adequate knowledge in theological and pastoral studies, coupled with the intellectual skill as well as practical pastoral abilities are required. It should be noted that inadequacy in the formation is more costly and harmful to the mission of the Church.

Specifically, the formation of African ecclesial leaders in view of building a synodal Church should be based on the systematic and critical reflection on the relational dimension of the theology of the Church as family of God which is articulated around the reciprocity of fraternal relationship. This relationship is neither dominion nor servitude, it is not a master-slave relationship but based on communal paternity, filiation, and fraternity. Thus, being a leader of brothers and sisters in the Church-Family of God, means being with brothers/sisters on the same scale. Not above them, not below them, but only with them. In other words, leadership is neither about a position of superiority nor of servitude: none is the oppressed nor the oppressor.

Thus, agents of evangelisation should theologically be formed within the African context to meet Christ in the neighbour, not behind him or above him; only this corresponds to love of incarnation and a true leadership of service. For the theology of the Church-Family of God cannot consider the struggle for pre-eminence and rank as being in accord with the will of God. Such a theology underscores the immediate implication of being-with-God. The filiation, the fraternity and the parenthood of God[3] radically command a relationship of equality and respect which does not allow any human creature to legitimately be considered superior, subordinate or inferior to another. This relational category, a fundamental condition for a synodal Church, is placed within Jesus Christ event, presented at once as a

---

[3]   D. J. Hall, *Etre image de Dieu. Le Stewardship de l'humain dans la création*, (Paris: Cerf, 1998), 233.

Trinitarian structure,[4] a perfect place and sign of exceptional revelation of the love of God, the Father. It is paramount to stress, from the perspective of the Church-Family of God, that such formation of builders of a synodal Church makes no alliance with any "form of ethnic tribalism, racial clannism, autonomist nationalism,"[5] else it would lead to a denial and destruction of the very foundation of its existence, namely, the Trinitarian love. It must be noted that there is paternity because there is filiation, and there is filiation because there is, through the Holy Spirit, communion with the only Son. In this sense, all racist discrimination,[6] all ethnocentrism,[7] in other words all depreciative and persecuted behaviour vis-à-vis the other, is contrary to the mission of the synodal Church, because it falls outside of Christian principles and norms regulating an authentic Christian fraternity. Consequently, the agents of evangelisation should be at the service of brothers and sisters through listening and dialoguing and bearing witness in taking and accepting risks towards building a synodal Church, which according to Pope Francis, is "bruised, hurting and dirty because it has been out on the streets, rather than a Church which is unhealthy from being confined and clinging to its own security."[8]

The Hierarchical Ministry

Within the context of the ecclesiology of the family of the People of God as taught by Vatican II, a paradigm dividing the

---

4   E. J. Penoukou, "Quel type d'Eglise pour quelle mission en Afrique ?" in *Spiritus* 123, (Mai 1991), 197.

5   J. Moltmann, "L'Eglise dans la force de l'Esprit. Une contribution à l'ecclésiologie" modern, (Paris: Cerf, 1980), 9.

6   M. Girod, *Penser le racism: De la responsabilité des scientifiques,* (Paris: Calmann-Levy, 2004), 1-5.

7   M. F. Kpakala, "The Church in Africa Today. Sacrament of Justice, Peace and Unity," in M. Brown, *African Synod, Documents, Reflections, Perspectives*, (New York: Orbis Books, 1996), 110-130.

8   Pope Francis, Apostolic Exhortation, *Evangelii Gaudium,* (Roma: Editrice Libreria Vaticana, 2013), 49.

Church into two levels, clergy and lay people,[9] should no longer be tolerated. The division of Church members into those who teach actively and with authority, and those who are taught in passive obedience (*ecclesia docens* vs. *ecclesia discens*) is thus overcome with an initial emphasis on the common dignity of the children of God who through baptism share in Christ's priestly, prophetic and kingly mission. It is the basis of this unity of the children of God that the diversification of various services takes place for the good of the whole body[10] and for the benefit of all who share the Christian dignity.

Pope Francis speaks about synodality as a constitutive dimension of the Church which manifests itself above all in listening to the supernatural sense of faith that the Holy Spirit arouses in every baptised person. In this perspective, it forms the "interpretative framework" for understanding the very hierarchical ministry in the Church. Synodality is a way of effectively expressing the fact that the whole People of God participate equally in Christ's prophetic mission and that true reform of the Church is a matter for all her members. For the synodal Church is nothing other than the journeying together of God's flock along the paths of history towards the encounter with Christ the Lord.[11] We must then understand that, within the Church, no one is raised higher than others. In principle all are servants to the Church-Family of God by our common fraternity and filiation.

Despite several efforts of the Second Vatican Council to integrate all into one big family of the People of God, and despite the theology of the Church as Family of God with its core constituents of paternity, filiation and fraternity in defining the manner of being Church in Africa, there is still counter-witness of the "*ecclesia-we*" *father's Church but* not our Church. Sometimes, the

---

9   Seecond Vatican Council, Dogmatic Constitution on the Church, *Lumen Gentium* 12.

10   *Lumen Gentium* 18.

11   Pope Francis, Synodality, as a Constitutive Dimension of the Church, "L'Osservatore Romano" 34 (2015), 11.

priest in a "Mr Know-all" attitude, fails to recognise and explore the talents and contributions the lay people can offer.[12]

In this perspective, the Church is admittedly clerical. This is witnessed by the fact that most of the books published by the church leaders do not have the lay people in mind as their target audience, even though basic inexpensive tracts, leaflets, and magazines can be produced in very simple languages, handed out to, and circulated among all. Sometimes the laity are regarded as unimportant, passive, and mere dots. The Leadership of the Church sometimes fails to seek opinions and consent of the laity. In spite of the canonical organs of administration and consultation, church leaders still impose their views on their flocks. A synodal Church is like a standard lifted up among the nations (cf. *Is* 11:12), while calling for participation, solidarity and transparency in public administration, the fate of entire people of the family of God cannot be consigned to the grasp of small but powerful groups. As a Church which journeys together, with men and women, sharing the drudgery of history, we come to the rediscovery of the inviolable dignity of peoples and function of authority as service. This brings us to evaluate the vocation and the responsibility of the laity in a synodal Church.

Lay Faithful's Vocation and Responsibility

The lay faithful and their participation in the mission of the Church and in the world are a significant force within the overall mission of the Church today; for they constitute the majority of Church membership. The mission of the Church is a communal mission, meaning all members of the Church have a duty to perform and a role to play. The contribution of each and every member of the Church towards the fulfilment of her mission in the world is indispensable and cannot be substituted.

---

12   I.K.E. Oraegbunam, "The Role of the Catholic Laity in Nigerian Nation Building" in *The Nigerian Journal of Theology*, 20, (June 2006), 134.

In the early Church, all were filled with the same eschatological expectation. The real distinction was not so much between clergy and laity, though, even in the absence of terminology such theologically important distinctions were never denied,[13] but rather between those called to the Kingdom and those not, between the holy People of God and the unredeemed world. "Laity" were hardly considered "of the world" as they are today. Lay persons were active in the early Church in liturgy and sacraments and participated with presbyters and Bishops in the corporate discipline of the Church. They shared in evangelising and the teaching of the faith and in the service of the whole community.[14]

By the middle of the third century, with the influx of many nominal Christians, the bond of unity was no longer the eschatological hope, but sacraments administered by the clergy. The understanding of the Church changed as it took on greater temporal form; greater distinctions were made between those willing to live and die as martyrs and those content to live by minimal gospel precepts.[15] Lay persons were gradually eased out of positions of financial authority in the Church in the fourth and fifth centuries. Pope Leo banned the laity from preaching, and Pope Gregory replaced all of his lay servants with clerics or monks.[16] With the end of the Empire, the cultural power of education became the exclusive province of the Church.[17] *Clericus* became synonymous with "literate" and *laicus* "illiterate." As C. Brooke puts it, "the view of the Church as the community of the faithful was not completely lost sight of by the theologians, but in the government of the Church and in everyday speech, the

---

13   G. H. Williams, "The Ancient Church", in Stephen Neill and Hans-Ruedi Weber eds., *The Layman in Christian History; a project of the department on the Laity of the World Council of Churches*, (London: SCM Press, 1963), 32.

14   E. Schillebeeckx, *The Mission of the Church* (New York: Seabury, 1973), 117-118.

15   G.H. Williams, "The Ancient Church", 29.

16   G.H. Williams, "The Ancient Church", 29.

17   C. M. Odahl, *Constantine and the Christian Empire*, (London: Routledge, 2004), 1.

Church was equivalent to the clerical order. The clergy were the shepherds, the laity sheep."[18] As an effect, the clergy became not only an ecclesial category but also a social class. The question that comes to mind is, how can social status supplant the dignity theologically acquired at baptism as Children of God sharing in the universal mission of Christ?

It is important to emphatically stipulate theologically that the laity is not ancillary to the clergy. With the clergy, they are ontologically the Church, sharing equally the divine nature of God through rebirth in baptism. Consequently, their participation in the building up of a synodal Church is not by convenience but by conviction. Synodality demonstrates this fundamental aspect of the lay faithful's vocation. As a convergent path of Christian life and the mission in transforming society, synodality conditions the life of the laity in the Church and outside the Church. It is the road on which the laity meets the world in its doubts, oppositions, indifferences, and sufferings.

Let me again emphasise and affirm that even though God granted the lay vocation to the vast majority of Christians, it does not mean that it is less valuable or less important than the others. To think in this way would be to despise the gifts of God, like throwing pearls to swine (cf. *Mt* 7:6). Thus, synodality would help the laity to be more conscious of their identity and the responsibility as Christians in the world. From the missionary mandate of the lay faithful, synodality is essential to maintain a proper relationship between the political community and the Church.[19] In addition to prayer and community life, synodality makes each Christian work actively for social justice, bringing the salvific Word of Christ to all and sundry.

---

[18] C. Brooke, "The Church of the Middle Ages," in Neill and Weber eds., *The Layman in Christian History*, 113.

[19] F. Appiah-Kubi & R. Yeboah, "The Nature and Missionary Role of the Lay People in the Light of Vatican II; Convenience or Conviction?", *E-Journal of Humanities, Arts and Social Sciences (EHASS)*, 1/ 1, (May 2020), 28-36.

Synodality as an Ecumenical Learning Process

The call to synodality is equally an invitation to discover the nature of the Church as a pilgrim community of faith. This is, moreover, contained in the very term journeying together. It means that we are not walking alone on this journey, but above all with God and also with those to whom we are bound by the bonds of sacramental communion. Walking together on the road to the Kingdom already means unity. And as Pope Francis says, if the Spirit of God works in them, (other Churches) then the area of application of synodality in the Church can also be the subject of exchange of gifts within the Christian ecumene.[20]

Synodality therefore, is a way of realising not only the gifts of the whole body of Christ through the service of mission, but also a way of healing the wounds of the Church itself. The more the Church can live a synodal life, the more it can be a sign to all peoples of the graced "fraternity" or solidarity that is the ultimate reality of humanity, which includes care for "our common home." Together with other religions and nations, whatever their governing philosophy and commitments, the Church is committed to working for the cultivating of a common home in which all have the means to flourish.

Faith helps us to journey together. When our relationships express our faith, we will be committed to each other on the journey, no matter how long or what difficulties may occur. Faith gives us the certitude not to be disoriented or diverted by conflicts and divisions, but to come to the understanding of our interconnectedness[21] as well as our dependency on the paternity of God. Similarly, hope fills us with creativity and opens new possibilities. It always allows us to begin again. It is not afraid of failure because it always opens to the future, which is God's gift.

---

[20]   Pope Francis, Apostolic Exhortation, *Evangelii Gaudium*, (Roma, Libreria Editrice Vaticana, 2013), 246.

[21]   E.P. Hahnenberg, "Common Discernment: A Catholic Perspective on The Church: Towards a Common Vision", *One in Christ*, 51/ 2, (2017), 218.

It has the power to learn from failure and to grow in understanding. The virtue of hope moves us to look always beyond ourselves to the One in whom we hope (God).[22] It gives us the courage to face reality and its truth without despair. When we are loved, we experience consolation and, when we love, we are ministers of Christ, the Consoler. Love has the power to overcome all hatred. Our love must inform us to understand the beauty and the grace of diversity; differences need not be a threat but rather a gift when it comes to love. When we journey together as a synodal Church in love, we can recognise the openness, reception, and vulnerability of the other and claim responsibility for them, for their truth, and the work of God.[23]

Synodality illuminates the ecumenical path of the Churches and the ecclesial communities to reach full and visible communion. The Church develops a deeper understanding of its own identity which, in turn, has informed its ability to engage in fruitful ecumenical exchange. Synodality sees the union of the Churches as primarily constituted by their inherent oneness as the locus of God's saving work and not primarily through external bonds such as the bonds of jurisdiction. The crucial challenges that the synodal Church has to face require a culture of encounter that demands sincerity of dialogue, service and co-operation. Walking on the path of evangelising reform, the Church can lead the "social *diakonia*" of synodality, to help cultivate justice, peace and care of our common home.

As an expression of an ecclesiology of communion, synodality requires an affirmation of and openness to a diverse range of voices within the Church and outside the Church. Attuning oneself to the diversity within one's own community creates greater possibilities for recognising the presence of the Holy

---

22   E. Hahnenberg, "Common Discernment", 218.

23   D. Bosch, *Transforming Mission: Paradigm Shifts in Theology of Mission,* (Maryknoll: Orbis, 1991). 211-221.

Spirit working in other communities.[24] As such, synodality is not only about becoming a "listening Church" which cultivates a posture of listening to its members, but also about becoming a "consulting Church" which actively seeks the input of faithful regarding its teaching and modes of governance.

Synodality: Relationality in Unity and Diversity in the Church-Family of God

The African society questions the Christian being on his contribution to the quest of sense, to the transformation of the world and to the construction of a community of peace and unity. In this line, the believers are called to respond to the hope that is in them by revealing and testifying to the nature of the bonds which link them to Christ and his Gospel. It is only through these bonds that a Church can be born as family, living space of communion. The Church as Family of God requires a radical decision of detachment for God. The choice is clear: God and his Kingdom or the world and its kingdom. Jesus himself left family, home and country, and made some people leave their families and social settings to constitute the Family of families, the Church. In view of the mission of the Church which is essentially pastoral and missionary, all historical, philosophical or anthropological media by which the message of the Gospel is transmitted, taking into account the needs and vicissitudes of each epoch, is relatively secondary. The image of the Church as family of God, first of all, places the Church in the plan of God which is realised through history. It unveils the gratuitous intervention of God, which connotes the ideas of incarnation, call, filiation, covenant, gathering and promises. It allows regaining the dynamic and missionary meaning of the Church that is journeying towards the Kingdom, the definitive hope.[25]

---

[24]   Pope Francis, *50th Anniversary of the Institution of the Synod of Bishops*, (Roma, Libreria Editrice Vaticana, 2015).

[25]   F. Appiah-Kubi, "Théologie de l'Eglise Famille de Dieu: Une évaluation critique",

The metaphor of the Church as Family of God is a notion pregnant with safe humanism of anthropological value. Despite the fact that it refers to the idea of a social structure, it equally refers to the functions played by each member at the service of this structure. This family is on a journey towards perfection, but it does not yet possess it fully. Its members, the sons and daughters of the Father, have therefore to purify and to reform themselves unceasingly. It is the Family of the families which journeys in the world and has as its goal, to gather together all the scattered children of God to bring them into the Father's house, the Kingdom. The Church is Family of God by nature, and fraternity by vocation, and nothing that concerns humanity, nothing that humanity looks for in its thinking and in its culture, through arts and sciences, nothing that humanity discovers in suffering or in happiness, is foreign to her.

For a synodal Church, the Church as Family of families invites us to reject all that damages humanity and disfigures God. The Church does not disclose itself through knowledge, but through signs. The real problem is to see how we are united to humanity. The mission of the Church, therefore, will be to anticipate the day of the great "Encounter" without failing to recognise the needs of this world.

Nonetheless, sometimes the traditional network of ethno-centrism or ethnicism, tribalism, favouritism, dent the image of the Church-Family of God. It is an ideology according to which a people naturally have the tendency to defend their identity in denigrating others, to the point of refusing to them, at least symbolically, their full quality as human beings.[26] Such behaviour is counter-productive to a synodal Church walking together in unison. The rejection of the other, of differences, can lead to a form of physical annihilation that sociologists qualify as ethno-

---

Spiritus, 215, (juin 2014), 201-202.

[26]   F. Appiah-Kubi, *L'Eglise famille de Dieu. Un chemin pour les Eglises d'Afrique*, (Paris: Karthala, 2008), 280-284.

cide or genocide, that tolerate the presence of the other only insofar as he/she allows himself/herself to be assimilated to the dominant culture. It would not be an exaggeration to notice that in Africa the cohabitation of ethnicities, traditions, languages, culture, not to say different religions, sometimes face racist and ethnocentric behaviours. The tribal oppositions sometimes endanger, if not peace, the pursuit of the common good of the whole society and thus create difficulties for walking together as a synodal Church.

I must emphasise that no reflection on the theology of the Church as Family of God, nor any elaboration of pastoral strategy in view of a deep evangelisation in today's Africa, can escape this thorny phenomenon which hinders every ecclesial action. It is up to the African Christians to be intimately convinced about their sacramental rebirth in God as brothers/sisters with God as our unique and common Father. It implies that the relationships that we should have with all, or the bonds that unite us, even in the political domain, must be in the order of charity. The idolatry of the ethnic group, with its violent consequences such as fratricide, the ethnic purification, tribalism and injustice should not find a place in the Church. Synodality should promote a Church rid of all the narrowness of clannism and ethnic tendencies. This is the real test for a synodal Church which aims at walking together with all and being Family of God in Africa.

Conclusion

All the five lessons discussed are in line with the vision of Pope Francis which is not to establish another structure in the Church but rather to implant an attitude, where the whole Church is involved in mission. If everyone is ontologically the Church, then no one should be a passive observer or spectator; all are sent on a mission. The entire family of People of God are involved in the synodal experience, albeit in different ways. This synodal process, as it has been analysed aims at reordering the internal mechanisms of the Church for in-depth discussions and reflections and helping to shape a new way for the Church to understand and articulate both her internal self-understanding and her mission of evangelisation. This is an effort to make the Church more mission-oriented, to make ordinary pastoral activity on every level more inclusive and open. Mission, for a synodal Church is not merely one of "going forth"; but more importantly one of listening, and walking together in the presence of the Spirit of God.

The Missionary Role of Communication in the Context of the Synodal Church Today

Lucio Adrian Ruiz

The Tomb Is Empty

He is risen. This is the great announcement that intrinsically changes history: he is not here, he has been raised (*Lk* 24:5). The metaphysics of history has changed, for if death, which put an end to all human history, no longer exists, not only does all human life take on a new meaning, but every thought, every feeling, every act, every word (cf. *Mt* 12:36) has its weight. Being part of the historical fabric, it is called to Eternal Life, like the flesh and history of Jesus (*Jn* 20:27).

He is not here is the centre of the Gospel message, the *Kerygma*, around which everything revolves and is built, and everything acquires a meaning and a form, even the sacraments, because they are the way to live the resurrection in history and are the means to reach the resurrection at the end of time. It is the proclamation of the resurrection that changes everything, that gives form and meaning to everything. It is, in short, the realisation of the prophecy: "Behold, I make all things new" (*Rv* 21:5). But if everything is "new", then it must be discovered and proclaimed. If everything is new because of the resurrection, then that is where our faith must be recreated, where our mission must begin, where communication must be born.

"He is not here, he has been raised" (*Mk* 16:7), and so he becomes the foundation of sending his disciples. They go because they are sent, and they go with a content. The community is therefore built around the Risen One and the mission to communicate to him. Thus, on the one hand, the resurrection is the centre of the message, on the other hand, it is the foundation of the mission, because it is an event that must be communicated, to be believed and lived, because it is the adherence that gives salvation: whoever believes in me will live (*Jn* 11:25).

We Cannot Not Speak

The disciples, with their transformed lives, with an inner movement, proclaim and announce. "It is impossible for us not to speak about what we have seen and heard" (*Acts* 4:20) is the response of the disciple who testifies: he has seen, he has heard, he cannot remain silent, and he goes out, he seeks, he announces, he is strong in the face of the contradiction of reality that rejects the new.

Believing leads to taking up the burden, to mission, and mission has as its goal to communicate it, to announce the *Kerygma*, to make new disciples, whom Jesus recognises as his own: "I pray not only for them, but also for those who will believe in me through their word" (*Jn* 17:20).

But the proclamation takes place in a communicative dynamic that appeals to the whole person: "...what we have heard, what we have seen with our eyes, what we have contemplated, what we have touched with our hands concerning the Word of Life, this we proclaim to you" (1 *Jn* 1:1). It is the story-changing experience of the disciples that generates the proclamation and the commitment.

This is why communication cannot be reduced to the processes, dynamics and strategies of the media and instruments of communication, and even less to technology. It is the most intrinsic reality of the dynamics of the Message to be communicated: received to be delivered. Proclamation and testimony are the vehicle for knowledge and discipleship. Thus, communication, rather than being media and technology, is proclamation and witness, from which all its effectiveness is born and strengthened, from which all strategic and technological activities are designed.

The Church Goes Out

The Church of Pope Francis essentially needs to rethink communication from the theology of *Kerygma*, as it constantly emerges from his Magisterium. For while he insists that he prefers *a wounded Church by going, not a sick Church by remaining locked up*, there is no doubt that this "going out" is in the context of the Announcement, that it must be carried to the culture, that it must transform all structures and life, and that it must create community.

But this Franciscan "show" does not remain a theoretical announcement, with a declaration of good intentions, but is concretised by reform and a synod. The first reform is that of the Roman Curia, where the title of the *Motu Proprio, Predicate Evangelium*, is programmatic and announces its structure and its dynamics of service and mission. This reform is a model and a call not only for all diocesan curias, but also for all ecclesial structures that must put themselves at the service of and in mission. The second is the Synod on Synodality, where the whole Church is placed in an attitude of "listening" to what the Spirit is saying to the Churches, which shows the necessary openness to dialogue in the whole People of God, with an openness and acceptance of diversity and confrontation.

If the reform puts the structures in the concept of mission, the Synod puts the people in an attitude of listening. Mission and listening are communicative dynamics, and they are the concepts from which all the communicative activities and strategies of the Church, in this culture of communication, must start and on which they must be based. But listening is not an isolated act with an end in itself, but requires a response, which is iconised in the figure of the Good Samaritan.

This is a fundamental element of Pope Francis's ecclesiology in a communicative concept, "Samaritanise." The parable of the Good Samaritan is an essential element of his Magisterium (we see it in *Fratelli Tutti*). There is nothing and no one that can stop the attitude of helping the "wounded of history," the "fallen on the way." Everyone has to open his eyes and heart to go towards the one who almost died on the road, and there is no excuse for not seeing him or not going towards him. This "samaritanisation of culture" draws the profile and attitude of the disciple, where the only possibility to look down on one's brother is when one "bends down to help him."

The attitude of listening described by the Synod, which is not an "event" but a "process", shows that it is a "way of exercising community" and a "way of being Church." It is, therefore, an ecclesiological concept built into a communicative concept.

The communicative dynamic of the "Resurrection" event, which from the beginning is contemplative/operative (seen, heard, contemplated, touched => announced) is repeated in the communicative ecclesiology of Francis (listening => samaritanising) which implies "flesh", "touch", because one cannot give alms without looking at the eyes, because one cannot be "brothers" without social and historical transformation.

To Sum Up

Communication thus becomes essentially missionary, because it is the proper and essential activity of the Church, which must proclaim Christ and transform the world from its newness. Communicative creativity will then come from missionary strength, and missionary strength will come from the conviction and adherence that in the resurrection, Christ makes all things new. In the context of a synodal Church, which goes out to meet every human person, communicative dynamics and strategies can only be effective in the perspective of mission with the commitment of the "flesh", with the *modus vivendi and operandi* of "listening" and "samaritanism", which models the community in the movement of "going" to heal wounds by "touching" them. Communication, understood from its theological roots, is the vehicle of *God's tenderness* towards man in the concrete reality of a transformed history.

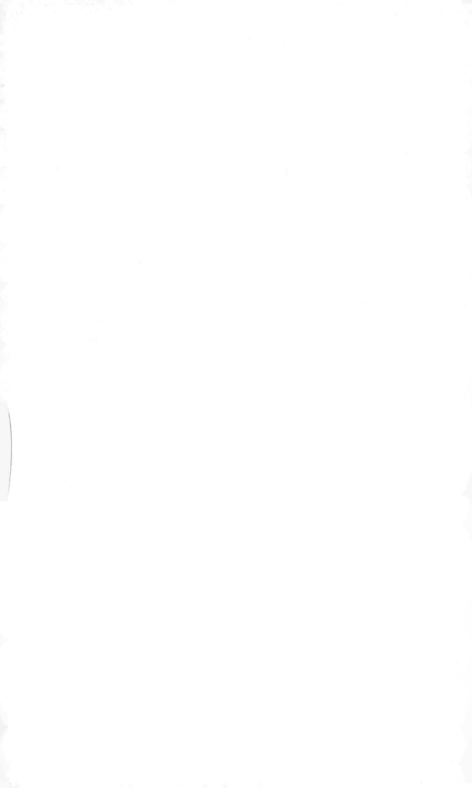

Selected Bibliography

Books and Online Media

Abela Antonio, «Abramo camina davanti al Signore (Esegesi di Gen 17)», Francesco Viatoni, éd, *Sangue e anthropologica biblica nella patristica,* I, (Roma, Edizioni Pia Unione Preziosissimo Sangue, 1982).

Achebe Chinua, *Arrow of God,* 2nd ed. (London: Penguin Books, 1964, 1974).

Adichie Chimamanda, "I Am Not Strong In The Face Of Grief" An Interview with TVC News, https://youtu.be/NZ--DQvMUIE.

Appel Kurt, "Reform and Renewal in Local Churches: Lessons from Rosmini and Pope Francis" in Stan Chu Ilo et al., eds., *Faith in Action,* vol. 1, (Abuja: Paulines Publications, 2020).

Appiah-Kubi, F., *L'Eglise famille de Dieu. Un chemin pour les Eglises d'Afrique,* (Paris: Karthala, 2008).

Arinze, Francis, *The Lay Person's Distinctive Role,* (San Francisco: Ignatius Press, 2013).

Azetsop, Jacquineau, *HIV & AIDS In Africa: Christian Reflection, Public Health, Social Transformation* (Maryknoll: Orbis Books, 2016).

Bacq, P. et Theobald, C., éd., *Passeurs d'Évangile. Autour d'une pastorale d'engendrement,* Bruxelles/Montréal/Ivry-sur-Seine: Lumen Vitae/Novalis/ Les éditions de l'atelier, 2008).

————, *Une nouvelle chance pour l'évangile. Vers une pastorale d'engendrement,* (Bruxelles/Montréal/Paris: Lumen Vitae/ Novalis/Les éditions de l'atelier, 2004).

Battle Michael, *Ubuntu: I in You and You in Me* (Cape Town: Church Publishing, 2009).

————, *Reconciliation: The Ubuntu Theology of Desmond Tutu* (Cleveland: The Pilgrims Press, 1997).

Benedict XVI, Pope, Post-synodal Apostolic Exhortation, *Africae Munus* (November 19, 2011).

Birago Diop, *Le souffle des ancêtres*, (Paris: Présence Africaine, 1960).

Bosch, J.D., *Transforming Mission: Paradigm Shifts in Theology of Mission.* (Maryknoll: Orbis, 1991).

Bujo, Bénézet. *The Ethical Dimension of Community: The African Model and the Dialogue between North and South.* Trans. Cecilia Nganda. (Nairobi: Paulines, 1998).

———, *Foundations of an African Ethic: Beyond the Universal Claims of Western Morality.* Trans. Brian McNeil. (Nairobi: Paulines, 2003).

Cartledge, Mark J. and Cheethman, David, eds., *Intercultural Theology: Approaches and Theme,* (London: SCM Press, 2011).

Casalla, Mario, *Razón y liberación. Notas para una filosofía latinoamericana.* (Buenos Aires: Siglo XXI, 1978).

Chukwu Donatus Oluwa, *The Church as the Extended Family of God: Toward a New Direction for African Ecclesiology* (Indiana: Xlibris Corporation, 2011).

Congregation for Institutes of Consecrated Life and Societies of Apostolic Life. *New Wine in new Wineskins: The Consecrated Life and its Ongoing Challenges since Vatican II.* Trans., Christina Cooley. (Vatican City: Libreria Editrice Vaticana, 2017).

Crowley, Paul, *From Vatican II to Pope Francis: Charting a Catholic Future,* (New York: Orbis Books, 2014).

Cuda, Emilce. *Para leer a Francisco, Teología, ética y política.* (Buenos Aires: Manantial, 2016).

Dreyer Jaco, Yolanda Dreyer, Edward Foley, Malan Nel, eds., *Practicing Ubuntu: Practical Theological Perspectives on Injustice, Personhood and Human Dignity* (Münster: LIT Verlag, 2017).

Ela Jean-Marc, *Le cri de l'homme africain,* Questions aux chrétiens et aux Églises d'Afrique, (Paris: L'Harmattan, 1980).

———, *Repenser la théologie africaine: Le Dieu qui libère* (Paris: Karthala, 2003).

Flannery Austin, ed., *Vatican Council II vol. 1: The Conciliar and Post Conciliar Documents,* New Revised Edition (Dublin: Dominican Publications, 1998).

Fortin-Melkevik, A., «L'interprétation croyante de l'existence», in G. Routhier, ed., *Évangélisation: Réflexions à l'occasion d'un synode,* (Ottawa: Novalis, 1993).

Foudriat, M., *La co-construction: Une alternative managériale,* (Paris: Presses de l'EHESP, 2019).

Francis, Pope, *Synodality, as a constitutive dimension of the Church,* "L'Osservatore Romano" 34, (2015).

———, *Apostolic Exhortation Evangelii Gaudium on the Proclamation of the Gospel in Today's World.* (Vatican City: Vatican Press, 2013).

———, *Encyclical Letter Fratelli Tutti on Fraternity and Social Friendship.* (Vatican City: Vatican Press, 2020).

Francisco SS Papa, Carta Encíclica *Laudato Si.* (24 May 2015).

———, Carta Encíclica *Fratelli Tutti.* (3 October 2020).

———, Exhortación Apostólica, *Evangelii Gaudium.* (24 November 2013).

———, *Un temps pour changer,* (Montréal, Flammarion Québec, 2020).

Fresia Iván Ariel, *Estar con lo sagrado: Kusch-Scannone en diálogo sobre pueblo, cultura y religión.* (Buenos Aires: Ciccus, 2020).

Gerald K. Tanye, *The Church-as-family and Ethnocentrism in Sub-Saharan Africa* (Münster: LIT Verlag, 2010).

Girod, M., *Penser le racisme: De la responsabilité des scientifiques,* (Paris: Calmann-Levy, 2004).

Hall, D.J., *Être image de Dieu: Le Stewardship de l'humain dans la création.* Original title: *Imaging God: Dominion as stewardship,* (Paris: Cerf, 1998).

Hankela Elina, *Ubuntu, Migration and Ministry: Being Human in a Johannesburg Church* (Johannesbourg: Brill, 2014).

Healy Joseph, *Building the Church as Family of God: Evaluation of Small Christian Communities in Eastern Africa* (Nairobi: CUEA, 2012).

Helder Camara, *Le Désert est fertile: Feuilles de route pour les minorités abrahamiques,* (Paris, Seuil, 1977).

Henri Mova Sakanyi, *Ubuntu et résilience des peuples africains* (Paris: L'Harmattan, 2021).

II Assemblée spéciale pour l'Afrique du synode des évêques, *Message au peuple de Dieu,* (Rome, 2019).

International Theological Commission, "*Sensus Fidei* in the Life of the Church" (2014). http://www.vatican.va/roman_curia/congregations/cfaith/cti_documents/rc_cti_20140610_sensus-fidei_en.html.

International Theological Commission, "Synodality in the Life and Mission of the Church" https://www.vatican.va/roman_curia/congregations/cfaith/cti_documents/rc_cti_20180302_sinodalita_en.html.

John Paul II Pope, Apostolic Exhortation, *Pastores dabo vobis.* (Roma: Libreria Editrice Vaticana, 1992).

———, Post-synodal Apostolic Exhortation, Vocation and Mission of the Lay Faithful, *Christifideles Laici* (1988).

Kaoma Kapya J., *God's Family, God's Earth: Christian Ecological Ethics of Ubuntu* (Kachere Series, 2014).

Karambai, Sebastian S., *Ministers and Ministries in the Local Church*, (Mumbai: The Bombay Saint Paul Society, 2015).

Kasper Walter, "Kirche ist Synode. 50 Jahre Limburger Synodalordnung" https://bistumlimburg.de/fileadmin/user_upload/Festvortrag_Kasper.pdf.

Khisi Maximian, *The Church as the Family of God and the Care for Creation*, (Mzuni Press, 2019).

Kpakala, M.F., "The Church in Africa Today: Sacrament of Justice, Peace and Unity," in M. Brown, *African Synod, Documents, Reflections, Perspectives*, (New York, Orbis Books, 1996).

Lemaire André, *Naissance du monothéisme: Point de vue d'un historien*, (Paris: Bayard, 2003).

Lonergan Bernard, *Method in Theology*, New York: Herder and Herder, 1972.

Mandivamba Rukuni, *Being Afrikan: Rediscovering the Traditional Unhu-ubuntu-botho Pathways of Being Human* (Mandala, 2007).

Marchadour Alain, *Genèse*, (Paris: Bayard/Centurion, 1999).

Marion Jean-Luc, *El fenómeno erótico*. (Buenos Aires: Literales, 2005).

Markham Ian, *Do Morals Matter? A Guide to Contemporary Religious Ethics*. (Malden; Oxford; Victoria: Blackwell, 2007).

Mathabane Mark, *The Lessons of Ubuntu: How an African Philosophy Can Inspire Racial Healing in America* (Skyhorse, 2018).

Mazzucato Mariana, *El valor de las cosas*. (Madrid: Taurus, 2019).

Mcunu Tobias Nhlanhla, *The Dignity of the Human Person: A Contribution of the Theology of Ubuntu to Theological Anthropology* (Pretoria: University of South Africa, 2004).

Midali Mario, *Practical Theology: Historical Development of its Foundational and Scientific Character*, (Roma: Libreria Ateneo Salesiano, 2000).

Mignolo, W. D., *La désobéissance épistémique: Rhétorique de la modernité, logique de la colonialité et grammaire de la décolonialité*, (Bruxelles: Peter Lang, 2015).

Mucherera Tapiwa N., Emmanuel Y. Lartey, *Pastoral Care, Health, Healing, and Wholeness in African Contexts: Methodology, Context, and Issues* (Wipf and Stock Publishers, 2017).

Ndongala Maduku, I., Mwana-Kitata, J., *Mots sur les maux du Congo: Le discours sociopolitique de Laurent Cardinal Monsengwo Pasinya*, (Paris: L'Harmattan, 2020).

Ndongala Maduku, I., «Résonances. Pour une approche décoloniale de la Parole de Dieu», dans A. Ngengi Mundele, E. Wabanhu, J.-C. Loba Moke (dir.), *Bible and Orality in Africa: Interdisciplinary Approaches*, (Nairobi, Bicam-Cebam Publications, 2021).

Ngomane Mungi, *Ubuntu, Je suis car tu es* (New York: Happer Collins, 2019).

Ngomane Nompumelelo Mungi, *Everyday Ubuntu: Living Better Together, the African Way* (New York: Random House, 2020).

Ngubane K., *Ubuntu: The Philosophy and Its Practice* (Durban: Mepho Publishers, 2015).

Nokukhanya Pearl Shabalala, *Truth and Reconciliation in Light of the Cross: Martin Luther's Theology of the Cross in Relationship to the Current Ubuntu Theology of Desmond Tutu* (Concordia Seminary, 2019).

Odozor Paulinus, *Morality Truly Christian, Truly African: Foundational, Methodological, and Theological Considerations.* (Notre Dame, Indiana: Notre Dame University Press, 2014).

Ogude James, *Ubuntu and the Reconstitution of Community,* (Indiana: University Press, 2019).

Paul, Samuel A., *The Ubuntu God: Deconstructing a South African Narrative of Oppression,* (Wipf and Stock Publishers, 2009).

Paul VI, *Populorum Progressio,* (16 March 1967).

———, *Evangelii nuntiandi,* (8 December 1975).

Piketty Thomas, *El capital en el siglo XXI.* (Ciudad de México: Fondo de Cultura Económica, 2014).

Pius XI Pope, *Pastor Bonus, Ad Catholici Sacerdotii*, Encyclical (Rome: Vatican, December 20, 1935; Wien: Priesterbruderschaft St. Petrus, 2011).

Poirier Jean-Michel, «"De campement en campement, Abraham alla au Negev" (Gen 12, 9). Le thème de la marche dans le cycle d'Abraham», Aguilar Chiu, José Enrique/O'Mahony, Kieran J./Roger, Maurice (éd), *Bible et Terre Sainte: Mélanges Marcel Beaudry,* (New York/Bern/Berlin/Bruxelles/Frankfurt am Main, Oxford, Wien, 2008).

Poucouta Paulin, *God'S Word in Africa,* (Nairobi, Éditions Paulines, 2015).

———, *Quand la Parole de Dieu visite l'Afrique: Lecture plurielle de la Bible,* (Paris: Karthala, 2011).

Quijano, A., «Colonialité du Pouvoir et Démocratie en Amérique Latine»., dans J. Cohen, H. Hirata et L. Gómez (dir.), *Amérique Latine: démocratie et exclusion,* (Paris, L'Harmattan, 1994).

Römer Thomas, «D'Abraham à la conquête. L'Hexateuque et l'histoire d'Israël et de Juda», *Recherches de Science Religieuse*, 103/1, janvier/mars 2015, 35-53.

Scannone Juan Carlos, *La ética social del Papa Francisco.* (Buenos Aires: Agape, 2018).

———, *Nuevo punto de partida de la filosofía latinoamericana.* (Buenos Aires: Guadalupe, 1990).

SCEAM, *Document de Kampala,* (Accra, La Croix Africa, 2020).

Ségal Abraham, *Abraham: Enquête sur un patriarche,* (Paris: Plon, 1995).

Segeja Nicholaus, "Pastoral Reflection on New Evangelization: A Call for *Communitas Christifidelium*" in John Lukwata and Others (eds), *Search for New Paradigms for Evangelization in the 21st Century: 15th Interdisciplinary Theological Session of the Faculty of Theology* (Nairobi: CUEA Press, 2013).

———, Pastoral Theology: New Understanding and Orientations, (Eldoret: AMECEA GABA Publications, 2020).

Sequeri Pierangelo, "An exemplary case of an authentic synodal exercise." *Avvenire.* (July 9, 2022). Accessed 12.08.2022. https://www.academyforlife.va/content/dam/pav/documenti%20pdf/2022/Etica%20Teologica/Sequeri%209%20luglio%20ITA%20ENG%20ESP%20POR/SEQUERI_ENG_Avvenire_An%20exemplary%20case%20of%20an%20authentic%20synodal%20exercise.pdf.

Ska Jean-Louis, «L'histoire d'Israël de Martin Noth à nos jours. Problèmes de méthodes», ACFEB, *Comment la Bible saisit-elle l'histoire ? XXIe congrès de l'Association catholique française pour l'étude de la Bible* (Issy-les-Moulineaux: 2005), (Paris: Cerf, 2007).

Stanley, J.-Samartha, "Scripture and Scriptures," in R. S. Sugirtharajah, (ed.), *Voices from the Margin: Interpreting the Bible in the Third World,* 2nd ed. (London: SPCK, 1995).

Sweeney, James *and others (eds), Keeping Faith in Practice: Aspects of Catholic Pastoral Theology,* (London: SCM Press, 2010).

Tchidimbo Raimundus, "Intervention in Congregatio generalis LII 21 October 1963." In Acta Synodalia sacrosanti concilii oecumenici Vaticani Secundi. Volumen II. Pars III. 150-152. Typis polyglottis Vaticanis MCMLXXII.

The Holy See, *The Code of Canon Law,* (Bangalore: Collins, 1983).

Tornielli Andrea, "Francis to Mexico's bishops" article in La Stampa. https://www.lastampa.it/vatican-insider/en/2016/02/13/news/francis-to-mexico-s-bishops-do-not-underestimate-challenge-drug-trade-represents-1.36564001.

Vatican II, Dogmatic Constitution on the Church, *Lumen Gentium,* (21 November 1964).

———, Pastoral Constitution on the Church in the Modern World, *Gaudium et Spes,* (7 December 1965).

———, Decree on the Apostolate of the Laity, *Apostolicam Actuositatem* (18 November 1965).

Vatican.va/roman_curia/congregations/cfaith/cti_documents/rc_cti_20140610_cerf-sensus-fidei_fr.html#:~:text=Dans%20la%20pensée%20du%20pape%20

François%2C%20comme%20d'ailleurs,tradition%20apostolique%2C%20 mais%20il%20aussi%20une%20valeur%20prospective.

Verstraeten, Johann (ed), *Scrutinizing the Signs of the Times in the Light of the Gospel*, (Leuven: Peeters, 2007).

Vico Giambattista, *Ciencia Nueva.* (Madrid: Tecnos, 2006).

Wijsen, Frans, et al., *The Pastoral Circle Revisited: A Critical Quest for Truth and Transformation*, (Nairobi: Paulines Publications, 2006).

World Council of Churches, *Churches and Moral Discernment—Volume 3: Facilitating Dialogue to Build Koinonia.* Faith and Order Paper. (Geneva: WCC Publications, 2021).

Journals

Allmen von D., "The Birth of Theology", *International Review of Mission*, 64, Issue 253, 1975.

Appiah-Kubi, F., "Théologie de l'Eglise Famille de Dieu: Une évaluation critique", *Spiritus,* 215, (Juin 2014), 201-202.

Appiah-Kubi, F. & Yeboah. R., "The Nature and Missionary Role of the Lay People in the Light of Vatican II; Convenience or Conviction?" *E-Journal of Humanities, Arts and Social Sciences (EHASS)*, Vol.1, Number 1, May 2020.

Bidima, J.-G., *La Palabre*, Paris, éd. Michalon, 1997; Diangitukwa, F., "La lointaine origine de la gouvernance en Afrique: l'arbre à palabre", *Revue Gouvernance* 11, (1), 2014. https://doi.org/10.7202/1038881ar.

Blanchard Yves-Marie, «synode et synodalité dans le Nouveau Testament», *Spiritus,* 245, (Décembre 2021), 409-421.

Bosch, J.D., "Currents and Cross Currents in South African Black Theology", *Journal of Religion in Africa*, 6 (1974).

Dell'Oro, Roberto, and M. Therese Lysaught. "Theological Ethics of Life: A New Volume by the Pontifical Academy for Life", Review Essay, *Journal of Moral Theology,* 11/2 (2022) 65-77.

Ejesu Onyemuche Anele, "Achebe's Arrow of God, the Anti-Promethean Figure and the Lukacs's Sociological Approach to Tragedy" in *Okike An African Journal of New Writing*, 52 (1), (November 2014).

Hahnenberg, E.P., "Common Discernment: A Catholic Perspective on The Church: Towards a Common Vision". *One in Christ*, vol. 51, no. 2, (2017).

Hinze Bradford, "Can We Find A Way Together? The Challenge of Synodality in a Wounded and Wounding Church". *Irish Theological Quarterly.* vol. 85, no. 3 (2020): 215-29. https://doi.org/10.1177/0021140020926595.

Korang Kwaku Larbi, "Homage to a Modern Literary Father" in *Project Muse, Research in African Literatures*, Vol. 42, No. 2, (Indiana: Indiana University Press, 2011): vi-xv.

Lafont Bertrand, «30 idées reçues sur la Bible», *Le monde la Bible*, 207, 2013.

Le Tourneau, D., «La prédication de la parole de Dieu et la participation des laïcs au *"munus docendi"*: fondements conciliaires et codification», *Ius Ecclesiae* 2 (1990): 101-125.

Lewis Maureen Warner, "Ezeulu and His God: An Analysis of Chinua Achebe's Arrow of God" in *Black world,* Journal 24/2, (Chicago: Johnson Publication, December 1974), 71-87. Available online at: https://books.google.at/ books?id=sbIDAAAAMBAJ&printsec=frontcover&source=gbs_ge_ summary_r&cad=0#v=onepage&q&f=false (accessed 07.01.2023).

Maina Wilson Muoha, "African Communitarian Ethics in the Theological Work of Bénézet Bujo." *Pacifica* 21, no. 2 (June 2008): 192-209. https://doi. org/10.1177/1030570X0802100205.

Martin John, "Participation of the Laity in the Teaching Function of the Church" in *African Christian Studies*, 26, no. 3 (September 2010), 50.

Mignolo, W., "Géopolitique de la sensibilité et du savoir. (Dé) colonialité, pensée frontalière et désobéissance épistémologique", dans *Mouvements* 73, 2013/1, 181-190.

Moltmann, J., "L'Eglise dans la force de l'Esprit. Une contribution à l'ecclésiologie" modern col. "Cogitatio Fidei" no. 102, (Paris: Cerf, 1980).

Penoukou, E.J., "Quel type L'Eglise? Pour quelle mission en Afrique ?" in *Spiritus* 123, Mai 1991.

Segeja Nicholaus, "Strategic Pastoral Planning for Deeper Evangelization: A Sign of vigilance of the Church in Africa" in *African Christian Studies*, 26, no. 2 (June 2010), 70–88.

———, "Reverential Dialogue-Based Evangelization in Africa: A New Icon Towards Fully Human Person Liberation" in *African Christian Studies*, 26, no. 4 (December 2010), 25-41.

———, "Contextualized Theological Reflection: A Pastoral Perspective" in *African Christian Studies*, 27, no. 1 (March 2011), 21-42.

———, "Reverential Dialogical Ministry: A Pastoral Paradigm for New Evangelization in the Parish Part I & II" in *African Christian Studies*, 28, no. 2 (June 2012), 45-88.

Addresses / Instructions / Homilies / Communiques

Commission Théologique Internationale, *La synodalité dans la vie et la mission de l'Église,* (Rome, 2018).

Commission Théologique Internationale, Le «sensus fidei» dans la vie de l'Église,

CONFÉRENCE ÉPISCOPALE DU ZAÏRE, *Présentation de la liturgie de la messe. Supplément au Missel Romain pour les diocèses du Zaïre,* (Kinshasa, Éditions du Secrétariat Général de la CEZ, 1989).

Congrégation pour le culte divin et la discipline des sacrements, Directoire sur l'homélie, Cité du Vatican, 2014. Microsoft Word - riformattato direttorio omiletico traduzione francese.doc (catholique.fr).

Francis Pope. "Address of His Holiness Pope Francis" (17 October 2015) http://www.vatican.va/content/francesco/en/speeches/2015/october/documents/papa-francesco_20151017_50-anniversario-sinodo.html.

François Pape, *Homélie*, Messe du 10 octobre 2021.

———, *Discours pour la Commémoration du 50ᵉ anniversaire de l'institution du Synode des Évêques,* 17 octobre. 2015. https://www.vatican.va/content/francesco/fr/speeches/2015/october/documents/papa-francesco_20151017_50-anniversario-sinodo.html

Secretaría del Sínodo, *Vademecum.*

Secretaría del Sínodo, *Documento Preparatorio.*

Primary/Unpublished References

400L students of the National Missionary Seminary of St Paul. "Responses to Questionnaire 'For a Synodal Church: Communion, Participation and Mission'." Abuja, n.d., 1-2.

Maryland Orphanage. "General Report on Synodal Church: Communion, Participation and Mission." Abuja, n.d., 1-6.

Theology 2 students of the National Missionary Seminary of St Paul. "Responses to Questionnaire 'For a Synodal Church: Communion, Participation and Mission.'" Abuja, n.d., 1-4.

Contributors

Emilce Cuda is a PhD holder in Theology from the Pontifical University of Argentina. She is currently a secretary at the Pontifical Commission for Latin America, Holy See, a member of the Pontifical Academy of Social Sciences and Pontifical Academy of Pro-Vita. She is an advisor of CELAM, and professor at Loyola University Chicago. She was also a visiting professor at Boston College (2016), Northwestern University (2011), and DePaul University (2019). Interim professor at St Thomas University of Texas (2020-2022), University of Buenos Aires (2017-2021), Pontificia Universidad Católica Argentina, and Universidad Nacional Arturo Jauretche (2011-2022). She is the author of *Para leer a Francisco: Teologia, ética y politica*, (Buenos Aires: Ediciones Manantial, 2016, also published in Italy by Bollati Boringhieri, 2018).

Francis Appiah-Kubi is a Professor at the Kwame Nkrumah University of Science and Technology, Kumasi, Ghana. He is a former Head of the Department of Religious studies and presently the Board Chairman of Procurement. He holds PhD degree from *Institut Catholique de Paris* and Catholic University, Leuven and Master's degree in Theology from Facultés Catholiques de Kinshasa, DR Congo. Currently, he is the Vice-Rector for Academics of the Spiritan University College in Ghana. He is also a visiting lecturer to the St. Gregory the Great Provincial Seminary, Kumasi and Institut Ecuménique Al Mowafaqa, Rabat Morocco. He is a Ghanaian Theologian specialised in Ecclesiology and African Traditional Religions.

Member of *Comitheol* at the service of SECAM. Among his publications is the *L'Eglise Famille de Dieu; Un chemin pour les Eglise d'Afrique,* Karthala, 2008.

Ignace Ndongala Maduku is associate professor at the Institute of Religious Studies at the University of Montreal (Canada). His current research focuses, on the one hand, on the posterity of the theologian Jean-Marc Ela, and on the other, on decolonial approaches in African theology. Author of several books and articles, he published in 2022, in collaboration with Dieudonné Mushipu Mbombo, at Éditions Karthala in Paris, *Les Églises d'Afrique entre fidélité et invention: Du synode romain de 1994 aux défis du XXIᵉ siècle,* and in 2021 at Éditions L'Harmattan in Paris, *Cultures africaines et modernités: Perspectives pour un dialogue prospectif.*

Ikenna U. Okafor is a priest of Nnewi diocese Nigeria, a senior research fellow in Intercultural Theology at the University of Vienna and a pastor in the Archdiocese of Vienna. His research interests include themes on fraternity, intercultural and interreligious theologies, and African theology. He is the author of *Toward an African Theology of Fraternal Solidarity: UBE NWANNE,* (Oregon: Pickwick Publications, 2014), and co-editor of *Faith in Action* Vols. II & III, (Paulines Africa, 2020). He is a member of the European Society for Catholic Theology (ESCT) and Pan-African Catholic Theology and Pastoral Network (PACTPAN).

John I. Okoye is from Owelli, Awgu LGA, in Enugu State, Nigeria. He is an alumnus of Bigard Memorial Seminary where he did his Philosophical and Theological studies from 1971 to 1978. He obtained his licentiate in Sacred Scriptures at the Pontifical Biblical Institute (Biblicum) Rome and his Doctorate in Biblical Theology at the Pontifical University of St Thomas Aquinas (Angelicum) Rome. After his doctoral studies, he taught Old

Testament Studies at Bigard Memorial Seminary where he successively functioned as Vice-Rector and Rector of the seminary. In September 29, 2005, he was ordained the pioneer Bishop of Awgu Diocese, Nigeria.

Josée Ngalula, from DR Congo, is a Sister of Saint Andrew community, Kinshasa and a professor of dogmatic theology at the Catholic University of Congo. Her fields of research include Christian Lexicology in African Languages, New Religious Movements in Africa, Religion and Violence, and African Theologies. She is currently the Director of the Observatory of Violence and Religious Fundamentalism in DR Congo (OVIRCO). She is also a visiting professor and member of the scientific board at the Ecumenical and Interreligious Institute "Al Mowafaqa" Rabat, Morocco, and a member of the following research groups: International Theological Commission (ITC), African Synodality Initiative (ASI), Pan-African Catholic Theology and Pastoral Network, and the ecumenical theological network "Tsena Malàlaka"

Her publications are available at: https://uccc.academia.edu/Jos%C3%A9eNGALULA/

Nicholaus Segeja is a Professor of Pastoral Theology and Director of the Catholic University of Eastern Africa (CUEA) Gaba Campus Eldoret, Kenya. He is a member of the International Theological Commission under the Congregation for the Doctrine of the Faith and a member of the Theological Commission under the General Secretariat for the Synod of Bishops. He is a Catholic Priest of the Archdiocese of Mwanza, Tanzania. His areas of research include the ecclesiology of reverential dialogue (*shikome*), Small Christian Communities and strategic pastoral planning. He is the Chief editor of "Good Shepherd – A Journey of Pastoral Theology", and has been globally giving seminars, workshops, and conference presentations.

Paulin Sébastien Poucouta is a priest of the Diocese of Pointe-Noire, Congo Brazzaville, Doctor in Biblical Theology from the Catholic Institute of Paris and Doctor in History of Religions from Paris/Sorbonne. He has taught in several theological training institutes both in Africa and in Europe. Honorary professor of Biblical Theology and African readings of the Bible at the Catholic Institute of Yaoundé (1992-2017), he currently directs the missionary review *Spiritus* in Paris. Member of several scientific associations (APECA, ATA, ACFEB, CEAFRI, ACADEMIE des Sciences Sociales, etc.), he is the author of *Quand la Parole de Dieu visite l'Afrique. Lectures plurielles de la Parole de Dieu*, Paris, Karthala, 2011. *God's Word in Africa*, Nairobi, Editions Paulines, 2015, and other publications.

Raymond Olusesan Aina (SThD/PhD) is a priest of the Missionary Society of St Paul, Nigeria. He is also the Vice-Rector and senior lecturer at the National Missionary Seminary of St Paul, Abuja, and visiting lecturer, at Veritas Catholic University, Abuja, Nigeria. His academic interests include restorative justice in peacebuilding, Catholic Social Thought, methodological issues in African thought, and Catholic sexual ethics. He is emeritus president of the Catholic Theological Association of Nigeria (CATHAN), and author of *Overcoming Toxic Emotions: A Christian Ethical Framework for Restorative Peacebuilding* (Wipf & Stock, 2022).

Stan Chu Ilo is a priest of Awgu diocese, Nigeria. He is a research professor of World Christianity, Ecclesiology, and African Studies at the Center for World Catholicism and Intercultural Theology, DePaul University, Chicago, USA. He is the Coordinating Servant of the Pan-African Catholic Theology and Pastoral Network, and a member of the Board of Editors of Concilium International Catholic Journal. He is the editor of the *Handbook of African Catholicism*.